Appearance as Capital

Appearance as Capital: The Normative Regulation of Aesthetic Capital Accumulation and Conversion

EDITED BY

OUTI SARPILA
University of Turku, Finland

IIDA KUKKONEN
University of Turku, Finland

TERO PAJUNEN
University of Turku, Finland

And

ERICA ÅBERG
University of Turku, Finland

United Kingdom – North America – Japan – India – Malaysia – China

Emerald Publishing Limited
Howard House, Wagon Lane, Bingley BD16 1WA, UK

First edition 2022

Reprints and permissions service
Contact: permissions@emeraldinsight.com

British Library Cataloguing in Publication Data
A catalogue record for this book is available from the British Library

ISBN: 978-1-80043-711-1 (Print)
ISBN: 978-1-80043-708-1 (Online)
ISBN: 978-1-80043-710-4 (Epub)

Printed and bound by CPI Group (UK) Ltd, Croydon, CR0 4YY

ISOQAR certified
Management System,
awarded to Emerald
for adherence to
Environmental
standard
ISO 14001:2004.

Certificate Number 1985
ISO 14001

INVESTOR IN PEOPLE

Table of Contents

List of Figures and Tables   *vii*

About the Contributors   *ix*

Acknowledgements   *xi*

Introduction   *1*
Outi Sarpila, Iida Kukkonen, Tero Pajunen and Erica Åberg

Part I Accumulating a Gendered Form of Capital

**Chapter 1   Physical Appearance as a Form of Capital: Key
Problems and Tensions**   *23*
Iida Kukkonen

**Chapter 2   Who Performs Appearance Work, and Who Believes
Appearance Works? Gendered Appearance Beliefs and Practices in
Finland**   *39*
Iida Kukkonen

**Chapter 3   The Metrosexual Who Never Visited Finland – The
Eternal Gender Gap in Appearance-related Consumption**   *57*
Outi Sarpila

**Chapter 4   Seeking Age-appropriate Appearance among Ageing
Men**   *71*
Hanna Ojala and Ilkka Pietilä

Part II Contested Conversions – Everyday (Re)workings of Aesthetic Capital

Chapter 5   Too Smart-looking for a Waiter? – Scripting Appearance Norms at the Theatre of Working Life   *87*
Tero Pajunen

Chapter 6   Generating Aesthetic Capital: Prospects from Autobiographical Narratives   *103*
Tero Pajunen

Chapter 7   The Ouroboros of Seeking Validation? Exploring the Interconnection of Appearance (Dis)satisfaction and Content Creation on Social Media   *117*
Erica Åberg and Aki Koivula

Chapter 8   Sofie's World: Resistance toward the Thin Ideal in Sofie Hagen's Fat Activist Online Content   *135*
Anna Puhakka

Chapter 9   Well-beshaved Women Rarely Make History – Exploring the Contestation of the Hairless Beauty Ideal with Case #Januhairy   *149*
Erica Åberg and Laura Salonen

Conclusion   *165*
Outi Sarpila, Iida Kukkonen, Tero Pajunen and Erica Åberg

Appendices   *173*

Index   *177*

List of Figures and Tables

Figure 2.1. Mean Daily Time (Minutes) Spent in Front of the Mirror by Age Group and Gender.   45

Figure 2.2. Belief in Appearance as Currency for Men and Women.   46

Figure 2.3. Mean Daily Time (Minutes) Spent in Front of the Mirror by Belief in Appearance as Currency.   47

Figure 3.1. 'I take good care of my physical appearance'.   65

Figure 3.2. Predicted Probabilities of 'Personal Hygiene and Beauty Care' Consumption Share of Total Consumption Expenditure. 67

Figure 7.1. The Likelihood of Creating Content on Social Media According to Appearance Satisfaction.   126

Figure 7.2. The Relationship between Creating Content and Body Satisfaction According to the Preferred Social Network Site.   127

Figure 7.3. The Relationship between Creating Content and Body Satisfaction.   128

Figure 9.1. Wordcloud Form the Comments According to the Themes 'Positive' Comments (Left) and 'Negative' Comments (Right).   157

Table 2.1.   Linear Regression of Daily Average Time (Min) Spent in Front of the Mirror.   48

Table 3.1.   Survey Data Analysed in This Chapter.   62

Table 3.2.   'I Take Good Care of My Physical Appearance'.   66

Table 7.1.   Descriptive Statistics of Applied Variables.   125

Table 9.1.   The Names and Quantities of the Themes of the Images.   156

Table 9.2.   The Names and Quantities of the Themes Rising
             from the Captions.   157
Table 9.3.   The Names and Quantities of the Sub-themes
             Rising from the Comments.   158
Appendix 1. Descriptive Statistics of Analytical Sample:
             Weighted Proportions of Categorical Variables,
             Weighted Means and Standard Deviations, as Well
             as Minimum and Maximum Values of Continuous
             Variables.   173
Appendix 2. Descriptive Statistics of Analytical Samples:
             Weighted Proportions of Categorical Variables,
             Weighted Means and Standard Deviations, as Well
             as Minimum and Maximum Values of Continuous
             Variables.   174

About the Contributors

Erica Åberg, PhD, works as a Senior Researcher at the INVEST flagship, sociology unit, University of Turku. In her doctoral dissertation, she examined the gendered norms of physical appearance, empirically focusing on social media, motherhood and ageing.

Aki Koivula, PhD, is a University Lecturer and Docent of Economic Sociology at the Department of Social Research, University of Turku.

Iida Kukkonen is a Senior Researcher at the Unit of Economic Sociology, Faculty of Social Sciences, University of Turku. Kukkonen's research interests revolve around physical appearance -related inequalities, gender and consumption. In her PhD thesis she studies gendered physical appearance -related inequalities in Finnish working life.

Hanna Ojala, PhD, is a University Lecturer in Gender Studies at the Faculty of Social Sciences, Tampere University, Finland. Her research has focused on intersections of age, gender and class in the various contexts of men's ageing, such as anti-ageing, exercise, health, retirement and communities.

Tero Pajunen is a Senior Researcher at the Unit of Economic Sociology, Faculty of Social Sciences, University of Turku, Finland. His research focuses on the meanings and meaning-making processes of physical appearance in various contexts.

Ilkka Pietilä, PhD, is Assistant Professor of Social Gerontology at the Faculty of Social Sciences, University of Helsinki, Finland. His work has covered topics such as ageing men and masculinities, health, ageing and embodiment as well as the use of anti-ageing products and services.

Anna Puhakka is a PhD Student in Gender Studies at the University of Jyväskylä, Finland.

Laura Salonen, PhD, works as a Senior Researcher at the INVEST flagship, sociology unit, University of Turku. In her dissertation she studied processes of long-term work disability and socioeconomic disparities. She has expertise in quantitative research methods and her research interests include social and health inequalities.

Outi Sarpila is an Adjunct Professor in Economic Sociology. She is currently working as a senior research fellow at the INVEST flagship, sociology unit, University of Turku. Her research interests include themes related to physical appearance and inequalities, and sociology of consumption.

Acknowledgements

This work was supported by the Academy of Finland, Decision Number: 325813 (Chapters, 1, 2, 5, 6, 7 and 9), the INVEST Research Flagship (Chapters 3, 7 and 9), the Finnish Cultural Foundation (Chapters 1 and 2) and Turku University Foundation (Chapters 1, 2, 5 and 6).

Introduction

Outi Sarpila, Iida Kukkonen, Tero Pajunen and Erica Åberg

Sara Sieppi is a former Miss Finland and current social media influencer. Despite the fact that Sieppi's posts are in Finnish and Finland is a small linguistic region, Sieppi has nearly 200,000 followers and her company makes a significant profit. In her Instagram account, she performs as an 'ambassador' of different beauty care brands, renting her beautiful looks to companies to enhance the sales of multifarious products and services. Therefore, Sieppi can be considered an example of today's aesthetic labourers, who have turned their physical appearance into cash flow. Young beautiful women around the world are nowadays using social media to exchange their aesthetic capital to economic capital. However, this does not please everyone. In December 2020, Sieppi was used as an example in a political column which tried to justify the monthly salary of the members of the parliament by comparing the salaries to Sieppi's monthly salary. The latter one was according to columnist, earned by presenting 'sponsored underwear and mint lemon chocolate muffins', whereas the former one by hard work (Parkkonen, 2020). The column was widely doomed misogynist and sexist. More generally speaking, it however shows how physical appearance as a form of capital, i.e. aesthetic capital, is normatively regulated and highlights the paradoxes related to the pivotal role of physical appearance in contemporary society.

Expectations to look good are increasing, and many people are under more pressure to look good and attend to their looks. In tandem with this, endeavours towards good looks and taking advantage of it are under strict normative regulation. In addition, this does not seem to apply only to female social media influencers, but people more generally. In fact, the salience of physical appearance as a form of capital is not just a novel trend generated by social media. On the contrary, the pervasiveness of the emphasis on physical appearance has increased steadily for a long period of time, making it an increasingly important, but normatively regulated, form of capital and hence a source of inequality.

Appearance as Capital, 1–19
doi:10.1108/978-1-80043-708-120210001

The Increasing Importance of Physical Appearance

Several cultural, economic, political and technological changes are contributing to the increasing institutional and individual focus on physical appearance.

First, scholars studying consumer culture have argued for decades that the physical appearance of the body serves as a source of individual pleasure and as a means of self-expression and identity formation. Desired bodily properties are produced through body modification; with the help of appearance-related commodities and services, consumers push their bodies towards the best version of themselves, constantly ready for new transformations (e.g. Bauman, 2007; Featherstone, 1982, 2007; Klesse, 1999). According to Euromonitor (2020), the global retail value of 'beauty and personal care' products increased by 28 percent, and 'clothing and footwear' by 40 percent, between 2009 and 2019. The power of consumer culture as a fuel for consumption related to appearance has been explained particularly with regards to the visual and performative character of consumer culture (e.g. Featherstone, 1982; Shilling, 2012; Turner, 2008). A central element of performing is the enhancement of the physical appearance, at least to some extent to gratify 'the audience'. The idea of the performing self is much the same as the concept presented by Goffman (1959). However, consumer culture emphasises 'onstage performances' in relation to 'backstage performances'.

Second, it can be argued that social media increases the amount of 'onstage performances' and has changed many individuals' relationships to physical appearance and self-presentations. Although social media is not just about selfies, it offers constant possibilities for photographing oneself and others (e.g. Featherstone, 2010). People are expected to be 'camera ready' everywhere they go, and virtual audiences are always ready to judge the 'appearance competence' of any person in a picture or video. Social media users are exposed to a constant flux of physical appearances, and they may be expected to present a variety of physical appearances. While social media has the potential for inclusion and widening the norms of physical appearance, on a global scale, it can also intensify and narrow appearance norms (e.g. Widdows, 2018). According to the logic of consumer capitalism, the majority of bodies that 'sell' are still mostly white, thin, young and able. Nevertheless, at an individual level, the possibility of empowerment on social media cannot be neglected (e.g. Barnard, 2016; Tiidenberg & Gómez Cruz, 2015). According to some interpretations, social media self(ie)-expression comes with a (dis)empowerment paradox: taking selfies may feel individually empowering while conforming and reifying existing oppressive and hegemonic beauty norms (Barnard, 2016).

Third, in recent interpretations, the cultivation of physical appearance has been associated with consumer-oriented wellness culture; physical appearance is seen as the embodiment of individuals' capabilities to make 'the right' lifestyle and self-care choices, including such practices as maintaining 'proper' sleeping and eating habits and engaging in physical and mental exercise (e.g., Grénman, 2019; Koskinen, 2020). Social media, with its army of influencers, amplifies trends, including the quest for 'wellness'. Also outside social media, people are encouraged to engage in various practices related to fitness, well-being and anti-ageing in order to enhance their physical appearance, productivity and status.

Fourth, individuals' physical appearance has become politicised, thus affecting the norms of proper looks. This also relates to the wellness discourse in a sense that taking care of one's physical appearance is no longer simply considered each individual's choice but a responsibility; as physical appearance is intertwined with health, physical appearance -related practices become increasingly considered necessary for everyone (cf. Sassatelli, 2010; Smith Maguire, 2008). This can be most clearly seen in discourses of body size. Individuals are nowadays expected to follow official eating and exercise recommendations, and the failure to do so is presumed based on external characteristics (Lupton, 1995; Shilling, 2007; Smith Maguire, 2008). A responsible citizen does not get fat and strain hard or public health care.

Fifth, the increasing importance of physical appearance and intensification of normative regulation relates to changes in labour market. According to several scholars, the expansion of the service sector and the emergence of new high-skilled and low-skilled performative occupations has, among other things, made good looks an occupational necessity. 'The right looks' play a pivotal role, facilitating individuals' entry into certain occupations (Smith Maguire, 2008; van den Berg & Arts, 2019). However, the institutionalised requirements to look 'right' do not apply only to those working in traditional services or new service sector occupations but to more or less all workers, regardless of their job titles (McDowell, 2009). Scholars view this as part of a broader post-Fordist development, where the service sector per se has expanded, but the so-called service logic has also spread throughout the labour market to all sectors and hierarchical levels (Parviainen et al., 2016). Simultaneously, precarity is becoming normalised in post-Fordist labour markets. As subsistence becomes increasingly uncertain and discontinuous, it necessitates continuous aesthetic adjustment and labour on 'looking right' and keeping up employable appearances (van den Berg & Arts, 2019). The precarisation of work blurs the lines between work and private life (van den Berg, 2019), and worker and consumer – proper workers also know how to consume 'properly' to maximise their own and their employers' competitive edge. Working on one's physical appearance may not only become more of an occupational necessity as competition for jobs increases (e.g., Sarpila & Erola, 2016), but it may also more generally serve as a means of appearing and feeling in control (Giddens, 1991; Shilling, 2012) and valuable under circumstances that are increasingly precarious for many (e.g., Hakim, 2018).

Capitalisation of Physical Appearance

The above-mentioned economic, cultural, political and technological changes have made physical appearance increasingly a normatively regulated form of capital and source of inequality. Numerous studies report that physical appearance, which is often conceptualised as attractiveness, is linked to various economic and social rewards including higher income (e.g., Brunello & d'Hombres,

2007; Cawley, 2004; Hamermesh & Biddle, 1994; Johnston, 2010), better employment opportunities and career advancements (e.g., Hamermesh, 2011; Hosoda et al., 2003), political success (e.g. Berggren et al., 2010), advantages in partner selection (e.g., Mathes & Kozak, 2008; McClintock, 2014) and increased socioeconomic status (Jæger, 2011). However, in economics and sociology, as well as in policymaking, the inequalities considered have been primarily socio-economic factors, while the role physical appearance has been largely neglected in 'serious' analyses of inequalities (Kuipers, 2019).

In this book, we develop the understanding of physical appearance as a form of capital and appearance-related inequalities by paying particular attention to normative regulations of the accumulation and conversion of this type of capital. We build on interdisciplinary research in the intersections of cultural sociology, economic sociology, sociology of consumption and everyday life, working life studies, gender studies and media studies.

The idea of physical appearance as form of capital stems particularly from recent sociological discussion on physical appearance and beauty and the role they play in formation of social divisions. During the past decade, sociologists have developed Pierre Bourdieu's ideas on capital further, incorporating physical appearance as an independent form of capital, or more specifically, as aesthetic capital (Anderson et al., 2010; Holla & Kuipers, 2015), erotic capital (Hakim, 2010) or physical capital (Shilling, 2004). Physical appearance as a form of capital can be understood as a combination of different resources or assets related to physical appearance including facial beauty and body shape, size and physique, as well as styles of grooming and clothing (Anderson et al., 2010). In this book, the idea of physical appearance as a form of capital is based on an assumption that physical appearance is, at least partly, an inherited quality, which does not fully conform to other social hierarchies (e.g. Edmonds & Mears, 2017). Furthermore, we assume that physical appearance as capital is convertible into other forms of capitals and that the value of these appearance-related assets varies from one field to another.

The perspective differs from the general approach adopted in the majority of other disciplines. Traditionally, beauty is considered a good thing, the consequences of which are mainly positive and the evaluation of which is based on shared ideals of beauty (for a review, see Anderson et al., 2010; Maestripieri et al., 2017). Thus, there seems to be a somewhat shared understanding of the logic of good looks, although the explanatory mechanisms differ. In economics, the principal mechanism through which beauty confers benefits is related to preferences: employers, customers and co-workers alike prefer beautiful people (Hamermesh, 2011). In social psychology, on the other hand, beauty is considered advantageous because people associate it with other desirable traits. This mechanism is often referred to as the physical attractiveness stereotype or 'what is beautiful is good' stereotype (e.g. Eagly et al., 1991; Langlois et al., 2000). Furthermore, evolutionary psychologists propose that it is the central role of physical appearance as a criterion for mate selection that accounts for the economic and social outcomes of beauty (Buss et al., 1990), whereas in sociology, Webster and Driskell (1983) regard physical attractiveness as similar to status characteristic as gender and race, and propose a mechanism they call 'beauty as status'. This approach, combined with Bourdieusian tradition, has recently been developed further in studies that consider physical appearance as a form of capital (Anderson et al., 2010). Feminists and theorists of aesthetic labour, who situate (dis)advantages of beauty in gendered status hierarchies (Elias et al., 2017; Wolf, 1990/2002), as well as more intersectional feminists, who highlight beauty as a site of struggle over class, race, colour, ethnicity, sexuality and able-bodiedness (e.g. Jha, 2016) have also made valuable contributions to these discussions.

In addition, certain recent studies in sociology and social psychology and organisational studies have questioned the universal logic related to beauty and its positive outcomes, particularly with regard to economic outcomes for women. Kuipers (2015) suggests that beauty standards are not universally shared, but instead multiple taste repertoires exist. Furthermore, men are less easily evaluated by strictly aesthetic standards than are women (Kuipers, 2015). In addition, strict social norms regulate the accumulation of economic advantage from one's physical appearance, particularly for women (Kukkonen et al., 2018; Sarpila et al., 2010). Indeed, it seems that the value of physical appearance in social exchange is not universal, but malleable, relational and contextual: always shaped in multiple, intersecting power relations. Furthermore, it is not just beauty or attractiveness that matters, but the logic of physical appearance in generating inequalities seems to be more complex than previously thought (see also van der Laan & Kuipers, 2016, p. 66).

To gain a better understanding of physical appearance -related inequality, it is crucial to pay particular attention to norms that regulate the accumulation and conversion of physical appearance as a capital. Norms are a core concept for sociologists, as they are relevant for understanding two fundamental issues of sociological thinking: order and inequality (e.g., Horne & Mollborn, 2020). Norms are 'the grammar of society' (Bicchieri, 2006). They guide people's actions by telling them what behaviour is normal, desirable or avoidable in particular contexts. They provide a map of how to value the social world. Yet norms are not predetermined and objectively 'out there' but are enacted, challenged and inter-preted by people; hence, they are in a constant flux (Horne & Mollborn, 2020; Xenitidou & Edmonds, 2014). Norms actualise through action, usually in the form of sanctions that may appear as penalisation or praise (Coleman, 1990). They, thus, operate and appear at both individual and collective levels (if that distinction is to be made in the first place).

At the level of the individual, norms appear as expectations of how others would evaluate behaviours (Hechter & Opp, 2001; Horne & Mollborn, 2020). They may appear as different emotions, like shame, admiration or disgust, which guide one's own behaviour and affect how one sanctions others. Thinking of physical appearance, norms also function as a moral obligation to, for example, aspire to having a fit body (e.g. Dworkin & Wachs, 2009) or invest in 'healthy ageing' (e.g. Lenneis & Pfister, 2017). Thus, the power of norms is internalised rather than always imposed by an identifiable other (see also Foucault, 1977). However, norms vary in their scale as well. Some norms are more long-standing, while others change. Certain norms may apply only in certain groups, while others may apply across a whole society or even the globe. While norms are the bread and butter of sociology, norms are often used as sociological explanations of actions and phenomena instead of taken as a subject of study. Yet, we argue, it is worth studying the forms and content of appearance norms and asking how they are created, applied, maintained, interpreted, negotiated and challenged in different contexts, by and for different people.

This Book's Approach

In this book, we ask in what kind of ways, to whom and in what types of context it is possible to accumulate and convert capital based on physical appearance. We call this capital aesthetic capital. We examine how norms of accumulating and converting aesthetic capital intertwine with gender, age and other forms of capital and play a role in shaping inequalities. The majority of the data analysed come from Finland. At the end of this introductory part, we present 'case Finland' and explain why Finland offers an interesting case to study physical appearance and inequalities. In addition, some chapters in this book use social media data, which is not bounded in any certain nation state context. The data include surveys, individual and group interviews and life stories, as well as visual and textual social media data. In this book, we employ a wide range of methodologies. We argue that the diversity of approaches and methodologies is beneficial for understanding the emergence, manifestation and reverberations of the social norms that regulate aesthetic capital.

This book examines the capitalisation of physical appearance and related normative regulations from two perspectives, accumulation and convertibility, and is divided into two main sections based on these perspectives. The first section deals with the logics of beauty and body work as, first and foremost, gendered ways to 'enhance' one's physical appearance -related assets. The second explores the social rules around the convertibility of these assets into social and economic resources.

Accumulating a Gendered Form of Capital

As does any form of capital, appearance-related capital accumulates. In an increasingly visual consumer culture, individuals are invited to engage in various aesthetic practices to accumulate, enhance and maintain their aesthetic assets. These practices range from mundane rituals such as washing, teeth cleansing, make-up application and hair removal and shaping to projects such as dieting and working out and interventions like aesthetic surgery or bodily implants. Social scientists have referred to the plethora of different aesthetic practices using various terms such as body modification (Featherstone, 1999) and dress work (van den Berg & Vonk, 2020), as well as beauty work, body work and appearance work (for reviews, see Gimlin, 2007; Kwan & Trautner, 2009; Mears, 2014). As the terminology suggests, many scholars have viewed these practices primarily as work rather than leisure. In the literature, a key distinction is often made between work performed on one's own body and work performed on the bodies of others (Gimlin, 2007; Mears, 2014). Further distinctions include the extent to which a practice happens slowly or whether it transforms the body directly, for instance, through cutting or inscribing (Featherstone, 1999). Gimlin argued in 2007 that sociology has in the past particularly ignored both the relevance of body work to experiences of working life and the more mundane forms of body work (Gimlin, 2007). Since then, the social sciences have seen a surge in interest in the importance of aesthetic labour: the labour of looking good and right at and for work (e.g., Boyle & De Keere, 2019; Mears, 2011; van den Berg & Arts, 2019; Williams & Connell, 2010). However, mundane forms of appearance work outside the labour market context remains a neglected field of study (although see Elias et al., 2017). As the research presented in the first section of this book show, mundane appearance work matters in social life beyond the labour market and is a highly gendered form of work.

The first section of this book, thus, situates physical appearance -related capital as a gendered form of capital in Finland from the perspective of appearance work as capital accumulation. In Chapter 1 of the book, Iida Kukkonen reviews the contributions of sociological research on appearance-related capital for the study of physical appearance and inequality. She highlights the Bourdieusian origins of the sociological conceptualisation of capital and shows how Bourdieusian thinking has, particularly in the past decade, inspired scholars to think about appearance-related inequalities. Crucially, however, the scholarship is highly variable in the extent to which it is faithful to Bourdieu's scholarship on culture and in the extent to which it incorporates (socio-)economics or extends or develops Bourdieusian thinking to consider feminist issues such as gendered labour and capital. Kukkonen teases out the tensions between capital as, on the one hand, a societal concept laden with economic value, and concomitantly, societal economic inequality, and as, on the other hand, a field-specific concept that is always implied in contextual and unequal power relationships, including those related to ethnicity, nationality, sexuality, gender, age and so forth. The chapter suggests the accumulation and conversion of appearance-related capital intertwine in shaping inequalities.

Chapter 2, also authored by Kukkonen, illustrates how appearance-related practices are not just driven by gendered norms but also by gendered beliefs about appearance as capital. While Finnish men and women equally hold the belief that appearances matter for success, the belief in appearance as capital does not seem to incite men to look into the mirror. And Finnish women who believe appearances matter for success engage in accumulating aesthetic capital more than women who do not.

Chapter 3, written by Outi Sarpila, further illustrates the gendered dimensions of aesthetic capital in the Finnish context by engaging with the figure of the metrosexual and by putting aesthetic consumption in a temporal context. The concept of the metrosexual arose in media culture to celebrate men who recognise their bodies and looks as capital worthy of investment and who take a step to engage in the pleasures offered by a consumerist appearance society. This trope, much adored and highlighted by the media, advertisement and commerce, is nowhere to be seen in the attitudinal and official statistics Sarpila delves into. In the light of these data, commercial masculinity appears an Anglo-Saxon phenomenon that is completely detached from the everyday lives of Finnish men. Despite all the talk of 'new masculinities', appearance-related capital accumulation still appears highly gendered in the Finnish context.

The problematic genderedness of appearance in society is further highlighted in Chapter 4, in which Hanna Ojala and Ilkka Pietilä interview elderly Finnish men regarding their appearance-related consumption. Their study shows how the contradictory norms regarding 'successful aging' and gendered norms of appearance work are brought together in the appearance-related practices of ageing men in Finland. They highlight how appearance work is not just aimed at gendered distinctions but also concerns class and, importantly, age. While elderly Finnish men may not buy into the idea of appearance as capital, they nevertheless employ appearance-related consumption as a way of fighting the marginalisation and invisibility that comes with old age.

Contested Conversions – Everyday (Re)workings of Aesthetic Capital

Like other forms of capital, aesthetic capital is convertible. Economics-inspired social scientific research on the outcomes of physical appearance commonly approaches conversions of aesthetic capital as 'beauty perks and penalties'. The assumption is that possessing aesthetic capital brings perks to individuals, while a lack of it brings penalties (see Anderson et al., 2010). This line of literature has largely focused on mapping the socio-economic outcomes of appearance (see, e.g., Hamermesh, 2011; Hosoda et al., 2003; Jæger, 2011), while also acknowledging that aesthetic capital is convertible to forms of capital beyond economic capital. While this research on socio-economic outcomes has focused on the overall quantitative regularities in the conversion of aesthetic capital to economic capital, other social scientists have investigated how the conversion of aesthetic capital happens on a particular social field, such as the modelling industry (Mears, 2011), the global party circuit (Mears, 2020) or beauty pageants (Balogun, 2020). This line of research has often used qualitative methods, including ethnography, to uncover a field's specific logics of valuation and exchange and to understand how these are navigated and negotiated in contexts where power is unevenly distributed. The second part of this book draws on both lines of scholarship and stresses the role of social norms for understanding capital conversion. This section considers both the workings and reworkings of aesthetic capital: how aesthetic capital structures and affects online and offline lives and what kind of struggles are involved in the evaluation and conversion of aesthetic capital. The chapters focus on mundane norms and mundane acts of resistance in everyday lives offline (Chapters 5 and 6) as well as on social media (Chapters 7, 8 and 9).

Working life is a crucial arena for capital conversion because labour is a field in which appearances may be, quite straightforwardly, economically rewarded or punished. In Chapter 5, Tero Pajunen brings out a Goffmanian lens and focuses it on Finnish working life, to look at how appearance norms are scripted in various fields of work. His study highlights how employees have to manage different field-specific appearance expectations in their everyday job. The look which works best with customers or clients is not necessarily the one employers recognise or reward. Pajunen, thus, shows that field-specific aesthetic capital may be misrecognised. This further complicates negotiations of appropriate appearances and the conversion of aesthetic capital in working life.

Chapter 6, also authored by Pajunen, shifts the outlook from working life to a wider perspective to investigate how individuals narrate the subjective benefits and penalties they have experienced in life from their appearance. The sanctions related in Finns' appearance-related autobiographies relate to making impressions as well as being included and excluded. Many of the 'objective' and tangible outcomes that are often the focus of research on physical appearance are missing in the narratives, which focus instead on the effects physical appearance has on one's life, conveyed in psychological terms. Pajunen's study elucidates the differences between research on the socioeconomic (dis)advantages of aesthetic capital and subjective (mis)recognition and remembrance of the effects looks have on lives. It highlights how researchers looking at society-level data see very different effects than individuals looking at the world from their spot in the data.

This tendency is further highlighted in Chapter 7, where Erica Åberg and Aki Koivula use population-level data from Finland to look at how satisfaction with one's appearance relates to creating content on social media. Åberg and Koivula suggest that especially for young females, social media in general, and Instagram in particular, may work as a never-ending cycle, in which lowered appearance satisfaction prompts the creation of more social media content, which in turn leads to lower appearance satisfaction. They illustrates how prevailing norms of aesthetic capital, value-seeking and content creation through self-presentation are gendered. They also suggest the value creation of aesthetic capital follows different normative logics on Instagram and Facebook. Chapter 8 of this book, thus, shows how visual social media may work as an amplifier of appearance society. In the social media context, where visibility is the marker of success, the need to be seen is urgent. Yet the need to present aesthetic capital online may drive behaviour that is not beneficial at the individual level.

Because social media is not restricted by national borders, Chapters 9 and 10 are not limited to Finnish social media phenomena but look international social media movements. As Chapters 9 and 10 of this book illustrate, social media are platforms where appearance norms can be contested and overthrown. Yet as both chapters show, contesting appearance-related norms is not an easy task, and it is not a task for which everyone is equally rewarded. In Chapter 8, Anna Puhakka explains how for Danish fat activist, Sofie Hagen, offencive resistance, doing fatness wrong and ambivalence are strategies that not only challenge prevailing norms but also allow for the valuation of non-normative bodies in a particular social field.

Finally, in Chapter 9, Erica Åberg and Laura Salonen look at a social media movement that contests the so-called 'last taboo' of female appearance: body hair. The movement's invitation to grow out one's body hair during January and post pictures and experiences of the process using the tag #januhairy can be likened to a breaching experiment à la Harold Garfinkel (Heritage, 2013). In breaching experiments, people break norms in order to examine the resulting reactions and sanctions. Åberg and Salonen elucidate how the reception of #januhairy posts is directly related to aesthetic capital: breaking an aesthetic norm is allowed for a person who already possesses significant amounts of capital.

Physical Appearance in the Finnish Context

Most articles in this book use data that are collected in Finland. Why particularly Finland, one may ask. Besides the fact that all the contributors of this book are Finns and experienced experts on the Finnish appearance culture, there are special characteristics in Finland's history that make it a unique and interesting laboratory in which to study the role of appearances. Because of its assumed egalitarian history, the differences in gender, age, class and context-dependent norms presented and discussed in this book are likely to be stronger in other national contexts. Thus, Finland can act as a 'baseline' for evaluating the importance of physical appearance in contemporary societies.

The Modest and Egalitarian Finns

Certain modesty has stereotypically highlighted appearance norms of the Finns. Finnish people have a tendency to downplay the significance of appearance to them, emphasising thriftiness and practicality as the cornerstones of their apparel (Autio, 2006; Wilska, 2002). According to several Finnish consumer culture researchers, frugality, caution and rationality have been the virtues traditionally cherished by Finnish consumers (e.g., Autio, 2006; Heinonen, 1998; Wilska, 2002). Compared to more-established consumer societies, such as the United Kingdom and United States, the history of Finnish consumer culture is somewhat shorter. It was not until the post-war period in the 1950s that Finnish consumer society began to flourish; prior to the 1950s and early 1960s, Finland was considered an agriculture-based society, which urbanised in the 1960s and 1970s (Heinonen, 2000; Heinonen & Pantzar, 2002). From the 1960s onwards, attitudes stressing the significance of saving money and self-sufficiency started to give way to more hedonistic consumer attitudes (Heinonen, 1998; Heinonen & Pantzar, 2002). According to empirical studies, modest attitudes towards consumption are still typical, particularly among representatives of the older generations (Huttunen & Autio, 2010; Räsänen, 2003; Wilska, 2002).

In terms of physical appearance, this downplay is also present in traditional Finnish sayings, emphasising the importance of modesty: 'modesty becomes you', as well as simple clothing: 'only ugly people parade with clothing' and 'a cake may look beautiful, but taste foul on the inside'. Finnish people are also known for their casual attitudes towards sporting outfits, calling themselves 'the nation of shell suits' (Vehkaoja, 2015). When looking at the streetscape on a typical cold and rainy autumn day, the mindset and the 'safety colours' of Finns seem impossible to miss. Various shades of grey and black coats are interwoven in the dull scenery under black umbrellas. Black is often said to be the favourite colour of the Finns. It is a safe choice as it is versatile and timeless, as well as ecological, because it never goes out of style (Viljanen, 2015).

Some of these stereotypes have their roots in Finnish history. When Finland was a part of the Kingdom of Sweden until 1809, the laws of Swedish estate society, which separated civics by their social status, were applied to Finland as well. One of those laws is the so-called 'luxury-act', which forbade lower estates from using certain luxurious clothing materials (such as silk, furs, tinsels). That law remained until 1816, seven years after the beginning of Finnish autonomy under the Russian Empire. In short, the official law controlled the appearances of the Finns to some extent at this point in history. The law enforced the idea that each person should look true to his or her social estate. At the same time, the church encouraged people to use simple and plain clothes that were preferably self-made. The Finns' appearance norms were explicitly regulated from above in the 1800s, although different local variations and sub-cultures with their unique appearance norms existed at the same time in different parts of Finland (Lempiäinen, 2016; Uotila, 2019, pp. 119–120).

Nowadays, the Finnish law does not divide people into groups by social status and define appearance norms for them, but the same spirit of being modest and 'not more than one is' still exists in the cultural heritage of Finns. Moreover, Finland's class structure is also more subtle and porous than that of the United Kingdom, for example. The elites have not developed class cultures to distinguish themselves from lower classes (Purhonen et al., 2010, p. 269). Rather, the elites generally avoid making conspicuous class distinctions, as this is seen as arrogant in Finland.

Another driving factor behind appearance norms underlining modesty is Finland's position as a highly egalitarian culture. Like other Nordic welfare states, Finland ranks high on gender equality indices (e.g. Crotti et al., 2020). Moreover, during discussions on the specific features of Nordic welfare states, their 'women-friendly' (Hernes, 1987) welfare policies are often brought up. These policies involve referring women to public care services, freeing women to enter the labour market and providing women with economic autonomy. The services also include universal social security system services and extensive public social care for reducing social inequality among Finnish women (e.g. Kangas & Palme, 2009; Virokannas et al., 2020). These aspects impact the general norms and moralities of the Finns, which probably also affect how appearance is seen and treated among Finns. For example, the general idea promoted in egalitarian societies is to treat people equally, which should apply to their visual appearances as well.

Geographical and Socio-demographical Peculiarities

The importance of aesthetics is often linked to urban culture and fashionable metropoles. Meanwhile Finland is known for its rather low population density

(18 persons per km^2), although it is slowly increasing as cities grow and rural areas wither (Worldometers, 2020). One could easily spot the differences in the appearances of Finns when one walks in the centre of Helsinki or Punkalaidun. Low population density seems to make a difference in terms of the appearance culture. For example, it means that fewer clothing shops are available for people living in rural areas. In addition, rural areas have fewer service occupations, in which the role of appearance is more pronounced, compared with urban areas. In urban areas with greater population density, more opportunities exist to consume appearance-related items. However, globalisation and the presence of online shops with free delivery have levelled the physical barriers of supply and created a wider spectrum of products available for Finns living in smaller regions in recent years. The Internet and mass media are significantly contributing to the global homogenisation of the conceptions of beauty. Moreover, today's appearance ideal is increasingly connected to social media (e.g. Tiggemann & Miller, 2010), especially for young people. Thus, the global range of acceptable appearances is becoming narrower, increasingly homogenised and globally aspirational (e.g. Jha, 2016; Widdows, 2018). Although the Finns previously emphasised their affinity for practicality and modesty, nowadays, they have also started to dress their children in expensive brands (e.g. Åberg & Huvila, 2019). In addition, some members of the younger generation like to distinguish themselves through the consumption of luxurious clothing (Blencowe, 2020).

In addition to possessing distinctive historical features, Finland has certain demographic peculiarities which play a role in shaping the normative landscape regarding physical appearance. Finland is a predominantly white country. A national myth about historic ethnic and cultural homogeneity exists but can be challenged (Tervonen, 2014). It is difficult to obtain reliable data on Finland's ethnic diversity, as the citizens' ethnicities are not registered in Finland (Nieminen, 2013). However, the lack of information on ethnicity can partly be supplemented with available information on first language and birth country. According to Statistics Finland, in 2019, only 8 percent of the Finnish population (by country of origin and language) has an origin other than a Finnish one (Statistics Finland, 2019). For example, in Sweden, about one-fifth of the population has a foreign origin (Statistics Sweden SCB, 2019). Although Finns' homogeneity is a myth, its population is ethnically less diverse compared with most European countries.

However, Finns' ethnic diversity is expected to increase in the future, as the fertility rate has been decreasing, and migration has been increasing in recent years. The discourse that highlights Finns' homogeneity and presents mainly white and otherwise normative appearances in the media has also been contested in recent years. For example, a nonprofit organisation, Ruskeat tytöt Ry ('brown girls registered association'), has successfully broadened the representations of 'brownness' in the field of culture, media and advertising, and it has advocated the diversity of the Finnish population. Moreover, the academic discussion regarding immigration and racism in Finland has been evolving since the beginning of the twenty-first century. Similarly, in recent years, Finnish universities have been encouraged to promote antiracist sensitivity in their curriculum content (Rastas, 2020).

Although Finland's streetscape is becoming less white, it is also becoming greyer. As in many other European countries, Finland's population is getting older. In 2019, Finland had one of the oldest populations in Europe with Germany, Italy, Portugal and Greece, which separates Finland from its Nordic neighbours, Sweden and Norway (Eurostat, 2019, p. 15). Younger people tend to pay more attention to appearance in general, and they face different types of appearance issues than older people do (Tiggemann & Slevec, 2012, p. 146). However, these differences do not necessarily reflect the more general appearance norms in society. Moreover, despite the fact that the population is growing older, the global consumer culture emphasises an ageless physical appearance, defining 'successful ageing' as ageing without giving the impression of doing so (Twigg, 2013). This discrepancy is also reflected in the anti-ageing industry, as older women especially respond to ageist social pressure to prevent the signs of ageing by investing in beauty interventions. These interventions include hair dye, make-up and surgical or non-surgical cosmetic procedures (Hurd Clarke & Griffin, 2007). It has been stated that Finland hardly differs from other countries in its attitudes regarding ageing (Ojala et al., 2016), so investing in anti-ageing practices and hiding the signs of ageing is expected, especially from women (Kukkonen et al., 2018). The appearance issues and norms of older people may achieve dominance in the culture if they are in the majority, but not this is not necessarily the case if the public imagery and discourse still favour presenting younger appearances more often.

Although some indicators show that the perceived importance of appearance has increased in recent years among Finns, they still see that looking good is a considerably less important value in life compared with work, a comfortable living, world peace or independence, for example (Sarpila et al., 2017). It may be conjectured that even urbanisation, globalisation and the Internet have not entirely caused the Finns to abandon their modest appearance ideals. However, little non-anecdotal data exist on the role of appearance in contemporary Finland and on the appearance relations of Finns. This book addresses these questions from various perspectives.

References

Anderson, T. L., Grunert, C., Katz, A., & Lovascio, S. (2010). Aesthetic capital: A research review on beauty perks and penalties. *Sociology Compass*, 4(8), 564–575. https://doi.org/10.1111/j.1751-9020.2010.00312.x

Autio, M. (2006). *Kuluttajuuden rakentuminen nuorten kertomuksissa*. Doctoral dissertation, University of Helsinki. http://hdl.handle.net/10138/20908

Balogun, O. M. (2020). *Beauty diplomacy*. Stanford University Press. https://doi.org/10.1515/9781503610989

Barnard, S. R. (2016). Spectacles of self (ie) empowerment? Networked individualism and the logic of the (post) feminist selfie. In L. Robinson, J. Schulz, S. R. Cotten, T. M. Hale, A. A. Williams, & J. L. Hightower (Eds.), *Communication and information technologies annual* (Vol. 11, pp. 63–88). Emerald Publishing Limited. https://doi.org/10.1108/S2050-2060201600000011014

Bauman, Z. (2007). *Consuming life*. Polity Press.

van den Berg, M. (2019). Precarious masculinities and gender as pedagogy: Aesthetic advice-encounters for the Dutch urban economy. *Gender, Place & Culture, 26*(5), 700–718. https://doi.org/10.1080/0966369X.2018.1551782

van den Berg, M., & Arts, J. (2019). The aesthetics of work-readiness: Aesthetic judgements and pedagogies for conditional welfare and post-Fordist labour markets. *Work, Employment & Society, 33*(2), 298–313. https://doi.org/10.1177/0950017018758196

Berggren, N., Jordahl, H., & Poutvaara, P. (2010). The looks of a winner: Beauty and electoral success. *Journal of Public Economics, 94*(1–2), 8–15. https://doi.org/10.1016/j.jpubeco.2009.11.002

van den Berg, M., & Vonk, L. (2020). The new discomforts of precarious workers: Wardrobe matter, insecurity and the temporality of calibration in dress work. *The Sociological Review, 68*(3), 574–589. https://doi.org/10.1177/0038026119892402

Bicchieri, C. (2006). *The grammar of society: The nature and dynamics of social norms*. Cambridge University Press.

Blencowe, A. (2020, March 10). Paljon sun outfit maksaa? Osa nuorista ja lapsista himoitsee 1 000 euron t-paitoja – "Tuntuu siltä, että jos ei ole merkkivaatteita, olet huonompi ihminen". Yle. https://yle.fi/uutiset/3-11247961

Boyle, B., & De Keere, K. (2019). Aesthetic labour, class and taste: Mobility aspirations of middle-class women working in luxury-retail. *The Sociological Review, 67*(3), 706–722. https://doi.org/10.1177/0038026119827753

Brunello, G., & d'Hombres, B. (2007). Does body weight affect wages? Evidence from Europe. *Economics and Human Biology, 5*(1), 1–19. https://doi.org/10.1016/j.ehb.2006.11.002

Buss, D. M., Abbott, M., Angleitner, A., Asherian, A., Biaggio, A., Blanco-Villasenor, A., & Ekehammar, B. (1990). International preferences in selecting mates: A study of 37 cultures. *Journal of Cross-Cultural Psychology, 21*(1), 5–47. https://doi.org/10.1177/0022022190211001

Cawley, J. (2004). The impact of obesity on wages. *Journal of Human Resources, 39*(2), 451–474. https://doi.org/10.3368/jhr.XXXIX.2.451

Coleman, J. S. (1990). *Foundations of social theory*. Cambridge, MA: Belknap Press of Harvard University Press.

Crotti, R., Geiger, T., Ratcheva, V., & Zahidi, S. (2020). *Global gender gap report 2020*. World Economic Forum. http://www3.weforum.org/docs/WEF_GGGR_2020.pdf

Dworkin, S. L., & Wachs, F. L. (2009). *Body panic: Gender, health, and the selling of fitness*. NYU Press.

Eagly, A. H., Ashmore, R. D., Makhijani, M. G., & Longo, L. C. (1991). What is beautiful is good, but: Meta-analysis of the beauty is good stereotype literature. *Psychological Bulletin, 110*, 109–128.

Edmonds, A., & Mears, A. (2017). Managing body capital in the fields of labor, sex, and health. In E. P. Anderson-Fye & A. Brewis (Eds.), *Fat planet: Obesity, culture, and symbolic body capital* (pp. 33–48). University of New Mexico Press.

Elias, A., Gill, R., & Scharff, C. (2017). Aesthetic labour: Beauty politics in neoliberalism. In A. S. Elias, R. Gill, & C. Scharff (Eds.), *Aesthetic labour: Rethinking beauty politics in neoliberalism* (pp. 3–49). Palgrave Macmillan.

Euromonitor. (2020). https://www.portal.euromonitor.com/portal/statisticsevolution/index

Eurostat. (2019). Ageing Europe - looking at the lives of older people in the EU. 2019 edition. https://doi.org/10.2785/811048

Featherstone, M. (1982). The body in consumer culture. *Theory, Culture & Society*, *1*(2), 18–33. https://doi.org/10.1177/026327648200100203

Featherstone, M. (1999). Body modification: An introduction. *Body & Society*, *5*(2–3), 1–13.

Featherstone, M. (2007). *Consumer culture and postmodernism*. Sage.

Featherstone, M. (2010). Body, image and affect in consumer culture. *Body & Society*, *16*(1), 193–221. https://doi.org/10.1177/1357034X09354357

Foucault, M. (1977). *Discipline and punish: The birth of the prison* [A. Sheridan (Trans.)]. London: Allen Lane Penguin.

Giddens, A. (1991). *Modernity and self-identity: Self and society in the late modern age*. Stanford University Press.

Gimlin, D. (2007). What is 'body work'? A review of the literature. *Sociology Compass*, *1*(1), 353–370. https://doi.org/10.1111/j.1751-9020.2007.00015.x

Goffman, E. (1959). *The presentation of self in everyday life*. Doubleday Anchor Books.

Grénman, M. (2019). *In quest of optimal self. Wellness consumption and lifestyle–A superficial marketing fad or a powerful means for transforming and branding oneself*. University of Turku.

Hakim, C. (2010). Erotic capital. *European Sociological Review*, *26*(5), 499–518. https://doi.org/10.1093/esr/jcq014

Hakim, J. (2018). 'The spornosexual': The affective contradictions of male body-work in neoliberal digital culture. *Journal of Gender Studies*, *27*(2), 231–241. https://doi.org/10.1080/09589236.2016.1217771

Hamermesh, D. S. (2011). *Beauty pays: Why attractive people are more successful*. Princeton University Press.

Hamermesh, D. S., & Biddle, J. E. (1994). Beauty and the labor market. *The American Economic Review*, *84*(5), 1174–1194.

Hechter, M., & Opp, K. D. (Eds.) (2001)., *Social norms*. Russell Sage Foundation.

Heinonen, V. (1998). *Talonpoikainen etiikka ja kulutuksen henki. Kotitalousneuvonnasta kuluttajapolitiikkaan 1900-luvun Suomessa [Peasant ethic and the spirit of consumption: From household advising to consumer policy in the 20th century Finland]*. Bibliotheca Historica 33. Suomen Historiallinen Seura.

Heinonen, V. (2000). Näin alkoi "kulutusjuhla": Suomalaisen yhteiskunnan rakenteistuminen. In K. Hyvönen, A. Juntto, & P. Laaksonen (Eds.), *Hyvää elämää – 90 vuotta suomalaista kulutustutkimusta* (pp. 8–22). Yliopistopaino.

Heinonen, V., & Pantzar, M. (2002). Little America: The modernization of the Finnish consumer society in the 1950s and 1960s. In M. Kipping & N. Tiratsoo (Eds.), *Americanisation in 20th century Europe: Business, culture, politics* (Vol. 2, pp. 41–59). Centre de Recherche sur l'Histoire de l'Europe du Nord-Ouest, Université Charles de Gaulle.

Heritage, J. (2013). *Garfinkel and ethnomethodology*. John Wiley & Sons.

Hernes, H. M. (1987). Women and the welfare state: The transition from private to public dependence. In A. S. Sassoon (Ed.), *Women and the state: The shifting boundaries of public and private* (pp. 72–92). Routledge.

Holla, S., & Kuipers, G. (2015). Aesthetic capital. In L. Hanquinet & M. Savage (Eds.), *International handbook for the sociology of art and culture* (pp. 290–304). Routledge.

Horne, C., & Mollborn, S. (2020). Norms. *Annual Review of Sociology*, *46*(4), 1–21. https://doi.org/10.1146/annurev-soc-121919-054658

Hosoda, M., Stone-Romero, E. F., & Coats, G. (2003). The effects of physical attractiveness on job-related outcomes: A meta-analysis of experimental studies. *Personnel Psychology*, *56*(2), 431–462. https://doi.org/10.1111/j.1744-6570.2003.tb00157.x

Hurd Clarke, L., & Griffin, M. (2007). The body natural and the body unnatural: Beauty work and aging. *Journal of Aging Studies*, *21*(3), 187–201.

Huttunen, K., & Autio, M. (2010). Consumer ethoses in Finnish consumer life stories–agrarianism, economism and green consumerism. *International Journal of Consumer Studies*, *34*(2), 146–152.

Jæger, M. M. (2011). "A thing of beauty is a joy forever"? Returns to physical attractiveness over the life course. *Social Forces*, *89*(3), 983–1003. https://doi.org/10.1093/sf/89.3.983

Jha, M. R. (2016). *The global beauty industry: Colorism, racism, and the national body.* Routledge.

Johnston, D. W. (2010). Physical appearance and wages: Do blondes have more fun? *Economics Letters*, *108*(1), 10–12. https://doi.org/10.1016/j.econlet.2010.03.015

Kangas, O., & Palme, J. (2009). Making social policy work for economic development: The nordic experience. *International Journal of Social Welfare*, *18*(s1), S62–S72. https://doi.org/10.1111/j.1468-2397.2009.00627.x

Klesse, C. (1999). Modern primitivism': Non-mainstream body modification and racialized representation. *Body & Society*, *5*(2/3), 15–38. https://doi.org/10.1177/1357034X99005002002

Koskinen, V. (2020). *Building skills for lifelong wellness: An empirical study on the wellness-oriented lifestyle.* University of Jyväskylä.

Kuipers, G. (2015). Beauty and distinction? The evaluation of appearance and cultural capital in five European countries. *Poetics*, *53*, 38–51. https://doi.org/10.1016/j.poetic.2015.10.001

Kuipers, G. (2019, March). 'Beauty and inequality' [keynote presentation], sosiologipäivät (the annual sociological conference), Turku, Finland.

Kukkonen, I., Åberg, E., Sarpila, O., & Pajunen, T. (2018). Exploitation of aesthetic capital–disapproved by whom? *International Journal of Sociology & Social Policy*, *38*(3/4), 312–328. https://doi.org/10.1108/IJSSP-09-2017-0116

Kwan, S., & Trautner, M. N. (2009). Beauty work: Individual and institutional rewards, the reproduction of gender, and questions of agency. *Sociology Compass*, *3*(1), 49–71. https://doi.org/10.1111/j.1751-9020.2008.00179.x

van der Laan, E., & Kuipers, G. (2016). How aesthetic logics shape a cultural field: Differentiation and consolidation in the transnational field of fashion images, 1982–2011. *Poetics*, *56*, 64–84. https://doi.org/10.1016/j.poetic.2016.01.001

Langlois, J. H., Kalakanis, L., Rubenstein, A. J., Larson, A., Hallam, M., & Smoot, M. (2000). Maxims or myths of beauty? A meta-analytic and theoretical review. *Psychological Bulletin*, *126*(3), 390–423.

Lempiäinen, P. (2016). *Vaatteet, muoti ja asema: Oululaisten pukeutuminen 1600-luvulla.* Master's thesis, University of Helsinki. http://urn.fi/URN:NBN:fi:hulib-201611293139

Lenneis, V., & Pfister, G. (2017). Health messages, middle-aged women and the pleasure of play. *Annals of Leisure Research*, *20*(1), 55–74. https://doi.org/10.1080/11745398.2016.1207091.

Lupton, D. (1995). *The imperative of health: Public health and the regulated body*. Sage.

Maestripieri, D., Henry, A., & Nickels, N. (2017). Explaining financial and prosocial biases in favor of attractive people: Interdisciplinary perspectives from economics, social psychology, and evolutionary psychology. *Behavioral and Brain Sciences, 40*: e19. https://doi.org/10.1017/S0140525X16000340

Mathes, E. W., & Kozak, G. (2008). The exchange of physical attractiveness for resource potential and commitment. *Journal of Evolutionary Psychology, 6*(1), 43–56. https://doi.org/10.1556/jep.2008.1004

McClintock, E. A. (2014). Beauty and status: The illusion of exchange in partner selection? *American Sociological Review, 79*(4), 575–604. https://doi.org/10.1177/0003122414536391

McDowell, L. (2009). *Working bodies: Interactive service employment and workplace identities*. Wiley-Blackwell.

Mears, A. (2011). *Pricing beauty: The making of a fashion model*. University of California Press.

Mears, A. (2014). Aesthetic labor for the sociologies of work, gender, and beauty. *Sociology Compass, 8*(12), 1330–1343. https://doi.org/10.1111/soc4.12211

Mears, A. (2020). *Very important people: Status and beauty in the global party circuit*. Princeton.

Nieminen, J. (2013). Etnisyystiedon merkitys kasvaamaahanmuuton lisääntyessä. *Hyvinvointikatsaus*. 3/2013. https://www.stat.fi/artikkelit/2013/art_2013-09-23_003.html?s=0

Ojala, H., Calasanti, T., King, N., & Pietilä, I. (2016). Natural(ly) men: Masculinity and gendered anti-ageing practices in Finland and the USA. *Ageing and Society, 36*(2), 356–375. https://doi.org/10.1017/S0144686X14001196

Parkkonen, T. (2020, December 27). Kumpi on auttanut enemmän koronaviruksen torjunnassa, Sara Sieppi vai kansanedustaja? *Iltalehti*. https://www.iltalehti.fi/politiikka/a/82e73d10-780e-406e-8f3d-469a9896f333

Parviainen, J., Kinnunen, T., & Kortelainen, I. (2016). Johdatus työruumiin tutkimukseen [An introduction to the study of the working body]. In J. Parviainen, T. Kinnunen, & I. Kortelainen (Eds.), *Ruumiillisuus ja työelämä: Työruumis jälkiteollisessa taloudessa* (pp. 9–75). Vastapaino.

Purhonen, S., Gronow, J., & Rahkonen, K. (2010). Nordic democracy of taste? Cultural omnivorousness in musical and literary taste preferences in Finland. *Poetics, 38*(3), 266–298. https://doi.org/10.1016/j.poetic.2010.03.003

Räsänen, P. (2003). *In the twilight of social structures: A mechanism-based study of contemporary consumer behavior*. Doctoral dissertation, University of Turku.

Rastas, A. (2020). Rasismikeskustelu suomalaisissa yliopistoissa. *Tieteessä tapahtuu, 38*(2), 45–49.

Sarpila, O., & Erola, J. (2016). Physical attractiveness—who believes it is a ticket to success? *Research on Finnish Society, 9*, 5–14.

Sarpila, O., Pajunen, T., Kekäläinen, S., & Åberg, E. (2017). Onko ulkonäön arvostus nousussa Suomessa? *Yhteiskuntapolitiikka, 82*(1), 86–93.

Sarpila, O., Räsänen, P., Erola, J., Kekki, J., & Pitkänen, K. (2010). *Suomi 2009. Tutkimusseloste ja aineistojen 1999–2009 vertailua*. Turun yliopisto/sosiaalitieteiden laitos.

Sassatelli, R. (2010). *Fitness culture: Gyms and the commercialisation of discipline and fun*. Palgrave Macmillan.

Shilling, C. (2004). Physical capital and situated action: A new direction for corporeal sociology. *British Journal of Sociology of Education, 25*(4), 473–487. https://doi.org/ 10.1080/0142569042000236961

Shilling, C. (2007). Sociology and the body: Classical traditions and new agendas. *The Sociological Review, 55*, 1–18. https://doi.org/10.1111/j.1467-954X.2007.00689.x

Shilling, C. (2012). *The body and social theory.* Sage.

Smith Maguire, J. (2008). *Fit for consumption: Sociology and the business of fitness.* Routledge.

Statistics Finland. (2019). *Population.* https://www.stat.fi/tup/suoluk/suoluk_vaesto_en. html. Accessed on November 18, 2020.

Statistics Sweden, SCB. (2019). Summary of population statistics 1960–2019. https:// www.scb.se/en/finding-statistics/statistics-by-subject-area/population/population-composition/population-statistics/pong/tables-and-graphs/yearly-statistics–the-whole-country/summary-of-population-statistics/. Accessed on November 18, 2020.

Tervonen, M. (2014). Historiankirjoitus ja myytti yhden kulttuurin Suomesta. In P. Markkula, H. Snellman, & AC. Östman (Eds.), *Kotiseutu ja kansakunta: Miten suomalaista historiaa on rakennettu* (pp. 137–162). SKS.

Tiggemann, M., & Miller, J. (2010). The Internet and adolescent girls' weight satisfaction and drive for thinness. *Sex Roles, 63*(1–2), 79–90. https://doi.org/10.1007/ s11199-010-9789-z

Tiggemann, M., & Slevec, J. (2012). Appearance in adulthood. In N. Rumsey & D. Harcourt (Eds.), *The Oxford handbook of the psychology of appearance* (pp. 142–159). Oxford: Oxford University Press.

Tiidenberg, K., & Gómez Cruz, E. (2015). Selfies, image and the re-making of the body. *Body & Society, 21*(4), 77–102. https://doi.org/10.1177/1357034X15592465

Turner, B. S. (2008). *The body & society* (3rd ed.). Sage Publications.

Twigg, J. (2013). *Fashion and age: Dress, the body and later life.* A&C Black.

Uotila, M. (2019). Kun talonpojat ryhtyivät kuluttamaan. Pukeutuminen miehen aseman ja varallisuuden ilmentäjänä 1800-luvun alun suomalaisessa maaseutuyhteisössä. In A. Niiranen & A. Turunen (Eds.), *Säädyllistä ja säädytöntä. Pukeutumisen historiaa renessanssista 2000-luvulle.* SKS.

Vehkaoja, M. (2015, March 22). Tämä nainen teki meistä tuulipukukansan. Seura. https://seura.fi/asiat/tutkivat/tama-nainen-teki-meista-tuulipukukansan/

Viljanen, K. (2015, December 14). Suomalainen rakastaa mustaa, sillä se suojaa häntä maailmalta. *Helsingin Sanomat.* https://www.hs.fi/kulttuuri/art-2000002872299.html

Virokannas, E., Salovaara, U., Krok, S., & Kuronen, M. (2020). Finnish welfare system from the standpoint of women in vulnerable life situations. In M. Kuronen, E. Virokannas, & U. Salovaara (Eds.), *Women, vulnerabilities and welfare service systems* (pp. 26–38). Routledge.

Webster, M., Jr, & Driskell, J. E., Jr (1983). Beauty as status. *American Journal of Sociology, 89*(1), 140–165. https://doi.org/10.1086/227836

Widdows, H. (2018). *Perfect me: Beauty as an ethical ideal.* Princeton University Press.

Williams, C. L., & Connell, C. (2010). "Looking good and sounding right": Aesthetic labor and social inequality in the retail industry. *Work and Occupations, 37*(3), 349–377. https://doi.org/10.1177/0730888410373744

Wilska, T. A. (2002). Me–a consumer? Consumption, identities and lifestyles in today's Finland. *Acta Sociologica, 45*(3), 195–210. https://doi.org/10.1177/ 000169930204500302

Wilska, T.-A. (2002). Me–a consumer? Consumption, identities and lifestyles in today's Finland. *Acta Sociologica, 45*(3), 195–210.

Wolf, N. (1990/2002). *The beauty myth: How images of beauty are used against women.* Harper Collins.

Worldomoters.info. (2020). Finland population. https://www.worldometers.info/world-population/finland-population/. Accessed on November 18, 2020.

Xenitidou, M., & Edmonds, B. (Eds.). (2014). *The complexity of social norms.* Springer.

Åberg, E., & Huvila, J. (2019). Hip children, good mothers–children's clothing as capital investment? *Young Consumers, 20*(3), 153–166. https://doi.org/10.1108/YC-06-2018-00816

Part I
Accumulating a Gendered Form of Capital

Chapter 1

Physical Appearance as a Form of Capital: Key Problems and Tensions

Iida Kukkonen

Introduction

> Beauty is having a moment in the social sciences.
>   (Mears, 2014, p. 1130)

Social scientists are increasingly turning to the body, and in particular its visual appearance, to understand social inequalities in contemporary societies. Many are finding the Bourdieusian metaphor of capital useful for understanding the connections between inequality and the body or physical appearance. In the past decades, scholars have variably referred to aspects of the body and its visual presentation as physical capital (Shilling, 1991, 2004), bodily capital (Connell & Mears, 2018; Wacquant, 1995), girl capital (Mears, 2015a, 2015b), aesthetic capital (Anderson et al., 2010; Balogun, 2020; Holla & Kuipers, 2015), sexual capital (Green, 2008, 2013, 2014; Martin & George, 2006) or erotic capital (Hakim, 2010, 2011).

In general, sociology suffers from what Neveu (2018) calls the 'shopping list syndrome' of capital. The symptoms of this syndrome appear as the Bourdieusian concept of capital is utilised loosely to refer to any single form of power, causing possible inflation the capital metaphor and, subsequently, an inflation of the whole Bourdieusian understanding of social class and structure. (Neveu, 2018). A glance at the shopping list of capital demonstrates that the Bourdieusian capital metaphor is often understood in a manner which promotes a neoliberal perspective of the self as a capital-accruing subject free of structural restraints rather than as a metaphor for class (re)production (see Connell & Mears, 2018).

Appearance as Capital, 23–37
Copyright © 2022 Iida Kukkonen
Published by Emerald Publishing Limited. These works are published under the Creative Commons Attribution (CC BY 4.0) licence. Anyone may reproduce, distribute, translate and create derivative works of these works (for both commercial and non-commercial purposes), subject to full attribution to the original publication and authors. The full terms of this licence may be seen at http://creativecommons.org/licences/by/4.0/legalcode
doi:10.1108/978-1-80043-708-120210002

It is, however, unclear whether contemporary social scientists concerned with the body and aesthetics are contributing to the shopping list syndrome of capital in adopting and employing the metaphor of capital. It is possible such social scientists are unearthing an important 'forgotten capital' to which Bourdieu failed to pay adequate attention – one that has to do with the body and aesthetics (Neveu, 2018).

A chief problem with understanding the physical and aesthetic as capital lies, according to Neveu, in that such capital would require its own specific laws of capital conversion. Writing specifically about erotic or sexual capital, Neveu points out many of the gains of erotic or sexual capital are labelled as sins and carry powerful stigmas (Neveu, 2018). Other forms of bodily or aesthetic capital are subject to powerful social supervision, too. In this chapter, I propose that it is particularly through paying careful scholarly attention to such social rules, or norms, that we can understand how physical appearances may or may not act as a form of capital, and as such contribute to social inequality. In sum, I (re-)claim the 'laws' of capital conversion depend on social norms, which may differ across social fields. I further suggest that such rules of capital conversion are structured by the social inequalities of these fields.

Some of the social norms steering capital conversion may be very localised, situational or temporary, others may be national, even global, and more enduring. As such, looking for universal laws of aesthetic capital conversion would be futile. Nevertheless, current scholarship on appearance-related capital has already identified certain commonalities, particularly in terms of how gender is implied in these conversions (e.g. Kukkonen et al., 2018; Sarpila et al., 2020).

A major problem with understanding the physical and aesthetic as capital lies in the underlying, ultimately reductionist understanding of social life as an exercise in capital exchange and of people, or subjects, as always being primarily interested in capital exchange. According to Skeggs, the idea of the capital-accruing subject is inherently middle class. Not everyone treats or understands themselves as projects of capital accumulation and exchange. Capital remains a useful metaphor, but it should not be reduced to an understanding of all people striving to maximise their capital (Skeggs, 2004).

This chapter focuses on how the capital metaphor has been employed to understand physical appearance -related inequalities. I commence with a brief overview of Bourdieu's understanding of capital and the body, and move on to scrutinising more contemporary conceptualisations of bodily or appearance-related capital. After that, I discuss how the content of what constitutes appearance-related capital has always been and will be in flux, and how not everyone considers their bodies as sites of capital investment. I then consider how conversions of capital are, overall, driven by social norms, after which I make a first draft of the grammar of the accumulation and conversion of what I call 'aesthetic capital'. Finally, I conclude with my thoughts on physical appearances a form of capital.

Bourdieu's Forms of Capital and the Body

While terms such as aesthetic, erotic or sexual capital are commonplace if not in everyday parlance then at least in sociological jargon, Pierre Bourdieu (1984,

2011/1986) did not directly consider the body or its appearance as a form of capital in itself. Bourdieu did have a keen interest in bodies, and his scholarship was beyond its years in foregrounding embodiment and the material – turns which humanism and social sciences only took in the 90s. For Bourdieu, bodies were the very loci of inequality: places where capital accrues, is made visible and appropriable.

In his early scholarship in the 60s, before developing his influential theory of the forms of capital, Bourdieu conducted ethnographic research among peasants. He described how in his childhood village of Béarn, the economic, social and cultural conditions had not just affected peasant men's bodies, but indeed, the agricultural labour was manifoldly inscribed on the bodies he studied. Not only were the peasant bodies physically shaped by labour, but the peasants also valued their bodies in terms of strength and durability. These bodies were, however, devalued as an asset in mating markets and appeared awkward to the peasants at the village dance. While peasant women from the village adopted fashions and movements from the town, peasant men with their peasant bodies and moves did not feel comfortable dancing. Bourdieu claimed many of the peasants he studied, thus, remained single (Bourdieu, 2004/1962).

Beginning in his early sociological works, Bourdieu was extremely preoccupied with bodies and the social, cultural and economic value inscribed on them. His sociology is corporeal. In his works, Bourdieu referred to the social, economic and cultural conditions inscribed on bodies using terms such as habitus, hexis, doxa and praxis (Bourdieu, 1984, 2013/1977). However, the perhaps strongest of the metaphors he used is that of capital. Along the lines of Marxist thinking, Bourdieu defined capital as 'accumulated labor (in its materialized form or its "incorporated", embodied form) which, when appropriated on a private, i.e., exclusive, basis by agents or groups of agents, enables them to appropriate social energy in the form of reified or living labor' (Bourdieu, 2011/1986, p. 81).

The most condensed version of Bourdieu's formulation of the forms of capital includes three forms of capital: economic, social and cultural. Economic capital refers to wealth that is directly convertible to money. Social capital is made up of the actual or potential benefits of belonging to certain social groups or networks. Cultural capital exists in an objectified state (e.g. books, pictures), an institutionalised state (e.g. educational qualifications) and, importantly, in an embodied state consisting of quite stable dispositions of the mind and body. Bourdieu also talks about symbolic capital, which is the form social, cultural and economic capital take when they are not perceived as capital, i.e. products of social labour, but rather as something 'innate', such as when accumulated labour is misrecognised as competence (Bourdieu, 2011/1986).

Bourdieu did not view capital as something that follows certain universal laws but as something that is always situated in social context, or what he referred to as a social field. For him, the way capital (re)produces social inequality is tied to social structure: '*The structure of the field, i.e., the unequal distribution of capital, is the source of the specific effects of capital*, i.e., the appropriation of profits and the power to impose the laws of functioning of the field most favorable to capital and its reproduction' (Bourdieu, 2011/1986, p. 84 [italics by Kukkonen]). While

Bourdieu regarded social fields as social spaces conditioned chiefly by economic, social and cultural capital, he did not think these are the only forms of capital that exist[1], but suggested rather these three were for him the 'three fundamental guises' of capital (2011/1986, p. 82).

Bourdieu mostly considered the body as the locus of inequality and not a form of inequality or capital in and of itself. Yet, he did also discuss, for example, *physical capital* in the context of sports (Bourdieu, 1978). He conceived of the development of such physical capital through sports as:

> [...] one of the few paths of upward mobility open to the children of the dominated classes; the sports market is to the boys' physical capital what the system of beauty prizes and the occupations to which they lead – hostess, etc. – is to the girls' physical capital [...].
>
> (1978, p. 832)

This very same idea – that bodily capital is not always just a simple sum of economic, social and cultural capital but instead has potential over and beyond these forms of capital – is echoed in *Distinction*, where Bourdieu notes how physical appearance sometimes challenges and shakes up the class system that is based on the forms of capital (1978, p. 193). This suggests that Bourdieu was aware of the fact that appearance may, in certain contexts, have exchange value that is independent of the three 'fundamental guises' (Bourdieu, 2011/1986, p. 82) or 'elementary forms' (Neveu, 2018) of capital.

Different Formulations of Appearance-related Capital

Overall, Bourdieu's ideas about the body, taste and capital have had a seminal impact on how scholars approach physical appearance as a form of inequality. Scholars have followed in Bourdieu's footsteps to varying extents, sometimes very explicitly and straightforwardly incorporating his ideas, and sometimes more subtly and implicitly referencing some of his conceptual tools without necessarily retaining the understanding of power and domination inherent in his theories. In this section, I briefly discuss different strands of scholarship that have looked at the body and its appearance as a distinct form of capital and labour in a Bourdieusian sense. By taking this focus, I regrettably exclude important studies that discuss appearance and cultural capital (e.g. Kuipers, 2015).

Physical, Bodily and Sexual Capital

Chris Shilling (1991) sought to elaborate on Bourdieu's theory through the concept of physical capital. He claimed the physical was too important to be reduced to a subform of capital. He was perhaps the first to claim physical capital is not just expressive of class location but actually magnifies social inequalities because people have different possibilities for converting physical capital into other forms of capital (p. 565). Loïc Wacquant, who studied under Bourdieu and collaborated with him, conducted ethnographic studies among boxers who cultivated their bodily capital. Crucially, Wacquant notes that this bodily capital was appropriated, owned and controlled by brokers; it was not just the boxer who benefited from their capital (Wacquant, 1995). Both Shilling and Wacquant focused on forms of appearance-related capital that are very physical and may be considered masculine: movement and strength. In the marriage markets of peasant fields of Béarn, these may not have constituted capital, but in boxing rings and athletic fields at school, movement and strength certainly matter.

The current trend of regarding the body as a somewhat distinct form of capital began with sociologists of sexuality, including Martin and George (2006) and Green (2008, 2013, 2014), who meticulously deployed and developed Bourdieu-sian concepts in their studies of sexual culture and fields. In Bourdieusian field theory, capital exchange happens in socially embedded markets or fields: actual social contexts in which people inhabit different locations, i.e. social positions. Adam Isaiah Green described this vividly, relating how he, as a doctoral student, had walked from Chelsea to the West Village, two districts on the small island of Manhattan located around 1.5 km from one another:

> In these settings [the gay scene of Chelsea], I grew keenly, often painfully aware of my body and its bearing, the fit of my clothing, the affect of my gait, the pump (or lack thereof) of my muscles, the expression on my face. [...] Walking south, below Fourteenth Street, I entered the West Village, and the change from one sexual field to another was abrupt and palpable, as if I had crossed into an entirely new geography. [...] The faces were less often white, the bodies less uniformly gym trained, the affect less controlled and more colorful, the clothing more varied, and the men typically older than I by at least a decade, often two.
>
> (2014, p. 3)

Fields are constituted by relationships between actors, and those relationships are not equal. People enter fields with different kinds of power resources, including, but not limited to, the 'fundamental' forms of capital. Age, gender, race, sexual orientation and related categorisations matter on social fields. It is on diverse fields that the value of capital is negotiated (more of less implicitly). Indeed, scholars of sexual capital and fields propose exchange value is a property of fields more than of individuals.

An Economist Approach to Capital

Economists have conducted quantitative research on appearance-related socio-economic inequalities for decades. Sociology was slow to catch up on the turn to appearances (Mears, 2014), and when it did, it incorporated much of the research in economics as a foundation and built research upon such scholarship. Socio-logical review articles on the topic of beauty and related inequalities (Kwan &

Trautner, 2009) and aesthetic capital (Anderson et al., 2010) took the totality of economic research as a starting point for their literature reviews. However, while economic research identifies the phenomenon of appearances being congruent with capital, it often turns to other sciences to explain it. In economics, aesthetic capital is often understood in terms of individual beauty, which has individual benefits: 'beauty pays' (Hamermesh, 2011). Sometimes it is understood as human capital, a concept which comes with the idea that human capital can, and should, be cultivated (for a discussion, see Holla & Kuipers, 2015).

The idea of aesthetic capital as a form of cultivable capital was popularised by Catherine Hakim, who published her 'theory of erotic capital' in 2010. The theory was deemed politically problematic but also internally inconsistent (Green, 2013), but it certainly caused a stir and popularised the idea of the (female) body as capital. Hakim (2010, 2011) believes appearance-related capital, or erotic capital as she calls it, is 'by nature' something that women possess more of. She urges women to accumulate and exploit this 'honey money' to remedy gender inequality. She suggests that while all women are not natural-born beauties, all females can benefit from beauty if they work on their appearance and dare to use beauty to their benefit.

Hakim's theory may be considered a prime example of what certain feminist critics consider postfeminism (Gill, 2017; McRobbie, 2009): a gendered neoliberal ideology which stresses female agency and power while obfuscating or disregarding structural inequalities, including class. Indeed, class-based physical differences are easily regarded as products of choices or lifestyle and in terms of individual responsibility (Vandebroeck, 2017, p. 232). Although Hakim's idea of erotic capital says to have its roots in Bourdieu's theory, it appears to have been largely inspired by economic theory instead. Hakim conceives of capital as if it were 'natural', meritocratic and individual rather than social and unequal, as if capital exchange happens on free markets according to the universal laws of supply and demand. Such a conceptualisation of markets is very different from the one held by scholars engaged in Bourdieusian field theory.

Gendered Capital and Labour

Bourdieu's theory of capital was, for some reason, not easy for feminists to engage with. While gender scholars working on the topic of bodies and appearances happily drew from other influential sociologists, importantly Foucault (e.g. Bartky, 1990; Bordo, 2003/1993), Bourdieu did not really trend among feminist scholars. As Adkins (2004) points out, the reason is not just that Bourdieu failed to include an understanding of gender in his theories (see, however, Bourdieu, 2001, 2013/1977). Foucault, too, dismissed gender in his ponderings. Nevertheless, most feminist thinking about the body took a Foucauldian direction (Adkins, 2004).

Meanwhile in the early 2000s, scholars of labour, organisation and gender turned to Arlie Hochschild's concept of emotional labour (Hochschild, 1983) to understand contemporary service economies but noticed that the labour they were studying was not just emotional but aesthetic as well. A new term, *aesthetic labour*, was coined (Warhurst & Nickson, 2001) to denote how in the service economy, workers' bodies are screened, cultivated and managed for commercial purposes, i.e. profit (for a review, see Mears, 2014). It is clear that aesthetic labour shares analytic similarities with theories of bodily capital (see Mears, 2014). However, the scholarship on aesthetic labour also involves a nuanced under-standing of power as more than just a sum of forms of capital. It incorporates discussions on the distribution of power in situated late-capitalist settings, where people face bodily expectations and norms chiefly as profit-producing entities in organisations as customers, employers, (potential) employees, entrepreneurs and freelancers (Boyle & De Keere, 2019; Entwistle & Wissinger, 2006; Hracs & Leslie, 2014; Pettinger, 2008; van den Berg & Arts, 2019). The scholarship has also paid particular attention to how the distributions of power, wherein appearances and their value at and for work depend on gender, sexuality, ethnicity and age, and how different aesthetic qualities related to such social categorisations, i.e. femininity, heterosexuality, whiteness and youthfulness, are invoked and curated for commercial benefit (van den Berg & Arts, 2019).

Recently, working with and beyond Bourdieu, scholars including Ashley Mears and Oluwakemi Balogun have used aesthetic or 'girl' capital as a lens through which to consider how women in the beauty and entertainment industries navigate such realms and the power imbalances involved in making the best of their capital, while at the same time maintaining standards of respectability. Both Mears and Balogun take seriously the agency of the women in their research, while at the same time highlighting how the exchange of female aesthetic capital is often reliant on male intermediaries and how a great deal of the profits involved actually accrue to these men (Balogun, 2020; Mears, 2020).

The Flux of Aesthetic Capital

In 2010, Anderson at al. reviewed the scholarship on beauty perks and penalties and proposed a working definition for aesthetic capital as combination of appearance-related resources, including facial traits, body shape, size and physique, hair, beard, styles of dressing and grooming (p. 566). This is, perhaps, a good start for a definition because it is indeterminate; it does not say what kinds of facial traits or body size constitute capital. This is crucial because capital can hardly be a list of traits; bodily traits and styles gain their exchange value in everyday social exchanges in various fields, where valuation, and indeed value, is in constant flux.

Hence, the bodily shapes, facial traits or fashions that are valued as resources today are different from those that could be exchanged and appropriated tomorrow. For example, the association between status and a slim and toned body is a relatively recent development (cf. Mennell, 1987). Looking at an old painting or reading a classic novel written in a time when food was not abun-dantly available, it becomes clear fat was beauty and it served as capital. It still does in certain parts of the world (see, e.g., Wiley, 2018 on Mauritanian beauty).

Another example which illustrates the social construction of appearance-related capital is the tanned (white) body, which became a status signifier and, hence, a resource at the time when it came to signify leisure instead of work in the fields. As more white people gained access to inexpensive flights to the south and solariums opened up even in the deepest heart of Lapland, tan lost its upper-status significance. These days, being too tanned or having too much fat is scorned – a prime example of this being reality television, which presents working-class bodies as abject and in need of transformation (McRobbie, 2009; Ringrose & Walkerdine, 2008; Skeggs, 2009).

In contemporary consumer culture, the concept of capital is often interpreted as if everyone has equal interest in and equal opportunity to accumulate aesthetic capital that is considered legitimate at that time and to exploit it. Connell and Mears (2018) criticise scholarship on bodily capital for endorsing such a neoliberal perspective of the self as a bundle of assets that can be used for personal gain and ignoring the structural inequalities that define beauty and guide the uneven distribution of what they call bodily capital (pp. 561–562). Indeed, the use of economic metaphors such as capital may be interpreted as reproductive of the very system of capitalist capital accumulation they wish to criticise.

Writing about the general concept of capital, Skeggs stresses the concept of the capital-accruing subject is inherently middle class and exchange value is a middle-class value (Skeggs, 2004). The so-called entrepreneurial self who rationally invests in their body and their self is arguably the ideal subject *of the middle classes.*

Working-class subjects may cultivate their own ideals that sometimes have nothing to do with accumulating exchange value, as Beverley Skeggs' empirical research suggests. Skeggs unpacks exchange value from use value: whereas exchange value bears potential for becoming economically valuable, use value carries possibilities for considering oneself valuable outside the system of middle-class values and ideals (Skeggs, 2004). Skeggs' thinking highlights how not all systems of value operate according to a simple standard of middle-class exchange value. In some fields, aesthetic practices carry different meanings and different values. For example, glamour can be inexpensively emulated and is, as such, quite democratic (Holliday & Taylor, 2006). Glamour does not necessarily aim at exchange for any socio-economic benefits; indeed it may be of little exchange value in, for example, labour markets. Nevertheless, it may carry use value.

Reducing all beauty practices to status-seeking and assuming everyone is equally interested in capital exchange is problematic. Overemphasising aesthetic capital as a strategic, meritocratic or universal resource fails to take into account that: first, not all agency is directed at capital accumulation (Skeggs, 2004); second, agency is structured by inequality (Schneikert et al., 2020); and third, agents are bound by social norms.

The Grammar of Exchanging Aesthetic Capital

Norms, essentially informal rules, comprise the 'grammar of society' (Bicchieri, 2006). Economic sociology and field theory both presuppose markets or fields are like any other social constellations in that they are bound by such social grammar. Indeed, a basic premise of economic sociology is that no free markets wherein exchange of capital happens exist because markets are always socially embedded (Swedberg, 2009).

Fields or markets can be very local (e.g. a particular bar or a subforum, or the online and offline market or field for collectors of particular items) and have their own local grammar or set of norms. While fields or markets may be very small or local and their unequal systems of value and exchange were very different one from another, this does not mean that there are no national or even global grammars. While different social fields constitute independent social contexts, they are nevertheless interconnected, as 'agents parlay their capital from one field to another' (Green, 2014, p. 13).

While at any given point, the social world can be divided into an infinite number of markets or fields, these bleed into and combine with one another; after all, a field or a market is a conceptual tool for delineating and studying a particular social constellation. Hence, social fields may be highly situational and temporary, as in a given nightclub or online chat room on a given night or a particular company at a given time. We may call the social norms that structure this field's micro-level norms. We can also draw the boundaries of a social field so that it constitutes a particular selection of people, such as Finnish people working in particular jobs. The norms that structure the conversions of capital in different occupational field might be considered meso-level norms. Finally, we can take a bird's view and look at, for example, the Finnish society as a whole, and consider the norms that structure the exchange of capital on such a large field, that is, macro-level norms.

The norms of any given field were shaped in the past and are shaped in the present in social interaction, in which people were never equal (as Bourdieu put it, 'the social world is accumulated history' (2011/1986, pp. 81)). People, thus, have different opportunities to define what constitutes value on a given field and to engage in exchange. However, norms do not only define the value of capital on a certain market but also govern the conditions of its exchange. They determine how and by whom capital may be exchanged.

Bourdieu referred to such social norms as 'the rules of the game' and highlighted how the upper classes with their accumulated capital are socialised to know these rules by heart and to know how to deploy them strategically. In a Bourdieusian sense, capital exchange is not just about carrying capital on a certain field, but it is also about how well one knows the system of value and exchange, and how well one is able to use this system to further one's accumulation of capital (Bourdieu, 1984, 2011/1986).

Bourdieu thought the rules of the game were rigged, particularly against the lower classes. It is somewhat peculiar that it did not really occur to Bourdieu that rules of exchange are unequal not only in terms of class but also in terms of other social categorisations that affect capital accumulation, including, for example, ethnicity and gender. Certain feminists have thought 'with and against Bourdieu' (Lovell, 2000) to understand the entanglement of class and gender (see also Adkins, 2004). Skeggs (1997) shows how femininity is inherently classed and also racialised. Moi (1991) suggests gender structures social fields. From this perspective, a player's position in the field is not the simple function of their habitus and their volume of different capitals, but other classifications also influence how one is inscribed in the grammar of capital exchange.

Thus, different people have different possibilities for exchanging aesthetic capital. The exchange of capital can be divided into the *accumulation* and *conversion* of aesthetic capital in social exchange (e.g. Sarpila et al., 2020). If we consider aesthetic capital a fourth 'elementary' capital (for a discussion, see Neveu, 2018) which compliments economic, social and cultural capital, then the accumulation of aesthetic capital means the exchange of economic, social or cultural capital for aesthetic capital. Likewise, the conversion of aesthetic capital means the exchange of aesthetic capital for economic, social and cultural capital.

Accumulation of aesthetic capital happens chiefly as a conversion of economic and cultural capital to aesthetic capital. The conversion of economic capital to aesthetic capital happens mainly through consumer practices, many of them laborious. That is, it is not enough to buy appearance-related consumer items, but these must be used (e.g. toothpaste, shampoo, trainers), applied (e.g. make-up, facial masks) and taken care of (e.g. ironing clothes) on a daily basis. Conversion is, thus, very time-consuming, even as much of the appearance work of consumers can be and is outsourced, as when a consumer visits a dental hygienist, a cosmetologists or hairdresser. The conversion of cultural capital to aesthetic capital happens through taste. As doing consumer practices 'right' requires cultural capital (Bourdieu, 1984), the successful accumulation and display of aesthetic capital strongly depends on cultural capital (Holla & Kuipers, 2015; see also Luna, 2019). Those endowed with more capital can 'afford' to engage in long-term, future-oriented and more subtle means of investing in their bodies and looks, while those with less capital tend to prefer practices of accumulation that produce quicker and more visible results (Vandebroeck, 2017). The subtler and more time-consuming forms of accumulation are particularly prone to being (mis) perceived as natural, innate differences and to be appraised as valuable symbolic capital.

The norms that guide conversions, which amount to the accumulation of aesthetic capital, are first and foremost gendered. Women are expected to accumulate aesthetic capital, while for men, such capital accumulation is less approved of (Kukkonen et al., 2018; Sarpila et al., 2020, see also Ojala and Pietilä, Chapter 4). Gimlin (2007) explains such gendered expectations by pointing out that while all bodies are required to work on their bodies in order to transform them from the 'natural' state to a 'cultural' state, groups traditionally associated with the 'nature' side of the nature/culture dichotomy (e.g. females, non-whites) need to work more on 'culturing' their bodies (see also Black, 2004).

Conversions of aesthetic capital are well documented (for reviews, see Anderson et al., 2010; Hosoda et al., 2003; Maestripieri et al., 2017) and can happen as conversion from aesthetic capital to social capital, such as when a person considered beautiful gains friends, potential or actual partners or, for example, followers on social media (a form of social capital that may quite easily be monetised, i.e. converted into economic capital). The conversion from aesthetic to economic capital happens chiefly on the labour market, for which there is plenty of evidence (Maestripieri et al., 2017) The conversion of aesthetic to cultural capital is evident, for example, in situations where a singer or artist's work is esteemed more highly because of their looks, or, generally, where a person who is deemed to possess aesthetic capital is rewarded in cultural fields (e.g. Dean, 2005; Hracs & Leslie, 2014).

The norms that guide the conversion of aesthetic capital are also gendered, particularly when it comes to exchanging aesthetic capital to economic capital in working life. Women who profit from their looks in working life are more disapproved of than men who do the same (Kukkonen et al., 2018; Sarpila et al., 2020).

Overall, the grammar of society appears to function such that those who are in subordinate positions in society (e.g. women, non-whites) are called upon to accumulate aesthetic capital yet are not necessarily allowed to benefit from it themselves. They are invited or even guided to exchange whatever capital they have for aesthetic capital and are promised upward mobility in exchange (see Kukkonen, Chapter 2). Arguably, even people who do not possess social, cultural or economic capital can train their bodies to be commercially viable at home, and supposedly, girls, in particular, ought to just learn to dress, behave and dance, notwithstanding their backgrounds (cf. Hakim, 2010). Such an overemphasis on the agency involved in the accumulation of aesthetic capital is misguided, as not everyone has equal opportunities for capital accumulation or conversion. As such, this promise of upward mobility by means of aesthetic capital appears a case of 'cruel optimism' (Adamson & Salmenniemi, 2017; on cruel optimism, see Berlant, 2011).

While aesthetic capital can be accumulated and converted in social exchange, it is also crucial to note that conversions do not always benefit the capital-accruing subject. As Wacquant (1995) and Mears (2015a, 2015b, 2020) have shown in their research on bodily capital, capital does not always benefit the person it is attributed to but can be appropriated by other actors in the field. Such actors may include individual persons who benefit from other people's aesthetic capital, but in most cases, it is economic actors, companies, that play a bigger role. The ways in which businesses cultivate, harness and benefit from employees' aesthetic capital and the aesthetic labour involved are well documented, particularly concerning the service sector (Boyle & De Keere, 2019; Williams & Connell, 2010; Witz et al., 2003). The appropriation of aesthetic capital and labour does not necessarily feel or look like appropriation of capital to the people involved, and indeed, this is key to the functioning of such unequal systems of exchange (Mears, 2015a, 2015b, 2020).

Conclusions

The social sciences have seen a veritable boom of interest in physical appearance in the past two decades, and many sociologists have turned to Bourdieu's scholarship to make sense of appearance-related social inequalities. In particular, scholars have conceptualised the body and its appearance using the metaphor of capital, in a more or less Bourdieusian sense, to explain and study such inequalities.

While the concept of capital has been used to suggest looks could or should be utilised as currency in social exchange on free markets, the majority of research on the subject suggests that insofar as we can conceive of a person's looks as capital, this capital ought to be situated in fields or markets that are unequal and governed by social norms. These social norms are not equal for everyone and differ by field or market. Even at a societal level, different people may face different rules of capital exchange, depending on their social position.

This should not be taken to mean that appearances could not constitute a veritable form of capital which has influence on our lives – quite the opposite. The idea that appearances act as a form of capital should be taken seriously. Considering appearance-related inequality from the perspective of norms and capital means recognising that the appearance-related inequalities of today were not always there, and importantly, they do not necessarily have to be there.

Note

1. Indeed, according to Neveu (2018, p. 368), Bourdieu wrote, '[t]here are as many forms of power (or capital) as existing fields (2011, p. 128)'.

References

Adamson, M., & Salmenniemi, S. (2017). 'The bottom line is that the problem is you': Aesthetic labour, postfeminism and subjectivity in Russian self-help literature. In A. S. Elias, R. Gill, & C. Scharff (Eds.), *Aesthetic labour* (pp. 301–316). Palgrave Macmillan.

Adkins, L. (2004). Introduction: Feminism, Bourdieu and after. In L. Adkins & B. Skeggs (Eds.), *Feminism after Bourdieu*. Blackwell Publishing.

Anderson, T. L., Grunert, C., Katz, A., & Lovascio, S. (2010). Aesthetic capital: A research review on beauty perks and penalties. *Sociology Compass*, 4(8), 564–575. https://doi.org/10.1111/j.1751-9020.2010.00312.x

Balogun, O. M. (2020). *Beauty diplomacy: Embodying an emerging nation*. Stanford University Press.

Bartky, S. L. (1990). *Femininity and domination: Studies in the phenomenology of oppression*. Routledge.

van den Berg, M., & Arts, J. (2019). The aesthetics of work-readiness: Aesthetic judgements and pedagogies for conditional welfare and post-Fordist labour markets. *Work, Employment and Society*, 33(2), 298–313. https://doi.org/10.1177/0950017018758196

Berlant, L. (2011). *Cruel optimism*. Duke University Press.

Bicchieri, C. (2006). *The grammar of society: The nature and dynamics of social norms*. Cambridge University Press.

Black, P. (2004). *The beauty industry: Gender, culture, pleasure*. Routledge.

Bordo, S. (2003/1993). *Unbearable weight: Feminism, western culture and the body* (10th anniversary ed.). University of California Press.

Bourdieu, P. (1978). Sport and social class. *Social Science Information*, *17*(6), 819–840.

Bourdieu, P. (1984). *Distinction: A social critique of the judgement of taste*. Harvard University Press.

Bourdieu, P. (2001). *Masculine domination*. Stanford University Press.

Bourdieu, P. (2004/1962). The peasant and his body. *Ethnography*, *5*(4), 579–599. https://doi.org/10.1177/1466138104048829

Bourdieu, P. (2011/1986). The forms of capital. In I. Szeman & T. Kaposy (Eds.), *Cultural theory: An anthology* (pp. 81–93). Wiley-Blackwell.

Bourdieu, P. (2013/1977). *Outline of a theory of practice*. Cambridge University Press.

Boyle, B., & De Keere, K. (2019). Aesthetic labour, class and taste: Mobility aspirations of middle-class women working in luxury-retail. *The Sociological Review*, *67*(3), 706–722. https://doi.org/10.1177/0038026119827753

Connell, C., & Mears, A. (2018). Bourdieu and the body. In T. Medvetz & J. J. Sallaz (Eds.), *The Oxford handbook of Pierre Bourdieu* (pp. 561–576). Oxford University Press.

Dean, D. (2005). Recruiting a self: Women performers and aesthetic labour. *Work, Employment and Society*, *19*(4), 761–774. https://doi.org/10.1177/0950017005058061

Entwistle, J., & Wissinger, E. (2006). Keeping up appearances: Aesthetic labour in the fashion modelling industries of London and New York. *The Sociological Review*, *54*(4), 774–794. https://doi.org/10.1111/j.1467-954X.2006.00671.x

Gill, R. (2017). The affective, cultural and psychic life of postfeminism: A postfeminist sensibility 10 years on. *European Journal of Cultural Studies*, *20*(6), 606–626. https://doi.org/10.1177/1367549417733003

Gimlin, D. (2007). What is 'body work'? A review of the literature. *Sociology Compass*, *1*(1), 353–370. https://doi.org/10.1111/j.1751-9020.2007.00015.x

Green, A. I. (2008). The social organization of desire: The sexual fields approach. *Sociological Theory*, *26*(1), 25–50. https://doi.org/10.1111/j.1467-9558.2008.00317.x

Green, A. I. (2013). 'Erotic capital' and the power of desirability: Why 'honey money' is a bad collective strategy for remedying gender inequality. *Sexualities*, *16*(1–2), 137–158. https://doi.org/10.1177/1363460712471109

Green, A. I. (2014). Toward a sociology of collective sexual life. In A. I. Green (Ed.), *Sexual fields: Toward a sociology of collective sexual life* (pp. 1–23). The University of Chicago Press.

Hakim, C. (2010). Erotic capital. *European Sociological Review*, *26*(5), 499–518. https://doi.org/10.1093/esr/jcq014

Hakim, C. (2011). *Honey money: The power of erotic capital*. Penguin.

Hamermesh, D. S. (2011). *Beauty pays: Why attractive people are more successful*. Princeton University Press.

Hochschild, A. (1983). *The managed heart: Commercialization of human feeling*. The University of California Press.

Holla, S., & Kuipers, G. (2015). Aesthetic capital. In L. Hanquinet & M. Savage (Eds.), *International handbook for the sociology of art and culture* (pp. 290–304). Routledge.

Holliday, R., & Taylor, J. S. (2006). Aesthetic surgery as false beauty. *Feminist Theory*, *7*(2), 179–195. https://doi.org/10.1177/1464700106064418

Hosoda, M., Stone-Romero, E. F., & Coats, G. (2003). The effects of physical attractiveness on job-related outcomes: A meta-analysis of experimental studies. *Personnel Psychology*, *56*(2), 431–462. https://doi.org/10.1111/j.1744-6570.2003.tb00157.x

Hracs, B. J., & Leslie, D. (2014). Aesthetic labour in creative industries: The case of independent musicians in Toronto, Canada. *Area, 46*(1), 66–73. https://doi.org/10.1111/area.12062

Kuipers, G. (2015). Beauty and distinction? The evaluation of appearance and cultural capital in five European countries. *Poetics, 53*, 38–51. https://doi.org/10.1016/j.poetic.2015.10.001

Kukkonen, I., Åberg, E., Sarpila, O., & Pajunen, T. (2018). Exploitation of aesthetic capital–disapproved by whom? *International Journal of Sociology and Social Policy, 38*(3/4), 312–328. https://doi.org/10.1108/IJSSP-09-2017-0116

Kwan, S., & Trautner, M. N. (2009). Beauty work: Individual and institutional rewards, the reproduction of gender, and questions of agency. *Sociology Compass, 3*(1), 49–71. https://doi.org/10.1111/j.1751-9020.2008.00179.x

Lovell, T. (2000). Thinking feminism with and against Bourdieu. *Feminist Theory, 1*(1), 11–32. https://doi.org/10.1177/14647000022229047

Luna, J. K. (2019). The ease of hard work: Embodied neoliberalism among Rocky Mountain fun runners. *Qualitative Sociology, 42*(2), 251–271. https://doi.org/10.1007/s11133-019-9412-8

Maestripieri, D., Henry, A., & Nickels, N. (2017). Explaining financial and prosocial biases in favor of attractive people: Interdisciplinary perspectives from economics, social psychology, and evolutionary psychology. *Behavioral and Brain Sciences, 40*. https://doi.org/10.1017/S0140525X16000340

Martin, J. L., & George, M. (2006). Theories of sexual stratification: Toward an analytics of the sexual field and a theory of sexual capital. *Sociological Theory, 24*(2), 107–132. https://doi.org/10.1111/j.0735-2751.2006.00284.x

McRobbie, A. (2009). *The aftermath of feminism: Gender, culture and social change.* Sage.

Mears, A. (2014). Aesthetic labor for the sociologies of work, gender, and beauty. *Sociology Compass, 8*(12), 1330–1343. https://doi.org/10.1111/soc4.12211

Mears, A. (2015a). Working for free in the VIP: Relational work and the production of consent. *American Sociological Review, 80*(6), 1099–1122. https://doi.org/10.1177/0003122415609730

Mears, A. (2015b). Girls as elite distinction: The appropriation of bodily capital. *Poetics, 53*, 22–37. https://doi.org/10.1016/j.poetic.2015.08.004

Mears, A. (2020). *Very important people: Status and beauty in the global party circuit.* Princeton.

Mennell, S. (1987). On the civilizing of appetite. *Theory, Culture & Society, 4*(2–3), 373–403. https://doi.org/10.1177/026327687004002011

Moi, T. (1991). Appropriating Bourdieu: Feminist theory and Pierre Bourdieu's sociology of culture. *New Literary History, 22*(4), 1017–1049. https://doi.org/10.2307/469077

Neveu, E. (2018). Bourdieu's capital(s). In T. Medvetz & J. J. Sallaz (Eds.), *The Oxford handbook of Pierre Bourdieu* (pp. 347–374). Oxford University Press.

Pettinger, L. (2008). Developing aesthetic labour: The importance of consumption. *International Journal of Work Organisation and Emotion, 2*(4), 327–343. https://doi.org/10.1504/IJWOE.2008.022495

Ringrose, J., & Walkerdine, V. (2008). Regulating the abject: The TV make-over as site of neo-liberal reinvention toward bourgeois femininity. *Feminist Media Studies, 8*(3), 227–246. https://doi.org/10.1080/14680770802217279

Sarpila, O., Koivula, A., Kukkonen, I., Åberg, E., & Pajunen, T. (2020). Double standards in the accumulation and utilisation of 'aesthetic capital'. *Poetics, 82*. https://doi.org/10.1016/j.poetic.2020.101447

Schneickert, C., Steckermeier, L. C., & Brand, L. M. (2020). Lonely, poor, and ugly? How cultural practices and forms of capital relate to physical unattractiveness. *Cultural Sociology, 14*(1), 80–105. https://doi.org/10.1177/1749975520905417

Shilling, C. (1991). Educating the body: Physical capital and the production of social inequalities. *Sociology, 25*(4), 653–672. https://doi.org/10.1177/0038038591025004006

Shilling, C. (2004). Physical capital and situated action: A new direction for corporeal sociology. *British Journal of Sociology of Education, 25*(4), 473–487. https://doi.org/10.1080/0142569042000236961

Skeggs, B. (1997). *Formations of class & gender: Becoming respectable.* Sage.

Skeggs, B. (2004). *Self, class, culture.* Routledge.

Skeggs, B. (2009). The moral economy of person production: The class relations of self-performance on 'reality' television. *The Sociological Review, 57*(4), 626–644. https://doi.org/10.1111/j.1467-954X.2009.01865.x

Swedberg, R. (2009). *Principles of economic sociology.* Princeton University Press.

Vandebroeck, D. (2017). *Distinctions in the flesh: Social class and the embodiment of inequality.* Routledge.

Wacquant, L. J. (1995). Pugs at work: Bodily capital and bodily labour among professional boxers. *Body & Society, 1*(1), 65–93. https://doi.org/10.1177/1357034X95001001005

Warhurst, C., & Nickson, D. (2001). *Looking good, sounding right: Style counselling in the new economy.* The Industrial Society. https://doi.org/10.1108/09604520510585370

Wiley, K. A. (2018). *Work, social status and gender in post-slavery Mauritania.* Indiana University Press.

Williams, C. L., & Connell, C. (2010). "Looking good and sounding right": Aesthetic labor and social inequality in the retail industry. *Work and Occupations, 37*(3), 349–377. https://doi.org/10.1177/0730888410373744

Witz, A., Warhurst, C., & Nickson, D. (2003). The labour of aesthetics and the aesthetics of organization. *Organization, 10*(1), 33–54. https://doi.org/10.1177/1350508403010001375

Chapter 2

Who Performs Appearance Work, and Who Believes Appearance Works? Gendered Appearance Beliefs and Practices in Finland

Iida Kukkonen

Introduction

Previous research shows that norms, consumption and practices related to physical appearance are thoroughly gendered and have a very different significance in the daily lives of women than in those of men. In particular, women face strict appearance norms and are expected to engage in various appearance-related practices.

Practices related to physical appearance may be considered as 'work that individuals perform on themselves to elicit certain benefits within a specific social hierarchy' (Kwan & Trautner, 2009, p. 50) – labour which I hereon will call *appearance work*. Through the metaphor of aesthetic capital, practices aimed at the maintenance and/or enhancement of aesthetic capital constitute practices where capital accumulates (see Kukkonen, Chapter 1). Hence, appearance work may be regarded as an accumulation of aesthetic capital (Sarpila et al., 2020) for fields or markets in which capital exchange happens (Bourdieu, 1984). In increasingly visual consumer societies, such work is increasingly in demand, and there are assumedly benefits for engaging in such work. Nevertheless, such work has rarely been empirically addressed.

While a rich scholarship details the social and economic benefits of physical appearance (for reviews, see, e.g., Hosoda et al., 2003; Maestripieri et al., 2017), less attention has been paid to the ideologies, beliefs and practices related to appearance as capital or currency. However, philosopher Heather Widdows has recently argued that the belief that being beautiful is a route to the good life is meaningful far beyond the question of whether beauty actually confers benefits

Appearance as Capital, 39–55

doi:10.1108/978-1-80043-708-120210003

(see also Requena, 2017). For beauty to be a dominant ideal that structures social life, it is crucial that individuals believe work on the body matters and are willing to work for beauty (Widdows, 2018). Similarly, Sarpila and Erola (2016) claim that the belief in the importance of physical attractiveness for success is important in itself, first because beliefs reflect the prevailing ideology of a society and second because beliefs are linked with behaviour through attitudes (Sarpila & Erola, 2016, pp. 5–6).

This study takes these suggestions into further scrutiny by drawing on feminist scholarship and studies on appearance and inequality to propose that the belief in appearance as currency may be a driver of daily appearance work. I propose that women as compared with men engage in a disproportionate amount of appearance work and that the belief in appearance as currency works as part of an ideology that keeps women engaged in appearance work.

Belief in Appearance as Currency

In a consumer culture, each individual is arguably invited to take responsibility over their body and appearance and called upon to invest in their looks (see Ghigi & Sassatelli, 2018). The invitation to work on one's looks comes with a promise of social and economic benefits; it entices people to believe in *appearance as currency*. Scholars of consumer culture, including Featherstone (2007) and Bauman (2007), have claimed that in an ever more widespread visual consumer culture, the body and particularly its surface become fluid and modifiable – a consumer object in their own right. Critics of neoliberalism such as Rose (1989) foresaw the rise of an entrepreneurial self who 'invests' in themselves. Consumer culture theorists such as Bauman (2007) took the thought further to describe the individual as akin to a well-branded and packaged product that is up for grabs on the market. In visual consumer culture, the packaging of a product may matter more than the content, or indeed, the packaging becomes the content. Physical appearance comes to be equated with the self (cf. Featherstone, 2007). As such, a rational individual living in a visual consumer culture will go to lengths to invest in an outer appearance that has market value.

Whereas everyone certainly is invited to modify their looks and 'invest' in their appearances, the invitation appears to be a euphemism when it comes to the realities that women face in front of the appearance-related norms of visual consumer societies. It can be argued that the ideology of appearance as currency does not just invite but compels women to work on their appearances.

According to such an argument, the belief in appearance as currency is inherently gendered. The analyses of consumer culture theorists fail to take into account that meticulous labour on the body and its appearance and movement is actually crucial for the production of femininity (Bartky, 1990). Feminist scholars including Sandra Lee Bartky claim femininity is an artifice that (re)produces a gendered social system (Bartky, 1990), wherein women's value lies in their dainty and beautiful looks whereas men's value is in their thoughts and deeds. Thus, while the ideology of physical appearance as currency may have appeared to scholars such as Bauman and Featherstone as a new social tendency, others suggest women's bodies have been subject to capitalisation, at least since the birth of capitalism (cf. Federici, 2004).

Beauty is considered a distinctly feminine asset and is often portrayed as a feminine source of power and social mobility. The ideology of beauty as a woman's asset has been contested by strands of feminism throughout the history of feminism (Kukkonen, 2019). By stressing the physical, bodily and visual as feminine, such an ideology reproduces problematic bifurcations inherent in Western thought: masculinity, mind and spirit versus femininity, body and nature (cf. Tseëlon, 1995). Such a gendered ideology is also sexist: considering that women are of the 'fairer sex' and are to be celebrated for it constitutes what Glick and Fiske (2001) call *benevolent sexism*, as does claiming that women are more compassionate and so naturally better at care work. Benevolent sexism complements the more hostile forms of sexism but is much more socially acceptable. Further, as benevolent sexism works by placing women on a pedestal, women as well as men can easily endorse it, and, thus, it helps conciliate resistance to gender inequality (Glick & Fiske, 2001). Calogero et al. (2017) suggest on the basis of their study on college students' gender activism that the belief in beauty as currency is connected to greater self-objectification in women and may work against social change.

In the early 90s, feminist writer Naomi Wolf referred to the belief in beauty as a form of feminine currency as 'the beauty myth'. She claimed that when women gain more access to power in society, the pressures for them to adhere to ever stricter appearance-based norms increase. The beauty myth implies that female beauty is inherently and naturally valuable for biological, sexual and evolutionary reasons, and hence women should do the best they can to harness theirs (Wolf, 2002/1990). Such a feminine beauty ideology posits appearance work as a principal activity for women. The work is never done, though (Calogero et al., 2017).

The belief in, or ideology of, beauty as an investment strategy is arguably highlighted in the contemporary postfeminist media culture (Gill, 2007, 2017), where the imperative to constantly develop oneself and one's 'assets' is directed particularly at young women (McRobbie, 2009). Women have always had to be 'desirable, presentable, consumable' (Ringrose & Walkerdine, 2008, p. 230), but in neoliberal or postfeminist culture, the feminine is increasingly the object and subject of commodification and consumption. Femininity is, thus, constructed as a site for endless transformation, change and makeover, and according to the neoliberal mythology, subjects capable of constant self-invention will gain success and possibilities for upward social mobility. Thus, for women, appearance work emerges as key path for presenting a subject of constant reinvention and succeeding in life (Ringrose & Walkerdine, 2008).

The Significance of Gendered Appearance Work

In the social sciences, labour on one's own body and its appearance has been discussed using terms such as grooming (e.g., Das & De Loach, 2011; Hamermesh, 2011), beauty work (Kwan & Trautner, 2009), body work and appearance work (e.g. Gimlin, 2007). Aesthetic labour, or labour on one's looks, particularly at or for waged labour, has also been a topic of increasing scholarly attention (e.g., Boyle & De Keere, 2019; Elias et al., 2017; Entwistle & Wissinger, 2006; Pettinger, 2008; Williams & Connell, 2010; Witz et al., 2003). I use the term appearance work, as I wish to highlight the labour involved (cf. 'grooming') but do not focus only on labour conducted at or for work (cf. 'aesthetic labour'). As I focus on daily routines in front of the mirror (in lieu of 'body work' which takes place beyond) and wish to refer to both masculine and feminine appearance-related labour, I find that the term appearance work functions best in this context.

In economics, appearance work may be designated as a 'non-market activity' (cf. Das & De Loach, 2011); it is an activity that happens outside formal economic markets. Other gendered non-market activities, notably housework and childcare, have been a focus of many studies (e.g. Bianchi et al., 2012; Treas & Tai, 2016), and such forms of non-market labour remain a constant political issue even in the Nordic countries, which are commonly praised for paying attention to the gender imbalances in such forms of labour. Appearance work, however, remains a gendered 'non-market' activity that lacks scholarly and political attention (Kukkonen & Sarpila, 2021). In studies of time use, appearance work has mostly been neglected; in national time-use surveys, it is subsumed under the category of personal care (cf. Eurostat, 2019). However, appearance work certainly matters beyond the general and the personal.

Studies show appearance work is demanded for employment (e.g., Warhurst & Nickson, 2007). Aesthetic labour (i.e., appearance work done at or for work) is increasingly demanded even in industries where physical appearances have little to do with the job in question. For example, in Finland, Kinnunen and Parviainen (2016) have shown how recruiters are on the watch for a 'certain look' even as they recruit for the IT industry, which is not well-known for being appearance-centred.

The appearance of an employee is of particular economic importance because the aesthetic capital of an employee may bring profits to an employer (e.g. Pettinger, 2008; Williams & Connell, 2010). Appearance-related capital is easily appropriated (Mears, 2015a, 2015b; Wacquant, 1995). Personal investments in aesthetic capital in terms of consumption and appearance work, hence, do not necessarily pay off for the individual engaging in them. Instead, appearance work may benefit the individuals' immediate social and economic surroundings (Wacquant, 1995).

Few studies have looked at how and to what extent appearance-related consumption or appearance work pays off for an individual. There are a few exceptions, though. Hamermesh et al. (2002) studied expenditure on appearances and found that money spent on appearance did slightly increase women's earnings and it did not pay for itself. Robins et al. (2011) found that taking grooming into account helps explain the relationship between attractiveness and income. Wong and Penner (2016) suggest that taking grooming into account explains the relationship between attractiveness and income for women but not for men. That is, for women, the estimation of attractiveness was contingent on grooming, whereas for men it was not. It has to be noted that Robins et al. (2011) and Wong and Penner (2016) used data for which both attractiveness and extent of grooming were measured by one interviewer.

Das and De Loach took a different approach and investigated whether time spent on grooming affects earnings. They found that the only group for whom time spent on grooming had a positive effect on wages was men in ethnic minorities. For women in ethnic minorities and non-minority men, time spent on grooming had no effect, whereas for non-minority women, time spent on grooming actually had a small negative effect. The authors suggested their results may have owed to groomed looks alleviating negative stereotypes often attached to men in minorities yet also aggravating negative stereotypes pertaining to non-minority women (Das & De Loach, 2011).

Indeed, appearance work may constitute a double bind for women. At the same time that women working on and with their looks risk activating negative feminine stereotypes, including frivolity, vanity and sexual promiscuity (Balogun, 2020; Kwan & Trautner, 2009; Mears, 2015b), the sanctions involved in not adhering to gendered appearance norms are also tangible. Living up to appearance norms is laborious and demands not only money but also, importantly, time, and the labour of looking good falls mostly on the shoulders of women (Mears, 2014). While work on appearances is outsourced to bodily labourers, including beauty professionals (cf. Mears, 2014), a great deal of it is ongoing and repetitive routine labour.

Daily appearance work is like any routine in that it has different meanings for different people. For example, some may experience their morning make-up routines as a revered moment of self-indulgence and calm, whereas for others, these routines may feel like a stressful waste of time (Ehn & Löfgren, 2009). This complexity of meanings attributed to gendered appearance work is mirrored in some of the feminist scholarship on the topic. While radical feminist scholars have for decades perceived femininity as an artifice achieved by continuous and meticulous appearance work that ultimately serves women poorly (e.g., Bartky, 1990; Dworkin, 1974), so-called liberal feminism and postfeminism emphasises beauty work as a joyous pathway to personal empowerment (e.g., Davis, 2003) or even power (Hakim, 2010) (for distinguishing empowerment and power, see Brown, 1995).

Against this background, I will first descriptively explore the amount of daily appearance work conducted by Finnish men and women (RQ1) as well as look at potential gender differences in the belief that beauty matters for success in life – i.e., *belief in appearance as currency* (RQ2). I will then move on to ask whether the belief in appearance as currency is linked to daily appearance work for men and women (RQ3).

Who Performs Appearance Work, and Do Beliefs Matter?

Data and Variables

Finland is supposedly one of the havens of gender equality (Crotti et al., 2020). Finland urbanised late. The country is located at a safe distance from any major fashion metropolis (cf. Kuipers, 2015). Finnish beauty culture has been described as modest and utilitarian (see Introduction). Hence, Finland provides an intriguing point of view into the gendered nature of daily beauty practices and ideologies. As more gender-equal countries are generally less sexist (concerning both benevolent and hostile sexism) (Glick & Fiske, 2001), gendered ideologies pertaining to social and economic attainment should matter less in countries such as Finland that are supposed to be relatively gender-equal. As highlighted by feminist scholars (Bartky, 1990; Dworkin, 1974; Federici, 2004) though, appearances and the (socio)economic significance of bodies are such profoundly or even inherently gendered issues that it is highly unlikely gender would not matter, even in comparatively gender-equal contexts. According to Wolf (2002/1990), appearance-related pressures on women actually pile up, particularly when and wherever women gain more power in society. Hence, my working hypothesis is that women compared to men engage in a disproportionate amount of appearance work and that the belief in appearance as currency works as part of an ideology that keeps women engaged in appearance work.

The data I use to explore my research questions come from a survey called 'Appearance and Everyday Life', which surveyed the everyday appearance-related norms, consumption and inequalities of the Finnish-speaking Finnish population. The survey was fielded in spring 2016 by the Unit of Economic Sociology at the University of Turku. Four thousand Finnish-speaking Finns were randomly sampled from the Finnish Population database and sent a postal survey with an option for online response. Six respondents could not be reached; hence, the final sample amounted to 3,994. The survey yielded 1,600 responses (1,320 postal, 280 online). The final response rate, thus, remained at 40%. While far from ideal, such a response rate is in line with current trends in survey research and may be considered sufficient (Koivula et al., 2016). Older women are somewhat overrepresented in the data, while younger men are underrepresented (Sarpila et al., 2016). However, these biases in the data are corrected for throughout the analyses by employment of weights designed to make the data correspond to the gender and age distribution of the Finnish population aged 15 to 74.

The main variable of interest in this study – and the dependent variable – is *daily time in front of the mirror*. It was measured by asking survey respondents to evaluate the number of minutes they spend in front of the mirror on a normal day, including during their morning and evening rituals. As such, the variable constitutes a subjective evaluation of time use rather than a more objective and orthodox time-use measurement (i.e., measurement by time-use diaries, such as in the Harmonised European Time Use Surveys). Nevertheless, I interpret this variable as a proxy for daily appearance work – as opposed to other related forms of everyday bodily labour, including body work (Gimlin, 2007) and dress work (van den Berg & Vonk, 2019). Time in front of the mirror is something respondents can easily grasp. Moreover, the measure is relatively gender-neutral, as it includes practices such as washing one's face and brushing hair and teeth (Kukkonen & Sarpila, 2021).

Secondly, I am interested in *the belief in appearance as currency*. In the survey, this belief was measured by asking respondents to what degree they agree or disagree with the statement 'I believe beauty and good looks are useful for succeeding in life'. This statement was part of a wider survey battery that explored respondents' attitudes concerning physical appearance on a 5-point Likert scale

(1 = completely disagree, 2 = somewhat disagree, 3 = neither agree nor disagree, 4 = somewhat agree, 5 = completely agree). This measurement has been previously utilised by Sarpila and Erola (2016), and a very similar measurement has been used by Requena (2017). Other scholars (Calogero et al., 2017) have previously used multiple-item constructs to tap into the issue; however, they have measured the belief in beauty as currency only in terms of female beauty.

The following descriptive and explanatory results are presented separately for men and women. In the survey, *gender* was measured dichotomously.[1] In Fig. 2.1 and for the explanatory models in Table 2.1, I utilise *age group*. I refrain from utilising age as a continuous variable, as the connection for women between age and daily time in front of the mirror is not straightforwardly linear. In the explanatory models, I also control for *area of living* (dichotomous: urban versus rural), *partner status* (partnered versus single) and *subjective class position*. I utilise subjective class position instead of a class categorisation inferred by the researcher (on the basis of occupation, education, income or a combination thereof) because I am chiefly interested in controlling for class as a cultural categorisation experienced by respondents. Finns are relatively aware of their class position (cf. Erola, 2010). Descriptive statistics for all the utilised variables are presented in Appendix 1.

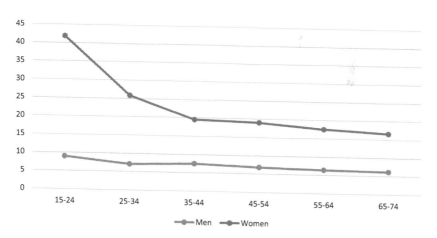

Fig. 2.1.   Mean Daily Time (Minutes) Spent in Front of the Mirror by Age Group and Gender.

Results

As beauty work is still somewhat at odds with the Finnish culture, which stresses modesty, practicality and equality (see Introduction), I expected the item would be particularly prone to social desirability bias, whereby respondents would downplay their beauty work so as to refrain from the 'vainness' traditionally attributed to beauty work in Finland. Yet despite the potential social desirability bias, we found Finns reported spending a significant amount of time in front of the mirror. Moreover, despite supposed 'gender equality', gender differences in time spent in front of the mirror are notable. Fig. 2.1 illustrates these gender differences by graphing the mean daily time spent in front of the mirror by gender and age group.

Indeed, Fig. 2.1 shows that differences in time spent on appearance work are notable not just in terms of gender but, particularly for women, in age as well. Women in the youngest age group (15–24) spend on average 42 minutes in front of the mirror on an average day. Women between the ages of 25 and 34 spend an average of 26 minutes in front of the mirror per day, and women in the age groups 35–44 and 45–54 spend an average of 19 minutes per day. In the older age groups, average time spent in front of the mirror daily is slightly lower (18 minutes for 55–64-year-olds, 17 minutes for 65–74-year-olds). In stark contrast, men in the youngest age group (15–24) spend on average nine minutes in front of the mirror on an average day. Men in older age groups spend slightly less time in front of the mirror: the average is between six and seven minutes in all age groups.

As Fig. 2.2 suggests, the belief in appearance as currency is equally common among men and women in Finland. The chi-squared for the cross tabulation is 0.96, and hence the minor differences in Fig. 2.2 are statistically insignificant.[2] This result differs from previous Finnish findings on belief in appearance as currency: a study by Sarpila and Erola (2016) which utilised data collected in 2011 – five years prior to the collection of this study's data – found that belief in appearance as currency was more common among women than among men. It is, however, worth noting that the survey Sarpila and Erola used was different and did not focus on physical appearance alone.

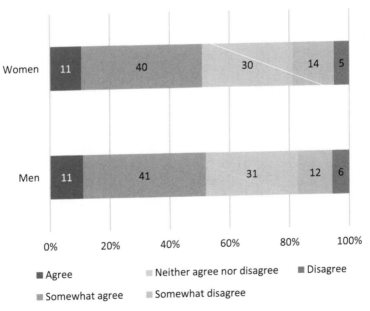

Fig. 2.2.   Belief in Appearance as Currency for Men and Women.

But does holding such a belief actually shape daily appearance work? Fig. 2.3 displays the mean daily time spent in front of the mirror by belief in appearance as currency.

Fig. 2.3 shows that for men, the mean daily time spent in front of the mirror on an average day does not vary greatly according to belief in appearance as currency. That is, whether men believe appearance matters for success in life or not, they engage in similar amounts of appearance work. Very interestingly, men who disagree with the statement that beauty and good looks matter for succeeding in life spend an equal amount of time in front of the mirror to what men who agree with the statement spend – ten minutes. On average, men who are less certain in their belief spend 6–7 minutes in front of the mirror on an average day.

Fig. 2.3 distinctly illustrates a trend whereby women who believe in appearance as currency spend more of their daily time engaged in appearance work. Women who disagree with the statement that they believe beauty and good looks matter for succeeding in life report spending on average 13 minutes in front of the mirror on an average day. Women who somewhat disagree spend more time (20 minutes), and women who neither disagree nor agree as well as women who somewhat agree with the statement spend 23 minutes facing the mirror daily. Women who agree that beauty and good looks matter for succeeding in life spend on average as much as 28 minutes a day in front of the mirror. The differences in

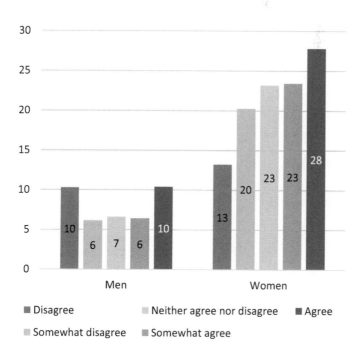

Fig. 2.3. Mean Daily Time (Minutes) Spent in Front of the Mirror by Belief in Appearance as Currency.

average time spent in front of the mirror, thus, differ significantly between women according to their belief in appearance as currency. Those who hold such a belief spend more than twice as much time in front of the mirror daily as those who do not hold such a belief.

To consider the statistical significance of these descriptive results, I ran two multinomial linear regressions – one for men and one for women – with daily time spent in front of the mirror as the dependent variable and belief in appearance as currency as the independent variable. Age group, area of living, partner status and subjective class position are controlled for in the models. The results of the regression models are presented in Table 2.1.

Table 2.1. Linear Regression of Daily Average Time (Min) Spent in Front of the Mirror. Separate Models for Men and Women.

	Model 1 Men	Model 2 Women
Belief in appearance as currency (*ref. disagree*)		
Somewhat disagree	−4.652** (1.532)	3.352 (3.145)
Neither agree nor disagree	−4.071** (1.358)	6.031** (2.896)
Somewhat agree	−4.591*** (1.341)	6.684* (2.857)
Agree	−1.215 (1.539)	11.46*** (3.271)
Age group (*ref. 15–24*)		
25–34	−2.668* (1.092)	−16.25*** (2.165)
35–44	−2.965* (1.163)	−21.40*** (2.230)
45–54	−2.212 (1.158)	−22.10*** (2.149)
55–64	−3.060** (1.122)	−23.08*** (2.117)
65–74	−3.125** (1.157)	−24.74*** (2.131)
Area of living (*ref. urban*)		
Rural	−1.665* (0.764)	−4.261** (1.462)
Partner status (*ref. partnered*)		
Single	−0.342 (0.777)	−0.0729 (1.419)
Subjective class position (*ref. upper/upper middle*)		
Lower middle class	−0.424 (0.784)	−3.455* (1.650)
Working class	−2.004* (0.823)	−1.980 (1.694)
None/other	−1.731 (0.955)	−2.085 (1.711)
Constant	14.53*** (1.639)	37.81*** (3.534)
N	622	847
R^2	0.0701	0.217

Note: Standard errors in parentheses* $p < 0.05$, **$p < 0.01$, ***$p < 0.001$.

Focussing first on Model 1, which concerns Finnish men, we can see that the descriptive results presented in Fig. 2.3 hold even after controlling for age group, area of living, partner status and subjective class position. That is, men who do not believe in appearance as currency actually engage in as much appearance work as men who do believe in it. Men who are more undecided spend four to five minutes less in front of the mirror on an average day.

Model 1 shows that men in the older age groups spend two to three minutes less in front of the mirror than men in the youngest age group (18–25) do. The differences are statistically significant with the exception of those for men aged 45–54, whose daily time in front of the mirror does not statistically significantly differ from that of the youngest age group. Men living in rural areas spend slightly less time in front of the mirror than do men living in more urban areas, and working-class men spend slightly less time in front of the mirror than do men who identify with the upper or upper middle class. Partner status appears to have no effect in this model.

In Model 2, which concerns Finnish women, we can see that the difference in time spent in front of the mirror between women who do not believe in appearance as currency and those who slightly disagree with the same view is not statistically significant. However, women who neither disagree nor agree with the statement identifying appearance as a currency spend six minutes more in front of the mirror than do women who disagree with the statement. Women who somewhat agree with the belief in appearance as currency spend on average seven minutes more in front of the mirror daily than women who do not agree with the belief do, and finally, the difference in time use between women who believe in appearance as currency and women who do not is 11 minutes, other factors being controlled for.

The differences in average daily time spent in front of the mirror definitely appear age-contingent, even when other factors are controlled for. The difference in time spent in front of the mirror between the age groups 15–24 and 25—34 is 16 minutes. As we proceed to consider the results from older age groups, time spent in front of the mirror shortens for each age group yet retains a difference of 21–25 minutes with comparison to the youngest age group. Women living in rural areas spend on average four minutes less time in front of the mirror than women living in urban areas do. There is no statistically significant difference in time spent in front of the mirror according to partner status. As compared to women who identify as upper class or upper middle class, women of the lower middle class spend three minutes more in front of the mirror on an average day. However, there are no statistically significant differences between women who identify as upper or upper middle class and women who identify with the working class, do not identify with any of the class options given in the survey, or do not view themselves as belonging to a class overall.

Discussion

While the belief in appearance as currency is held equally by men and women in Finland, its practical daily implications are different between those groups.

Women who believe appearance matters for success in life engage in appearance work significantly more than women who do not. However, men who believe in appearance as currency overall do not work much more on their appearance than men who do not hold such a belief.

This result certainly mirrors the normative outlook whereby appearance work is considered a means of capital accumulation for women and men who engage in appearance work may be disapproved of for paying too much attention to their appearance. Sarpila et al. (2020) found, however, that daily appearance work is equally acceptable for Finnish women and men; a man who does not want to leave the house without being well-groomed is no more disapproved of than a woman who feels daily grooming is necessary for leaving the house. Hence, it appears that the reason men do not engage in further daily grooming does not necessarily have to do with normative societal disapproval of men who do appearance work. Instead, it is possible that men never even consider further appearance work a possibility, as they are not socialised to engage in appearance work (just as they are not socialised to engage in care work). Perhaps this is the reason why the belief in appearance as currency does not imply lengthy daily investment in aesthetic capital in terms of daily appearance work for men.

However, it has to be noted that men who believe in appearance as currency appear to spend an equal time in front of the mirror to that spent by men who do not believe in it, and it is men who have more moderate beliefs about appearance as currency who invest more time in their looks. Could it be that certain men acknowledge that their appearances matter but do not feel the need to enhance their looks, as they already benefit from their looks and thus do not feel a need to enhance their looks by further grooming? As results from previous studies such as ones by Robins et al. (2011) and Wong and Penner (2016) would suggest, women's attractiveness is evaluated on the basis of their level of grooming, whereas the attractiveness of men is evaluated more independently of grooming.

Relatedly, the result can be read as a sign that the belief in appearance as a currency is in itself gendered; that is, people believe it matters more for women than for men. Read as such, the result suggests that Finnish men and women both believe appearances matter for success in life, but they also believe that they matter mostly for women and that it is women who can gain benefits from their appearances. As scholars have pointed out, the ideology of appearance as an asset worthy of investment is an extremely gendered ideology (Gill, 2007; Wolf, 2002/1990). One of the problems of this ideology (for more, see, e.g., Green, 2013) is that, in reality, the socioeconomic gains to be had on the basis of appearance appear to be equally prevalent among men and women. The overall status quo of social stratification research suggests women do not necessarily gain any more profits from their looks than men do (for reviews, see, e.g., Hosoda et al., 2003; Maestripieri et al., 2017); that is, this form of capital is not more convertible into other forms of capital for women than for men. Further, appearance-related gains (e.g., in the labour market) are more disapproved of for women than for men (Sarpila et al., 2020). Hence, women are stuck in a limbo where they are told their appearance matters and are bombarded with the idea that investing in appearances is a good deal, but if they ever actually profit from their appearances economically, they may well be scorned at (Sarpila et al., 2020; see also Balogun, 2020; Mears, 2015a, 2015b). The profits of female investment in beauty mainly accrue to the beauty industrial complex (Wolf, 2002/1990). As for the labour market, scholarship on aesthetic labour shows that the appearance of an employee truly matters, but it also suggests it is the employer who has the power to benefit from employees' appearance work. However, many women expected to do appearance work actually enjoy it, notwithstanding its few tangible perks.

Indeed, problematising the gendered nature of appearance work always comes with questions of female agency. Certainly, many women enjoy spending time in front of the mirror, and doing so is an individual's choice and pleasure. Many women also enjoy taking care of children, but childcare is nevertheless considered a political issue, and in many welfare states, including Finland, societal arrangements are made so that men as well as women can enjoy taking care of their children. Appearance work appears radically gendered, just as care for children is, but it is never even considered as a political issue; similarly to other forms of 'feminine' labour, appearance work is not considered work. Meanwhile, consumer societies including Finland are becoming increasingly visual and service-based, thus requiring an increasing amount of appearance work – by women in particular – in 'real life' as much as on social media.

Future studies could approach appearance-related work in a more holistic sense by also taking into account other forms of appearance-related labour and aesthetic capital accumulation, including body work and dress work. Comparative time-use data from different European countries could be used to garner a better understanding of appearance-related work among other forms of daily 'non-market' labour. The most recent release of the Harmonised European Time Use Studies (HETUS) is from 2010. While a new survey round was scheduled for 2020, the collection of data appears to have stalled (Eurostat, 2020). Data on time use are, however, crucial for researching daily lives and particularly for keeping track of gendered 'non-market' labour, which may include appearance work.

The main limitation of this study is that the belief in appearance as currency was measured as a non-gendered item, while, as the results show, this belief clearly has gendered dimensions. It is quite possible that some people believe beauty and good looks are useful for succeeding in life for women but not for men. Future studies with a survey methodology should use a split-ballot design (cf. Kukkonen et al., 2018; Rijken & Liefbroer, 2016; Sarpila et al., 2020) to further investigate the extent to which the belief in appearance as a currency is gendered.

Acknowledgements

I am deeply indebted to Laura Salonen, whose brilliant suggestions made the whole chapter! I am also grateful for all the people who commented on the manuscript in different seminars. In particular, I would like to thank Pasi Pohjolainen for his insights.

52   *Iida Kukkonen*

Notes

1. I acknowledge that measuring and treating gender as a binary is highly problematic and encourage all future survey designs to take into account non-binary people.
2. In the test, data are unweighted.

References

Balogun, O. M. (2020). *Beauty diplomacy: Embodying an emerging nation.* Stanford University Press.
Bartky, S. L. (1990). *Femininity and domination: Studies in the phenomenology of oppression.* Routledge.
Bauman, Z. (2007). *Consuming life.* Polity.
van den Berg, M., & Vonk, L. (2019). The new discomforts of precarious workers: Wardrobe matter, insecurity and the temporality of calibration in dress work. *The Sociological Review, 68*(3), 574–589. https://doi.org/10.1177/0038026119892402
Bianchi, S. M., Sayer, L. C., Milkie, M. A., & Robinson, J. P. (2012). Housework: Who did, does or will do it, and how much does it matter? *Social Forces, 91*(1), 55–63. https://doi.org/10.1093/sf/sos120
Bourdieu, P. (1984). *Distinction: A social critique of the judgement of taste.* Harvard University Press.
Boyle, B., & De Keere, K. (2019). Aesthetic labour, class and taste: Mobility aspirations of middle-class women working in luxury-retail. *The Sociological Review, 67*(3), 706–722. https://doi.org/10.1177/0038026119827753
Brown, W. (1995). *States of injury: Power and freedom in late modernity.* Princeton University Press.
Calogero, R. M., Tylka, T. L., Donnelly, L. C., McGetrick, A., & Leger, A. M. (2017). Trappings of femininity: A test of the "beauty as currency" hypothesis in shaping college women's gender activism. *Body Image, 21*, 66–70. https://doi.org/10.1016/j.bodyim.2017.02.008
Crotti, R., Geiger, T., Ratcheva, V., & Zahidi, S. (2020). *Global gender gap report 2020.* World Economic Forum. http://www3.weforum.org/docs/WEF_GGGR_2020.pdf
Das, J., & De Loach, S. B. (2011). Mirror, mirror on the wall: The effect of time spent grooming on earnings. *The Journal of Socio-Economics, 40*(1), 26–34. https://doi.org/10.1016/j.socec.2010.06.005
Davis, K. (2003). *Dubious equalities and embodied differences: Cultural studies on cosmetic surgery.* Rowman & Littlefield.
Dworkin, A. (1974). *Woman hating.* Dutton.
Ehn, B., & Löfgren, O. (2009). Routines-made and unmade. In E. Shove, F. Trentmann, & R. Wilk (Eds.), *Time, consumption and everyday life: Practice, materiality and culture* (pp. 99–112). Berg.
Elias, A., Gill, R., & Scharff, C. (2017). Aesthetic labour: Beauty politics in neoliberalism. In A. S. Elias, R. Gill, & C. Scharff (Eds.), *Aesthetic labour: Rethinking beauty politics in neoliberalism* (pp. 3–49). Palgrave Macmillan.
Entwistle, J., & Wissinger, E. (2006). Keeping up appearances: Aesthetic labour in the fashion modelling industries of London and New York. *The Sociological Review, 54*(4), 774–794. https://doi.org/10.1111/j.1467-954X.2006.00671.x

Erola, J. (2010). Luokkarakenne ja luokkiin samastuminen Suomessa [Class structure and class idenfification in Finland]. In J. Erola (Ed.), *Luokaton Suomi? Yhteiskuntaluokat 2000-luvun Suomessa* [*Classless Finland? Social class in 21st century Finland*] (pp. 27–44). Gaudeamus.

Eurostat. (2019). How do women and men use their time – Statistics. https://ec.europa.eu/eurostat/statistics-explained/index.php?title=How_do_women_and_men_use_their_time_-_statistics

Eurostat. (2020). Harmonised European time use surveys (HETUS) – Overview. https://ec.europa.eu/eurostat/web/time-use-surveys

Featherstone, M. (2007). *Consumer culture and postmodernism.* Sage.

Federici, S. (2004). *Caliban and the Witch.* Autonomedia.

Ghigi, R., & Sassatelli, R. (2018). Body projects: Fashion, aesthetic modifications and stylized selves. In O. Kravets, P. Maclaran, S. Miles, & A. Venkatesh (Eds.), *The Sage handbook of consumer culture* (pp. 290–315). Sage.

Gill, R. (2007). Postfeminist media culture: Elements of a sensibility. *European Journal of Cultural Studies, 10*(2), 147–166. https://doi.org/10.1177/1367549407075898

Gill, R. (2017). The affective, cultural and psychic life of postfeminism: A postfeminist sensibility 10 years on. *European Journal of Cultural Studies, 20*(6), 606–626. https://doi.org/10.1177/1367549417733003

Gimlin, D. (2007). What is 'body work'? A review of the literature. *Sociology Compass, 1*(1), 353–370. https://doi.org/10.1111/j.1751-9020.2007.00015.x

Glick, P., & Fiske, S. T. (2001). An ambivalent alliance: Hostile and benevolent sexism as complementary justifications for gender inequality. *American Psychologist, 56*(2), 109–118. https://doi.org/10.1037/0003-066X.56.2.109

Green, A. I. (2013). 'Erotic capital' and the power of desirability: Why 'honey money' is a bad collective strategy for remedying gender inequality. *Sexualities, 16*(1–2), 137–158. https://doi.org/10.1177/1363460712471109

Hakim, C. (2010). Erotic capital. *European Sociological Review, 26*(5), 499–518. https://doi.org/10.1093/esr/jcq014

Hamermesh, D. S. (2011). *Beauty pays: Why attractive people are more successful.* Princeton University Press.

Hamermesh, D. S., Meng, X., & Zhang, J. (2002). Dress for success—Does primping pay? *Labour Economics, 9*(3), 361–373. https://doi.org/10.1016/S0927-5371(02)00014-3.

Hosoda, M., Stone-Romero, E. F., & Coats, G. (2003). The effects of physical attractiveness on job-related outcomes: A meta-analysis of experimental studies. *Personnel Psychology, 56*(2), 431–462. https://doi.org/10.1111/j.1744-6570.2003.tb00157.x

Kinnunen, T., & Parviainen, J. (2016). Rekrytointikonsulttien tuntuma "hyvästä tyypistä" [Recruitment consultants' feel of a "good fellow"]. In J. Parviainen, T. Kinnunen, & I. Kortelainen (Eds.), *Ruumiillisuus ja työelämä: Työruumis jälkiteollisessa taloudessa* [*Embodiment and working life: The working body in the postindustrial economy*] (pp. 59–75). Vastapaino.

Koivula, A., Räsänen, P., & Sarpila, O. (2016). Internet- ja paperilomakkeiden täyttäjät: Vastaustavan muutoksen ja merkityksen arviointia hyvinvointitutkimuksessa [Web and survey respondents: Response mode effects in wellbeing research]. *Yhteiskuntapolitiikka, 81*(2), 54–65.

Kuipers, G. (2015). Beauty and distinction? The evaluation of appearance and cultural capital in five European countries. *Poetics, 53*, 38–51. https://doi.org/10.1016/j.poetic.2015.10.001

Kukkonen, I. (2019). Aikaa, jonka voisi käyttää myös paremmin? Feministisiä näkökulmia kauneuskäytänteisiin [Time, that might have better uses? Feminist perspectives on beauty practices]. In I. Kukkonen, T. Pajunen, O. Sarpila, & E. Åberg (Eds.), *Ulkonäköyhteiskunta: Ulkonäkö pääomana 2000-luvun Suomessa* (pp. 123–136). Into.

Kukkonen, I., Åberg, E., Sarpila, O., & Pajunen, T. (2018). Exploitation of aesthetic capital–disapproved by whom? *International Journal of Sociology and Social Policy, 38*(3/4), 312–328. https://doi.org/10.1108/IJSSP-09-2017-0116

Kukkonen, I., & Sarpila, O. (2021). Gendered experiences of appearance-related perks and penalties in Finnish labor markets. *Nordic Journal of Working Life Studies.* forthcoming.

Kwan, S., & Trautner, M. N. (2009). Beauty work: Individual and institutional rewards, the reproduction of gender, and questions of agency. *Sociology Compass, 3*(1), 49–71. https://doi.org/10.1111/j.1751-9020.2008.00179.x

Maestripieri, D., Henry, A., & Nickels, N. (2017). Explaining financial and prosocial biases in favor of attractive people: Interdisciplinary perspectives from economics, social psychology, and evolutionary psychology. *Behavioral and Brain Sciences, 40.* https://doi.org/10.1017/S0140525X16000340

McRobbie, A. (2009). *The aftermath of feminism: Gender, culture and social change.* Sage.

Mears, A. (2014). Aesthetic labor for the sociologies of work, gender, and beauty. *Sociology Compass, 8*(12), 1330–1343. https://doi.org/10.1111/soc4.12211

Mears, A. (2015a). Working for free in the VIP: Relational work and the production of consent. *American Sociological Review, 80*(6), 1099–1122. https://doi.org/10.1177/0003122415609730

Mears, A. (2015b). Girls as elite distinction: The appropriation of bodily capital. *Poetics, 53*, 22–37. https://doi.org/10.1016/j.poetic.2015.08.004

Pettinger, L. (2008). Developing aesthetic labour: The importance of consumption. *International Journal of Work Organisation and Emotion, 2*(4), 327–343. https://doi.org/10.1504/IJWOE.2008.022495

Requena, F. (2017). Erotic capital and subjective well-being. *Research in Social Stratification and Mobility, 50*, 13–18. https://doi.org/10.1016/j.rssm.2017.04.001

Rijken, A. J., & Liefbroer, A. C. (2016). Differences in family norms for men and women across Europe. *Journal of Marriage and Family, 78*(4), 1097–1113. https://doi.org/10.1111/jomf.12310

Ringrose, J., & Walkerdine, V. (2008). Regulating the abject: The TV make-over as site of neo-liberal reinvention toward bourgeois femininity. *Feminist Media Studies, 8*(3), 227–246. https://doi.org/10.1080/14680770802217279

Robins, P. K., Homer, J. F., & French, M. T. (2011). Beauty and the labor market: Accounting for the additional effects of personality and grooming. *Labour, 25*(2), 228–251. https://doi.org/10.1111/j.1467-9914.2010.00511.x

Rose, N. (1989). *Governing the soul: The shaping of the private self.* Routledge.

Sarpila, O., & Erola, J. (2016). Physical attractiveness—Who believes it is a ticket to success? *Research on Finnish Society, 9*, 5–14.

Sarpila, O., Koivula, A., Kukkonen, I., Åberg, E., & Pajunen, T. (2020). Double standards in the accumulation and utilisation of 'aesthetic capital'. *Poetics, 82.* https://doi.org/10.1016/j.poetic.2020.101447

Sarpila, O., Sandell, R., Koivula, A., & Kukkonen, I. (2016). *Arkielämä ja ulkonäkö -kyselyn tutkimusseloste* [Research report on the Physical appearance and everyday life -survey]. Working papers in Economic Sociology. University of Turku. https://www.utu.fi/sites/default/files/public%3A//media/file/Arkiel%C3%A4m%C3%A4_ja_ulkon%C3%A4k%C3%B6_kyselyn_tutkimusseloste.pdf

Treas, J., & Tai, T. (2016). Gender inequality in housework across 20 European nations: Lessons from gender stratification theories. *Sex Roles, 74*(11–12), 495–511. https://doi.org/10.1007/s11199-015-0575-9

Tseëlon, E. (1995). *The masque of femininity: The presentation of woman in everyday life.* Sage.

Wacquant, L. J. (1995). Pugs at work: Bodily capital and bodily labour among professional boxers. *Body & Society, 1*(1), 65–93. https://doi.org/10.1177/1357034X95001001005

Warhurst, C., & Nickson, D. (2007). Employee experience of aesthetic labour in retail and hospitality. *Work, Employment and Society, 21*(1), 103–120. https://doi.org/10.1177/0950017007073622

Widdows, H. (2018). *Perfect me: Beauty as an ethical ideal.* Princeton University Press.

Williams, C. L., & Connell, C. (2010). "Looking good and sounding right": Aesthetic labor and social inequality in the retail industry. *Work and Occupations, 37*(3), 349–377. https://doi.org/10.1177/0730888410373744

Witz, A., Warhurst, C., & Nickson, D. (2003). The labour of aesthetics and the aesthetics of organization. *Organization, 10*(1), 33–54. https://doi.org/10.1177/1350508403010001375

Wolf, N. (2002 [1990]). *The beauty myth: How images of beauty are used against women.* Harper Collins.

Wong, J. S., & Penner, A. M. (2016). Gender and the returns to attractiveness. *Research in Social Stratification and Mobility, 44,* 113–123. https://doi.org/10.1016/j.rssm.2016.04.002

Chapter 3

The Metrosexual Who Never Visited Finland – The Eternal Gender Gap in Appearance-related Consumption

Outi Sarpila

Introduction

Over two decades ago, we were introduced to a new form of masculinity, '*the metrosexual*'. Originally, the term was coined by journalist Mark Simpson in 1994. However, it was not until 2002 that the term gained global publicity as Simpson published his essay remarks online (Coad, 2016). Simpson's original term referred to young single men living or working in the city, who were not only interested in but also had monetary possibilities to invest in their looks (Simpson, 1996).

The journalist welcomed the new word echoing all around the Western, that masculinities were under a huge change. In Finland, different reports were made: 'Men's cosmetic industry is booming in Finland' (Markkinointi ja mainonta [Marketing and advertising], 1999) and 'Men got enthusiastic about their looks' (Talouselämä [Economy], 2004). Only few wanted to ruin the party by claiming that the change, in the example of the sale of men's cosmetic products, was rather imperceptible, or 'cosmetic', as noted in *Markkinointi ja mainonta* (a trade journal in the field of media and marketing) in 2005. In Finland, metrosexuality got media attention partly because the practices related to metrosexuals felt distinctively different from the ones associated with Finnish men in particular. In other words, the metrosexuality was seen to challenge the conventional gender norms of appearance-related consumption.

However, little academic effort was made to empirically analyse the 'real nature' of these possible normative changes. Instead it seems that the metrosexual phenomenon has always generated more popularity than academic interest. This means that academic research on metrosexuality is and has been scant. Hall

Appearance as Capital, 57–70

doi:10.1108/978-1-80043-708-120210004

argues in his book *Metrosexual Masculinities* (2014) that the lacking interest among academics stems from the popular connotations that the term 'metrosexual' has. Originally 'metrosexual' was a popular term, not an academic concept, and has thus been avoided by the academics. The small body of academic research that has taken up the challenge and dealt with metrosexuality has mainly been done in the field of cultural studies and concentrated on analysing metrosexual representations in popular culture (Coad, 2008; Miller, 2006; Schugart, 2008). More recently, research on the topic has expanded to encompass the study of men's own perceptions of metrosexuality, receiving the attention of a growing number of sociologists and psychologists as well (Casanova et al., 2016; Hall & Gough, 2011; Kaplan et al., 2017). The scant interest in the topic seems surprising considering that discussion about metrosexuality is, first and foremost, a discussion of the changing norms of masculinities. In terms of this book, the topic is relevant as it directly relates to gender norms of accumulation of aesthetic capital.

The main idea behind 'the metrosexual phenomenon' is indeed *change* or even 'crisis' in masculinity, which is manifested in changing consumption practices and self-presentations of men (e.g., Shugart, 2008). However, both affirmative and critical discussions about the metrosexual phenomenon have revolved around sales figures of men's fashion, accessories, grooming products, body/fitness goods and plastic surgery operations (Miller, 2006); the story is limited. What if it is not just male consumers who have adopted more 'feminine' consumption practices as 'masculinity hypothesis' suggests? In the realm of contemporary consumer and the emphasis put on good looks and accumulating it, shouldn't we expect to see an increase in interest in physical appearance both among men and women?

To the best of my knowledge, there has not been a previous study that analysed changes from both attitudinal and monetary-spending perspectives using gender comparisons. In this chapter, the analysis's time frame is 20 years. The aim is not to reject or support some kind of 'metrosexual hypothesis'. However, this chapter sets the discussion on 'the metrosexual phenomenon' into a wider context.

This chapter analyses the hypothetical change in men's consumption practices from the attitudinal and monetary expenditure perspectives. In my analysis, I compare men and women to see whether the possible changes in men's attitudes and monetary spending are in line with changes in women's attitudes and spending. I argue that this type of examination is important to see whether physical appearance -related attitudes and spending has actually changed in a way that is peculiar to men. Simpson (2014) himself has argued that there is no need to talk about metrosexuality anymore since it has 'died' in a sense now that it has become a norm. However, my analysis shows that, despite all the talk, nothing has really changed dramatically during the past 20 years. Metrosexuality has certainly not become a norm. I ask: Can something die if it never lived?

The chapter proceeds as follows. First, I introduce previous literature on the metrosexuals. After that, I introduce the data and methods used in this chapter. Then I present the results and make some concluding remarks.

Who Is or Was a Metrosexual?

First and foremost, metrosexuality has been related to fashion and grooming consumption. Compared to other types of masculinities, metrosexuality is associated with a more open interest in physical appearance and consumption, which involves conspicuous elements (e.g., Hall, 2014; Casanova et al., 2016). These types of 'definitions' or descriptions are typically the ones presented in the popular media. For example, Wickman (2011) has noted that in addition to this 'aesthetic' aspect (i.e., appearance-related consumption), there is also an 'erotic' aspect of metrosexuality. The latter one refers to the erotisation of the male body in popular media and certain open-mindedness to the 'male-on-male' gaze (Wickman, 2011). Thus, in the realm of metrosexuality, men are themselves the objects of and for consumption (Schugart, 2008). Although scholars have debated whether the term applies only to heterosexual men (for discussion, see Wickman, 2011), research on metrosexuals has concentrated more on the aesthetic, not what Wickman (2011) called the 'erotic' aspects of metrosexuality.

In regard to this aesthetic aspect, Schugart (2008, p. 283) has argued that there was nothing new about metrosexuality. Instead metrosexuality was just one 'manifestation of commercial masculinity', a descendant of the 1980s' 'yuppie'. In the most critical discussion, both have been considered marketing devices aimed at manipulating young men's consumption desires (for a discussion, see Schugart, 2008).

More broadly speaking, several scholars in masculinity studies have analysed how the 1980s was a time for reconstructing masculinities (at least in Anglo-Saxon countries) (e.g., Edwards, 1997; Nixon, 1996). According to Beynon's (2002) summary of the era, the commercial masculinity was a second strand in this reconstruction; the first strand offered men a new role as nurturers, and the second strand as narcissistic conspicuous consumers. The 'new man' was born. Although through the history of consumer culture, men have participated in consumption practices conventionally associated with femininity, especially from the 1980s onwards, new male aesthetics were presented in the media. Men's glossy lifestyle magazines in particular gave the so-called new man a boost in the United Kingdom and the United States (Edwards, 1997; Nixon, 1996).

That being said, men have been actually offered various, even conflicting roles under the concept of the 'new man', i.e., a narcissist and a nurturer. In the same vein, Kaplan, Rosenmann, and Shuhedler (2017) stated that, on one hand, there has been the new man discourse rising from the therapeutic cultural discourses of authenticity and holistic self-awareness. On the other hand, popular media in particular promotes the consumerist discourse of masculinity, underlining the importance of consumption practices related to physical appearance in constructing self-identity. Although there is no consensus on what constitutes the 'new man', there seems to be an agreement on how the new man conflicts with the so-called 'traditional man' or 'traditional masculinity' (Kaplan et al., 2017). Unlike the traditional man, the new man is argued to be connected with his 'feminine side' either through his emotions or by appearance-related consumption practices (see Harrison, 2008 for a review). Thus, in the early 2000s, the new man was presented as someone not only willing to attend to his appearance but also ready to adopt more gender and sexual egalitarian views (Clarkson, 2005).

Although some marketing scholars have been inclined to argue that metrosexuality can be interpreted as a sign of increasing gender equality (cf. Mitchel & Lodhia, 2017; Salzman et al., 2005), within sociology and gender studies this has not been the case. On the contrary, neither the metrosexual representations of masculinity in the media (Alexander, 2003; Harrison, 2008; Shugart, 2008) nor the practices and attitudes of self-identified metrosexuals challenge, but rather they maintain the traditional gender order (Anderson, 2005; Casanova et al., 2016; Kaplan et al., 2017). The metrosexual representations and consumption practices can broaden the normatively accepted ways to perform masculinity. However, metrosexuality has its roots in the rejection of femininity and homosexuality, and thus both practices and representations of metrosexuality first and foremost privilege straight men over gay men and women (e.g., Anderson, 2005; Casanova et al., 2016; Kaplan et al., 2017; Shugart, 2008).

Although for decades media and marketing industries have striven to socialise both men and women to become full members of the appearance-centred society, in regard to men, the task has been much more difficult to complete. In Rosenmann and Kaplan's (2014) analysis on masculine body ideologies, the so-called metrosexual consumerist body ideology appears in sharp contrast to the unattended, functional body ideology associated with traditional masculinity (Rosenmann & Kaplan, 2014). However, in the media representations, using grooming products has been 'masculinised', underlining the 'corrective' instead of the 'beautifying' nature of cosmetics as well as the 'scientific' and 'technical' background of these products (Harrison, 2008). Several products and services have also been reinvented with a masculine label on them as Hall (2014, p. 16) pointed out:

> Indeed, even traditional feminine activities and items now have male counterparts and labels. For example: Brazillian bikini waxing becomes a boyzillian or manzillian; eyeliner becomes guyliner; handbag becomes manbag; makeup is mankup; non-head body hair removal is termed manscaping; mascara changes to manscara; pantyhose become mantyhose; panties are reworked to manties and there are many more.

The changing aesthetic codes of masculinity fit even more uneasily with the notions of the traditional Finnish man, at least in the beginning of the 2000s when the debate on metrosexuals was at its height. At the same time, as men's lifestyle magazines where booming in the United Kingdom, the magazines launched in Finland and in Finnish (e.g., *Cosmos, Men's Health, Miesten Gloria, Slitz*) struggled to find their Finnish audience. The lifespan was short and all the magazines were buried only a couple of years after they were launched. Afterwards, the target group was considered to be too small in Finland, and buying these types of magazines fit relatively uneasily with the idea of traditional Finnish men's consumption habits (Jokinen, 2003). For example, according to Hakala's

(2006) comparative study on representations of men in advertising in Finland and in the United States, the objectification of men had surprisingly not increased in neither of the two countries between 1973 and 2003. In a similar vein, Sarpavaara (2004) concludes in his study on the presentations of embodiment in TV advertisement by saying that 'most of the representations repeat the notions of the traditional gender system'. Although men were represented as objects to be looked at and also subjects who look after their physical appearance, these types of roles were assigned to women in the great majority of cases. Similarly, in the Finnish edition of *Slitz*, the young men's lifestyle magazine, the impression and representation of the male-to-male gaze was strictly avoided. Instead, the ideal man in *Slitz* was a playboy who took care of his physical appearance to appeal (i.e., to be good looking) to women and for whom the good-looking women were merely status symbols (Jokinen, 2003).

More recently, several masculinity scholars in Finland have argued that masculinities have become more hybrid in the sense that such elements as bodily strength, emotional restraint and orientation towards paid work have been supplemented with features typically related to femininity and marginalised masculinities (for a discussion see Hyvönen, 2019). This type of hybridisation can be seen, for example, in how Finnish men legitimise a non-traditional masculine practice with traditional masculine reasoning. In Ojala et al.'s (2016) study of men's anti-ageing practices, men wanted to distance themselves from femininity and women by rationalising these practices as something that promotes health and performance (see also Ojala & Pietilä, Chapter 4).

In sum, the previous literature on metrosexuals and changing masculinities suggests that men would have adopted more 'feminine' consumption practices. Next, I move on to analyse whether there is support for these claims when looking at national-level consumption expenditures and attitudinal data from Finland.

Data and Methods

Data

In this chapter, the main interest lies in analysing the gendered changes in physical appearance -related attitudes and consumption. My attitudinal examination is based on nationally representative survey data collected every 5 years between 1999 and 2019. I study the possible changes in monetary consumption by analysing Statistics Finland's Household Budget Survey data from 1998 to 2016. The data collection frequency of the Household Budget Surveys has fluctuated during the years. However, I have chosen five cross-sectional data points that, to some extent, match data collection points of attitudinal surveys. In my analysis, I adopt a gender-comparative perspective to assess whether men's consumption practices, i.e., attitudes and consumption expenditure, have actually changed and how the possible changes are comparable.

To analyse attitudinal changes, I use Finland 1999, Finland 2004, Finland 2009, Finland 2014 and Finland 2019 consumption and lifestyle surveys. The Sociology/Economic Sociology unit at the University of Turku conducts the surveys on a 5-year basis. All samples were random and drawn from the Central Register of Population. The data represent the Finnish-speaking 18–74-years-old population in Finland. The data for 1999 and 2004 were solely collected via postal questionnaires. From 2009 onwards, the respondents were also given the opportunity to complete the survey online. The sample sizes have fluctuated from 2,500 to 6,000 and, according to the general trend, response rates have declined (For more information, see data collection reports Saari et al., 2019; Koivula et al., 2015; Sarpila et al., 2010). The number of respondents and response rates for each survey year is shown in Table 3.1.

The five Finnish Household Budget Surveys I analyse in this chapter were conducted by Statistics Finland in 1998, 2001, 2006, 2012 and 2016. The surveys concentrated on a household's expenditure on goods and services. The data sets are comparable over time and are nationally representative. The surveys are sample surveys of Finnish households, the consumption expenditure of which is collected by telephone interviews and consumption diaries kept by the households, and from purchase receipts and administrative registers. Table 3.1 shows the number of households in the final original data and their response rates. In addition, it shows the exact number of cases used in the analysis. In the surveys, the unit of analysis is household. This means that to analyse differences between men and women, I have to restrict my analysis to single households. In other household types, it is not possible to examine consumption expenditure at an individual level (for more detailed description, see Statistics Finland, 2020).

Table 3.1. Survey Data Analysed in This Chapter. Number of Respondents (Response Rates in Parentheses).

Attitudinal Data	Finland 1999	Finland 2004	Finland 2009	Finland 2014	Finland 2019
Original data	2,417 (60%)	3,574 (60%)	1,202 (49%)	1,354 (46%)	1,742 (44%)
Number of households analysed	1,907	2,856	801	960	1,249

Consumption Expenditure Data	Household Budget Survey 1998	Household Budget Survey 2001	Household Budget Survey 2006	Household Budget Survey 2012	Household Budget Survey 2016
Original data	4,359 (63%)	5,495 (63%)	4,007 (52%)	3,551 (43%)	3,673 (46%)
Number of households analysed	642	828	588	546	723

Measures

To analyse changes in men's consumption practices from the gender-comparative perspective, I analyse two different dependent variables. The attitudinal changes is examined using an attitudinal variable called 'perceived care of one's physical appearance'. The respondents were asked to what extent they agreed with the statement: 'I take good care of my physical appearance'. The answers were given on a 5-point Likert scale that ranged from 'Definitely agree' = 1 to 'Definitely disagree' = 5. Note that the original scale can be considered 'reversed' (a smaller number indicating agreement and not vice versa) and in that sense it is atypical. However, I decided not to further revise the scale, which is a typical procedure in these types of cases to help interpretation. I consider this solution to be in line with using generalised ordered logit where operationalisations are taken less for granted. More particularly, it could be argued that people would answer differently to the question if it would be indicated that 'Definitely agree' equals a value of 1 when compared to the situation where it is indicated that 'Definitely agree' equals a value of 5. Thus, the scale cannot be revised autocratically (see Williams, 2016). Independent variables include gender (female/male) and research year (1999/2004/2009/2014/2019). I restrict my analysis to under 65-year-old household respondents to make the age range correspond to one I am obligated to use with the Household Budget Survey data.

In my analysis on appearance-related consumption expenditure, I analyse one dependent variable: the proportional share of yearly consumption expenditure on 'personal hygiene and beauty care' of the total consumption expenditure. As stated, I restrict my analysis to single households with an under 65-year-old household reference person. Again, my independent variables include gender (female/male) and research year (1998/2001/2006/2012/2016). My control variables include education (academic/non-academic), age as a continuous variable and place of residence (Helsinki metropolitan area/other). Furthermore, I must note that income is certainly associated with consumption expenditure. However, as I analyse proportional shares, there is no need to control for income. A descriptive overview of the variables applied is shown in the supplementary appendix.

Methods

The analysis on both attitudinal and consumption expenditure data starts with a descriptive overview on changes in the gender gap. After that, I will conduct a multivariate analysis of each dependent variable. For attitudinal data, I use ordinal regression analysis. I use linear regression (OLS) for the Household Budget Survey data. As I am interested in the changes in men's consumption expenditure and the possible peculiarities compared to women's consumption expenditure, I test interactions between gender and research year.

In terms of attitudinal data, the models are estimated with the gologit2 software in Stata (Williams, 2006). The generalised ordered logit is suitable method for analysing ordinal outcomes, if the so-called parallel regression assumption (also known as proportional odds assumption) is not met (Hardin & Hilbe, 2012).[1] However, this is not the only reason for using generalised ordered logit. As Williams (2016) has pointed out, using generalised ordered logit should be theoretically reasoned as well. Here, I leave space for the possibility that men and women may use different thresholds in classifying their attitudes towards attending to their physical appearance.

Results

In the first stage of my analysis, I use Finland Consumption and Lifestyle Surveys to examine the gender gap in attitudes between the years 1999 and 2019. The respondents were asked to evaluate to what extent they agreed or disagreed with the statement, 'I take good care of my physical appearance' (on a scale from 1 to 5). Fig. 3.1 shows the proportions of responses for each response category for men and women by research year. It indicates that the distributions of responses to five response categories seem to be quite stable over time. Neither men's nor women's attitudes towards taking care of their looks seem to have changed dramatically.

The figure shows how approximately half – varying from 47% to 55% – of the women have either strongly or slightly agreed with the statement that they take good care of their looks (values '1' and '2'). The rate of male respondents who agree with statement is clearly lower, varying from 27% to 36% during 1999–2019.

Next, I used generalised ordered logit models to examine the possible interactions between gender and survey year. The idea is to examine whether association between response year and the 'perceived attendance of physical appearance' is different for men and women. On the basis of discussion on metrosexuals, presumably men's attitudinal changes are somewhat different compared to changes among women. For these analyses, I combined the categories '4' and '5' as the number of cases in the category '5' was small, particularly for women. Table 3.2 presents the results for partial proportional odds model. As neither of the explanatory variables meet the proportional odds assumption, there are three coefficients for each explanatory variable. Results are presented as average marginal effects.

The table shows that gender differences in all outcome levels are significant (7–10% points difference between men and women). Attitudinal changes are rather modest and show no clear pattern. The analyses shows there is no significant interaction between gender and survey year. This indicates that the modest attitudinal changes have been similar among men and women.

Finally, I turn to examine gender differences in appearance-related consumption with Household Budget Surveys. The figure shows the predicted probabilities for the share of personal hygiene and beauty care out of total consumption.[2] The predicted probabilities are presented separately for men and women. I compared the OLS models with and without the interaction term. With regard to consumption expenditure on 'personal hygiene and beauty care', the interaction between gender and survey year was significant. However, the

18-64 year-old men (%)

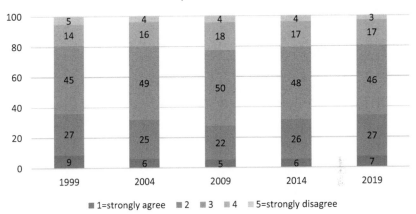

■ 1=strongly agree   ■ 2   ■ 3   ■ 4   ■ 5=strongly disagree

18-64 year-old women (%)

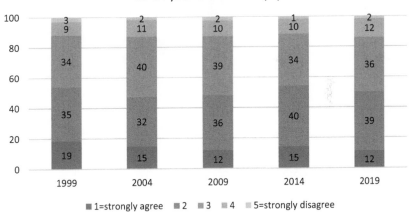

■ 1=strongly agree   ■ 2   ■ 3   ■ 4   ■ 5=strongly disagree

Fig. 3.1.   'I take good care of my physical appearance', responded to on a 5-point Likert scale, 1 = strongly agree; 5 = strongly disagree, 18–64 year-old men and women in 1999, 2004, 2009, 2014 and 2019 (%). *Note*: Please note the atypical formulation of the Likert scale.

predicted probabilities with 95% confidence intervals presented in Fig. 3.2 show only slightly different trends for men and women. Thus, the assumption that men's consumption behaviour has gone through a dramatic change is not supported by the Household Budget Survey data either.

Table 3.2. 'I Take Good Care of My Physical Appearance', Average Marginal Effects.

	Outcome 1			Outcome 2			Outcome 3			Outcome 4 + 5		
	AME	P-value	95% CI	AME	P-value	95% CI	AME	P-value	95% CI	AME	P-value	95% CI
Explanatory Variables												
Year (ref 1999)												
2004	−0.031	0.001	−0.050 −0.013	−0.025	0.065	−0.051 0.002	0.050	0.001	0.021 0.078	0.006	0.394	−0.015 0.028
2009	−0.050	0.000	−0.075 −0.026	−0.014	0.317	−0.052 0.023	0.030	0.106	−0.011 0.071	0.0344	0.038	0.002 0.070
2014	−0.044	0.000	−0.068 −0.020	0.036	0.064	−0.002 0.074	0.017	0.272	−0.022 0.057	−0.009	0.372	−0.038 0.020
2019	−0.042	0.000	−0.066 −0.019	0.031	0.084	−0.004 0.066	0.004	0.562	−0.032 0.040	0.007	0.418	−0.020 0.034
Gender (ref female)												
Male	−0.079	0.000	−0.093 −0.066	−0.091	0.000	−0.112 −0.070	0.095	0.000	0.073 0.118	0.075	0.000	0.058 0.092
Age categories (ref older)												
Young	0.019	0.028	0.002 0.037	0.107	0.000	0.082 0.133	−0.073	0.000	−0.099 −0.047	−0.054	0.000	−0.073 −0.035

Note: controls; age*gender.

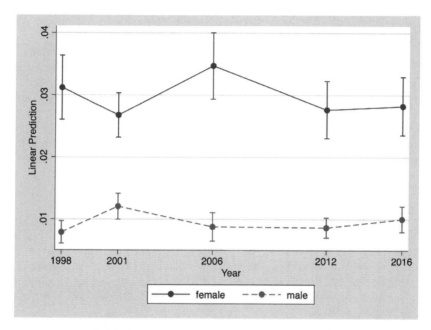

Fig. 3.2.   Predicted Probabilities of 'Personal Hygiene and Beauty
Care' Consumption Share of Total Consumption Expenditure. For men and
women under 65 years of age, single households, years 1998, 2001, 2006,
2012 and 2016. With 95% confidence intervals. *Note*: controls; age,
education, place of residence.

Conclusions

In this chapter, I reviewed academic discussions on the metrosexuality. The
discussion relates directly to understanding gendered norms concerning accumulation of aesthetic capital in contemporary consumer culture. Some scholars
have perceived metrosexual as an embodiment of commercial masculinity,
which takes different forms and is given different names in different times
(Shugart, 2008). However, metrosexuality is associated with a change in men's
appearance-related consumption practices and norms. Previous research has
analysed critically the pervasiveness of metrosexuality among different population
groups of men and gender-egalitarian views related to the phenomenon (Casanova
et al., 2016). However, previous studies are mainly conducted in Anglo-Saxon
countries, where change in the men's consumer practices per se has been taken for
granted more easily, although the reasons behind change towards metrosexuality
have remained debatable. In this chapter, I have shown that even the change in
consumption practices cannot be taken for granted. At least not in Finland.

In the introductory part of this chapter, I asked: Can something die if it
never lived? As a cultural discourse, the metrosexual seems to be nearly dead;
its heyday was clearly in the early 2000s (Casanova et al., 2016). However, the
empirical 'proofs' of the existence of 'metrosexuals' can only be collected and

analysed now, i.e., 20 years after the term was introduced. Simpson (2014), who introduced the term, has claimed that the metrosexual is dead, as grooming practices typical of certain groups of men have become a general norm among all men. According to Simpsons, this logic, i.e., all men have become metrosexuals, the metrosexual cannot be referred to as its own species anymore. Although this might be an idea not only Simpson adopted but, for example, also US white-collar men (Casanova et al., 2016), it is not supported by population-level data collected in Finland and covering the past 20 years. Either men's attitudes have not changed or there has been no change in the proportional share of the yearly consumption expenditure on 'personal hygiene and beauty care' of total consumption expenditure. Furthermore, the gender gap seems to be extremely stable. It might very well be that David Beckham is the only metrosexual who has ever visited Finland (he had knee surgery in Finland in 2010).

As I write this, the Finnish lifestyle magazine *Image* drops through my letterbox. The magazine is covered with a rustling plastic, which hides inside a sample of men's facial cream. The package is black and silver. A perfect free gift for a magazine's target group of a 28–50-years-olds working and having an urban and consumerist lifestyle. It feels that, during the past 20 years, I have seen this same 'masculine-coloured' men's cosmetic product several times before. It seems that nothing has really changed in this respect either. Although there is no talk about metrosexuals in the media anymore, the metrosexual or his inheritor is still expected to take human form sooner or later. From consumer capitalism's point of view, this is understandable, as the potential market is huge. In light of the current figures, it appears more profitable to tap into women's appearance-related insecurities (see also Kukkonen, Chapter 2).

Moreover, very recent studies (e.g., Hakim, 2018) suggest that appearance as a form of capital can be particularly important among men who lack other forms of capital. Unlike in metrosexuality, it is thus the most subordinated men for whom the very traditional masculine bodywork techniques, i.e., not those connected with metrosexuality, provide a way of creating value (Hakim, 2018). This, combined with my analysis in this chapter, tells a story of men and their relationship to their physical appearance. It seems that this story cannot be easily rewritten despite all the black and silver facial cream packages mailed 20 years from now.

Notes

1. Thus, the model allows the explanatory variable to have a different effect on the odds at the different levels of the outcome variable (Hardin & Hilbe, 2012). I used the Wald test to test the parallel regression assumption. It showed that the assumption does not hold for my data.
2. For simplicity of interpretation, the results are presented without logarithm transformations. I, however, run the models with logarithm transformation which did not change the results.

References

Alexander, S. M. (2003). Stylish hard bodies: Branded masculinity in Men's Health magazine. *Sociological Perspectives*, *46*(4), 535–554. https://doi.org/10.1525/sop.2003.46.4.535

Anderson, E. (2005). Orthodox and inclusive masculinity: Competing masculinities among heterosexual men in feminized terrain. *Sociological Perspectives*, *48*(3), 337–355. https://doi.org/10.1525/sop.2005.48.3.337

Beynon, J. (2002). *Masculinities and culture*. Open University Press.

Casanova, E. M. de, Wetzel, E. E., & Speice, T. D. (2016). Looking at the label: White-collar men and the meanings of "metrosexual". *Sexualities*, *19*(1–2), 64–82. https://doi.org/10.1177/1363460715583607

Clarkson, J. (2005). Contesting masculinity's makeover: Queer eye, consumer masculinity, and 'straight-acting' gays. *Journal of Communication Inquiry*, *29*, 235–255. https://doi.org/10.1177/0196859905275234

Coad, D. (2008). *The metrosexual: Gender, sexuality, and sport*. State University of New York Press.

Coad, D. (2016). Metrosexual. In *The Wiley Blackwell encyclopedia of gender and sexuality studies* (pp. 1–2). The Wiley Blackwell. https://doi.org/10.1002/9781118663219.wbegss497

Edwards, T. (1997). *Men in the mirror: men's fashion, masculinity and consumer society*. Cassell.

Hakala, U. (2006). *Adam in ads: A thirty-year look at mediated masculinities in advertising in Finland and the US*. Turku School of Economics.

Hakim, J. (2018). 'The Spornosexual': The affective contradictions of male body-work in neoliberal digital culture. *Journal of Gender Studies*, *27*(2), 231–241. https://doi.org/10.1080/09589236.2016.1217771

Hall, M. (2014). *Metrosexual masculinities*. Springer. https://doi.org/10.1057/9781137404749

Hall, M., & Gough, B. (2011). Magazine and reader constructions of 'metrosexuality' and masculinity: A membership categorisation analysis. *Journal of Gender Studies*, *20*(01), 67–86. https://doi.org/10.1080/09589236.2011.542023

Hardin, J. W., & Hilbe, J. (2012). *Generalized linear models and extensions* (3rd ed.). Stata Press.

Harrison, C. (2008). Real men do wear mascara: Advertising discourse and masculine identity. *Critical Discourse Studies*, *5*(1), 55–74. https://doi.org/10.1080/17405900701768638

Hyvönen, H. (2019). Men's work-related self-care in the Finnish Media. *Research on Finnish society*, *12*, 7–22. http://finnresearch.fi/RFS2019_Hyvonen.pdf

Jokinen, A. (2003). Sisäsiistiä seksismiä: Slitz ja miehen kriisi. In A. Jokinen (Ed.), *Yhdestä puusta. Maskuliinisuuksien rakentuminen populaarikulttuureissa*. Tampere University Press.

Kaplan, D., Rosenmann, A., & Shuhendler, S. (2017). What about nontraditional masculinities? Toward a quantitative model of therapeutic new masculinity ideology. *Men and Masculinities*, *20*(4), 393–426. https://doi.org/10.1177/1097184X16634797

Koivula, A., Räsänen, P., & Sarpila, O. (2015). *Suomi 2014 – kulutus ja elämäntapa: Tutkimusseloste ja aineistojen 1999–2014 vertailua*. Turun yliopisto / sosiaalitieteiden laitos.

Miller, T. (2006). A metrosexual eye on queer guy. *Lesbian and Gay Studies*, *11*(1), 112–117.

Mitchell, V., & Lodhia, A. (2017). Understanding the metrosexual and spornosexual as a segment for retailers. *International Journal of Retail & Distribution Management*, *45*(4), 349–365. https://doi.org/10.1108/IJRDM-05-2016-0080

Nixon, S. (1996). *Hard looks. Masculinities, spectatorship & contemporary consumption*. UCL press.

Ojala, H., Calasanti, T., King, N., & Pietilä, I. (2016). Natural(ly) men: Masculinity and gendered anti-ageing practices in Finland and the USA. *Ageing & Society*, *36*, 356–375. https://doi.org/10.1017/S0144686X14001196

Rosenmann, A., & Kaplan, D. (2014). Masculine body ideologies as a non-gynocentric framework for the psychological study of the male body. *Body Image*, *11*(4), 570–580. https://doi.org/10.1016/j.bodyim.2014.07.011

Saari, H., Koivula, A., Sivonen, J., & Räsänen, P. (2019). *Suomi 2019 – kulutus ja elämäntapa. Tutkimusseloste ja koodikirja*. Turun yliopisto / sosiaalitieteiden laitos.

Salzman, M., Matathia, I., & O'Reilly, A. (2005). *The future of men*. Palgrave Macmillan.

Sarpavaara, H. (2004). *Ruumiillisuus ja mainonta. Diagnoosi tv-mainonnan ruumiillisuusrepresentaatioista*. Tampere University Press.

Sarpila, O., Räsänen, P., Erola, J., Kekki, J., & Pitkänen, K. (2010). *Suomi 2009. Tutkimusseloste ja aineistojen 1999–2009 vertailua*. Turun yliopisto / sosiaalitieteiden laitos.

Schugart, H. (2008). Managing masculinities: The metrosexual moment. *Communication and Critical/Cultural Studies*, *5*(3), 280–300. https://doi.org/10.1080/14791420802206833

Simpson, M. (1996). *It's a queer world*. Vintage.

Simpson, M. (2014). The metrosexual is dead. Long live the 'spornosexual'. http://www.telegraph.co.uk/men/fashion-and-style/10881682/The-metrosexual-is-dead.-Long-live-the-spornosexual.html

Statistics Finland. (2020). Household budget surveys: General information about the data collection. Retrieved March 25, 2020, from https://www.stat.fi/keruu/kul/yleista_en.html

Wickman, J. (2011). Review of *The Metrosexual: Gender, Sexuality and Sport* by David Coad. *Men and Masculinities*, *14*(1), 117–119. https://doi.org/10.1177/1097184X09352176

Williams, R. (2006). Generalized ordered logit/partial proportional odds models for ordinal dependent variables. *The Stata Journal*, *6*, 58–82. https://doi.org/10.1177/1536867X0600600104

Williams, R. (2016). Understanding and interpreting generalized ordered logit models. *The Journal of Mathematical Sociology*, *40*(1), 7–20.

Chapter 4

Seeking Age-appropriate Appearance among Ageing Men

Hanna Ojala and Ilkka Pietilä

Introduction

Ageing is risky in contemporary Western societies. The ageing body and its physical manifestations of older age (e.g. wrinkles, grey hair, changing body composition and skin elasticity) are socially recognised as signs of less valued personhood. As Hurd Clarke, Repta, and Griffin (2007, p. 71) put it, in appearance-obsessed Western societies, 'individuals are constantly bombarded with the ageist message that youth is attractive, healthy, and desirable, whereas old age is unattractive and synonymous with poor health.' Bodies that appear to be old are not socially valued and may draw rejection and rebuke, which exemplifies widespread appearance-based ageism in many contemporary societies (Hurd Clarke & Griffin, 2008, p. 670).

Although ageing cannot be prevented, it can be controlled, or so the present thinking goes. In his classical text, Mike Featherstone (1982, pp. 21–22) states that consumer cultures emphasise the individual's responsibility to 'adopt instrumental strategies to combat deterioration and decay' of the body, and that the consumer culture relies on the 'idealised images of youth, health, fitness and beauty'. Both mid- and later-life bodies are characterised by decline in terms of youthful energy, vitality, virility and physical attractiveness (Lodge & Umberson, 2013, p. 225). As a result, people are expected to engage in appearance work to distance themselves from ageist stereotypes and maintain one's own aesthetic capital through beauty work, physical activity, diet and clothing. Technologies aimed at enhancing youth and beauty have become increasingly normalised and a natural requirement of especially feminine body work (Hurd Clarke & Griffin 2007, p. 190).

Managing an ageing body is based on maintaining (youthful) aesthetic capital through various bodily techniques to protect the self's social value and ensure ageing in a socially 'respectable' way (Skeggs, 2004). However, social demands for

Appearance as Capital, 71–83

doi:10.1108/978-1-80043-708-120210005

preserving youthful appearance, ideals of an ageing body and forms of appearance work are different for women and men, and thus body management practices are gendered (Calasanti et al., 2018; Sarpila & Erola, 2016; Sarpila et al., 2020). Interest in appearance has primarily been regarded as a woman's concern. Several studies (e.g. Hurd Clarke & Griffin, 2008, pp. 668–669) have shown that 'the social fixation on youthful bodies' leads particularly older women to lose self-esteem, experience insecurity in relationships, employment-related discrimination and perceived social invisibility.

Although research has largely focused on women's anti-ageing practices, it is important to bear in mind that men live in the same ageist culture as women, and are thus not immune to the dictate of fighting the visible signs of growing old. Therefore, in this chapter we explore ageing men's appearance work and consumption for managing their (masculine) aesthetic capital. Drawing on Bourdieu's (1986) conceptualisation of the body and capital, and Shilling's (2011) ideas of producing physical capital, we approach aesthetic capital as a combination of given features and achieved qualities by appearance work, which can be used as an individual resource to act appearance-wise in 'appearance-obsessed Western society'. Our primary interest is in how men relate their appearance-related practices to gendered and age-based appearance norms, and deal with potential cultural conflicts between masculinity and appearance work. In our analysis, we focus on an appearance work related to skin care, hair, physical exercise, diet and clothing.

In this chapter, we first aim to show that men are indeed interested in physical appearance, work for their appearance and are engaged in appearance-related consumption. However, we argue the ideals and norms that guide body management practices are shaped by intersectional differences, such as social class and generation. Age-based collective consciousness, or generational habitus as Simpson (2015) calls it, has a major effect on men's possibilities to grow older in a socially 'respectable' way (Skeggs, 2004) in terms of appearance. We conclude that appearance is a crucial factor in people's attempts to avoid a marginalised position of old age in contemporary societies.

Ageing, Gender and Appearance-related Consumption

Body management and appearance-related consumption include notably gendered features. Previous research (e.g. Hurd & Mahal, 2019; Hurd Clarke & Korotchenko, 2011; Hurd Clarke, Currie, & Bennett, 2020; Lodge & Umberson, 2013; Twigg, 2020) suggests that older men tend to be more positive about their bodies and are less concerned about their appearance compared to younger men and older women. Twigg (2020) interviewed older men and concluded that men's clothing choices were marked by continuity both with men's younger selves and with mainstream masculinity. Thus, men did not report any experiences of the *changing room moment*, by which Twigg (2013, p. 62) referred to women's consciousness that, by ageing, their clothes or styles were starting to look 'too young', which is why they had to abandon those clothes. Men did not see dress through the lens of age in such a direct way that most women did (Twigg, 2020, p. 113). There were men in the Twigg's study who tried to avoid the 'too old' look. This was about keeping upbeat or not allowing oneself to slip into negativity and dullness.

Despite this, men experience pressures related to taking care of their appearance when they grow older, but instead of attractiveness, which they relate to femininity, men think about their bodies more in terms of activity and performance (Calasanti et al., 2018; Hurd Clarke, Currie, & Bennett, 2020; Ojala et al., 2016). Therefore, body shape is a particular subject causing dissatisfaction for men as many of them wish to stay muscular and toned and maintain an athletic figure when they grow older (Hurd & Mahal, 2019, p. 13). For men in middle and later life, control over the ageing body and maintaining aesthetic capital revolve around able-bodiedness and preserving an athletic figure (Calasanti et al., 2018; Hurd Clarke & Korotchenko, 2011), alongside holding on to an active sexual life (Hurd Clarke & Lefkowich, 2018). Therefore, body management practices and appearance-related consumption are primarily based on exercise and diet. Physical exercise enables men to grow older in desirable ways (Hurd Clarke, Currie, & Bennett, 2020, p. 133) and manifests in three ways of men's understanding of physical activity: maintaining health, feeling good and getting tougher. Physical activity is positioned as an essential practice for demonstrating the 'will to health' (Higgs et al., 2009, p. 687).

Despite gender differences, there are also similarities in women's and men's body management practices and appearance-related consumption. For both ageing women and men, an essential issue in maintaining physical appearance is to keep the balance between means that are thought of as either natural or unnatural (Hurd Clarke & Griffin, 2007; Ojala et al., 2016). Keeping a natural body image is important to both women and men. However, as Hurd Clarke and Griffin (2007, p. 198) suggest, 'rather than being natural per se, the natural look entailed passing for a normal, unmodified, and youthful body even as it was the product of skilful artifice and covert technological interventions'. (Non)-surgical cosmetic interventions are currently viewed as normative and required aspects of especially female beauty work (Hurd Clarke & Griffin, 2007), but also increasingly of male's (Atkinson, 2008). The cultural demand for maintaining natural body images affects people's appearance-related choices, as looking unnatural may be socially more stigmatising than looking old.

A central feature in people's attempts to maintain natural body images and 'authenticity' (Simpson, 2015) is to avoid falling 'into the trap of denying their ageing' (Tulle, 2007). Based on Bourdieun-derived theory of capitals (cf. Kukkonen, Chapter 1), Simpson (2015, 2016) calls this sort of *cultural logic* as an ageing capital. Ageing capital 'consists of the emotional, cognitive and political resources developed over time through experience in various realms of existence' (Simpson, 2016, pp. 370–371). It indicates an increasing awareness of self and a sense of self-acceptance as one grows older (Simpson, 2015, p. 33). Ageing capital can be deployed as a resource to negotiate with cultural and social demands for maintaining a naturally ageing body. It also offers discursive resources through which middle-aged and older men can verbalise their accounts for physical appearance and appearance-related consumption.

Material and Methods

The empirical analysis of this chapter is based on 22 face-to-face open-ended interviews with Finnish men aged 56–77 years in 2017. Ten of the interviewed men had a middle-class background and 12 a working-class one. Thirteen men were retired and nine were working. All men were Caucasian, heterosexual and partnered, and lived economically stable lives when interviewed.

The data come from a larger qualitative longitudinal study on men's ageing (*MANage* study). The original interviews (three personal interviews and two focus groups for each man) were made in 2010 and 2011, and the follow-up interviews (one personal interview for each man) were in 2017. The interviews covered several themes that ranged from ageing employees' position in the labour market, retirement as a period of change in a man's life, health-related behaviours and psycho-social well-being to impacts of ageing on appearance, age-related consumption and anti-ageing practices. All interviews were digitally recorded with signed informed consent from the interviewees, transcribed verbatim by a professional transcription service and validated by the study investigators to ensure accurate and complete transcription. All names used in the data excerpts are pseudonyms.

The preliminary analyses led us to note that men primarily approached appearance-related issues from the perspective of bodily functionality and instrumentality that they attached to the masculine performative body and distanced from feminine aesthetic values – a divide reported in many previous studies (Calasanti & King, 2018; Calasanti et al., 2018; Gill et al., 2005; Hurd Clarke, Currie, & Bennett, 2020; Lodge & Umberson, 2013). A recurrent feature in the interaction was that the word *appearance* in the interviewer's questions systematically activated a traditional masculine discourse among the interviewees resulting in responses, in which they underscored their disinterest in aesthetics that they attached to feminine vanity (cf. Sarpila, Chapter 3). Lodge and Umberson (2013, p. 230) have called this a distancing strategy. Distancing from femininity especially may be seen as a response to a culturally mediated fear that ageing leads to men's de-masculinisation.

However, this does not mean that men have no interest in their appearance or appearance-related consumption. In their study on young British men's talk about their bodies and bodily practices, Gill et al. (2005, p. 43) noted that men's appearance talk was drawn on by a very limited range of discourses, independently of their age, class, race and sexuality. The same applies to the older men of our studies. Therefore, we focused on discursive practices that the men utilised for justifying their attempts to control their bodily ageing and balancing the potentially 'effeminate' effects of appearance consumption. In other words, our primary interest was in how men discursively manage the contradictory cultural demands of maintaining a 'not old' look while avoiding any practices or their verbalisations that could be considered feminine. Alongside this, we analyse the ways in which men from different occupational groups construct their versions of (masculine) aesthetic capital; while previous research has concluded that 'able-bodiedness' is a key element of this capital for ageing men, class-based and generation-related values and norms may have an effect on both the interpretations of able-bodiedness and which kind of role consumption plays in preserving it. Therefore, we analyse our male interviewees' descriptions of their body management practices from the perspectives of gender, class and generation.

Analysis

Taking Distance to Femininity: Skin Care and Hair

Our previous study (Ojala et al., 2016) on men's use of and thoughts about anti-ageing products, which was based on interviews with the same men in 2010/2011, showed that while men considered it important to maintain a youthful appearance, they opposed any means that they considered to belong to women and thus have 'effeminate' effects on them. At its core, their thinking was to maintain good looks in 'natural ways' and thus avoid any cosmetics or commercial anti-ageing products and services that they attached to multinational companies that they thought were cheating people. As reviewed above, men also often deny having any ambition to care about their appearance in an aesthetic sense, but underscore healthy and performative looks.

While in the earlier study none of our interviewees had dyed their hair and most expressed negative stands towards it, in the 2017 interviews, the attitudes were not as strict. Although in the earlier study the working-class men had the strongest negative views about using anti-ageing products, including hair dyeing, in the 2017 interviews, one of them said he had dyed his hair a few times. Quite interestingly, his main reason for doing so was because 'other men have started to dye their hair', which both underlines the importance of the norms shaping men's appearance-related consumption and seems to indicate a certain change in them. Despite this potential change, most of our interviewees did not find hair dyeing as something they would do themselves. Particularly for the older participants, having grey hair was considered a sign of their age that should not be 'artificially' concealed. Younger interviewees subscribed to this idea, even though they did not feel that 'getting grey' was pleasant.

The working middle-class group of men had the most positive attitudes towards taking care of one's looks and appearance-related consumption. Their interviews echoed somewhat different perspectives to grey hair as it was also viewed to create some advantage instead of being an entirely bad thing. As Teppo (59 years) jokingly put it, 'Let the experience be seen'. For middle-class men working in expert positions, grey hair is not only a negative sign of ageing but also may be taken to display accumulated knowledge and skills.

As reviewed above, men justified their use of skin care products with functional reasons, such as preventing dry skin. From this perspective, an excerpt from Asko's interview includes interesting features when the interviewer points to these functional goals as a reason for Asko's use of skin care product.

Excerpt 1

Asko (72 years): When I shave, I've used for 10 years such a new gel, which contains vitamins. It's new on the market. First I used another shaving gel, such as white gel. And it always – I don't use aftershave, I use that gel a lot. And now when there's one with vitamins – I used to have barber's itch here [under his chin] every now and then, when it got dry. Now when I shave I always spread it here and a bit there too [pointing to his face]. And you know my skin has completely changed. You can notice it right away.

Interviewer: So it's not that dry?

Asko: Yeah, it's not dry and it's – it's like so bright and sort of, I'm not sure if even the wrinkles have [become smooth]. But there's not plenty of them yet anyway. I really recommend it, like if older men could be persuaded to use such [products]. But many [think] 'it's just such that women fuss about' when they use night creams and day creams [laughing].

Interviewer: So you indeed think about your *appearance*, and take a look at –.

Asko: No, no but – well of course I see myself from the mirror every morning. But anyway I've noticed that [the gel] helps with my skin, in principle. And when it includes vitamins; I can get those dry spots away. Therefore I've liked it.

After Asko's description of the gel he uses, the interviewer offers a functional explanation for his use of a skin care product ('So it's not that dry?'). At this point, Asko more or less ignores this interpretation and accentuates the 'brightness' of his skin and possible smoothing of wrinkles. This leads the interviewer to make another question: 'So you indeed think about your appearance?' It is striking that after this comment Asko gets back to the 'functional' explanation and praises the gel for helping him in getting rid of his dry skin. In our interpretation, the reference to thinking about appearance seems to refer to aesthetic motives for the use of skin care products in Asko's mind, which makes him get back to the functional argument. The exchange showcases the oscillating stands that the men express in interviews about appearance and consumption, and evince the existence of norms that regulate the ways in which men can talk about their appearance work.

Idealisation of Performative Masculinity: Physical Exercise and Diet

In our interviews, men accentuated the importance of physical exercise in controlling the effects of ageing on their bodies (see also Calasanti et al., 2018; Hurd Clarke, Currie, & Bennett, 2020). In describing their preferences of exercise, many men said they considered everyday physical work to be the best way to keep themselves in good condition, referring to such daily tasks as gardening, chopping firewood or having walks with their dogs, instead of sports. Those who were engaged in sports type of exercise preferred traditional forms of sports, such as swimming, riding a bicycle or cross-country skiing. Only a few said they go to a gym. Another important feature of their thinking about exercise was that their motives for exercising were related to maintaining good health and functional ability, which was distanced from the motives relating to aesthetic control of an ageing body (see also Hurd Clarke, Currie, & Bennett, 2020). Men's descriptions of physical exercise thus largely followed the same logic as with skin care. For them, an ideal way of having physical exercise involves other functional purposes (such as moving from one place to another or making firewood), it is a 'natural' way to be physically active and does not cause extra costs and the goals of exercise are distanced from aesthetic purposes that are considered feminine.

Although the men underscored that they did not engage in physical exercise for aesthetic reasons, they acknowledged that their physical activeness was partly aimed at avoiding negative changes in their appearance. An ageing (or old) man's body was often described in terms of sagging and softness, with frequent references to a 'beer belly', that men wanted to avoid. A slim body was regarded as healthy and 'not aged'.

Excerpt 2

> Interviewer: Last time [in 2011] we met, we talked about appearance. So how do you think about your *appearance* now?
>
> Olli (57 years): That's a tough question. I don't know [laughs]. Like as such, I don't really – I don't [think about it] in such a way that I would pay particular attention to my looks. So I don't, no I don't really, I don't think about it very much. But of course there's – I certainly have a clear purpose to keep myself slim in the future. So I take care of it and I think I have such a strong self-discipline that I think I also can do it and keep it. So in a certain way that's such a thing to me that I want to stick to it.

A notable feature in Olli's description is his inability to first choose his perspective and discourse in responding to the interviewer's question, which includes the word 'appearance', which often provoked oscillating responses for our interviewees (cf. Excerpt 1). This is manifested in his frequent expressions of 'I don't' and difficulties to formulate coherent sentences. After these difficulties, his main argument is that his efforts to maintain a slim body requires strong self-discipline. Keeping the body slim through physical exercise and diet certainly requires willpower, as Olli points out. However, at the same time, bodily control of ageing is aimed at modifying the body to represent the self-discipline of its carrier; while a slim body signifies a controlled self with sufficient self-discipline to meet the goals, a soft and sagging body represents a lack of control and willpower.

Most of our interviewees did not consider appearance to be an important motive for doing exercise. Those who acknowledged the importance of looks, as Olli did, most often described the importance of appearance in general terms without a specific context with identifiable people who would assess their bodies. In this respect, 57-year-old Timo's case was an exception. When he was single, being physically fit related to more concrete aesthetic capital of (sexualized) attraction in the 'market' of coupling. For Timo, appearance was a modifiable element of the self that he felt increased his exchange value in embodied interaction in bars. Both examples above highlight that alongside symbolic value, aesthetic capital also yields more concrete exchange value both in the labour market and coupling.

Externalised Forming of Aesthetic Capital: Clothing

Most our interviewees did not buy their clothes themselves, but their partners either bought them or selected suitable clothes after which the couples went together to a shop to buy them. Some men said they go to shop only when their wives 'order' them to do so. The partners also controlled men's dress by judging what clothes men should wear in various situations, while the interviewees underlined that comfort and durability were the main, and often only, criteria for the clothes they wore.

The men expressed two different stances towards their wives' domineering behaviour regarding their clothing. Some of them attached this eagerness to buy new clothes to women's vanity and complained that their wives were constantly 'pressing' new clothes and new ideas regarding clothing to them, which the men regarded as completely dispensable. This stand was based on an idea that the interviewees were still satisfied with their old clothes and buying new clothes 'just for fun' was simply a waste of money. These interviewees often accompanied their descriptions with notably critical views on any form of consumption in regards to their looks, which they thought was unnecessary. On the other hand, several men's descriptions included features of a certain pride they felt in having wives who took care of their dress. These men praised their wives' good taste and sense of colour, and thought that their wives knew exactly what kinds of clothes the men themselves wanted to wear.

While the majority of our interviewees actively expressed various levels of disinterest in clothing, the working-aged engineers were clearly the only group of men who showed both interest and knowledge regarding clothes, even fashion, which was a pet peeve for most other interviewees. When asked which kind of an effect clothing has on how people assess a person's age, Teppo gives a rather detailed answer.

Excerpt 3

> Teppo (59 years): It has a major effect if you're wearing braces and baggy trousers. [...] I've switched to mainly using these slim cut B shirts because I sort of noticed that, hey, I can wear these and they

look a lot better. I used to have such baggy shirts, I had those C cut shirts for some reason. [...] And then tighter jeans or tighter trousers, they look better than those that are comfortable. And well, then you should have good shoes, nice-looking shoes, so I've started to pay a little bit attention to such issues. [...] For example, I bought these slacks. They're my favourites, and then I bought this coat. And then I bought such outdoor jacket made of polyester, which has been really comfortable, I've used it at work and travel, it's nice-looking, blue, such a basic stuff. I've bought jeans. I mainly go [to clothes shop] abroad because there I sometimes have time to do it and then, for instance in Germany, they are a lot cheaper. I never buy designer clothes, unless they just pop up and are good-looking and inexpensive.

Teppo's account includes elements of both fashion-conscious consideration of clothes and a slightly resistant attitude towards clothing-related consumption. He expresses his awareness of how tighter clothes have become trendy and that he has modernised his clothing so as not to look outdated. He even says that he buys tighter jeans that are not comfortable but look better. On the other hand, he underscores that he never buys designer clothes, prefers inexpensive clothes and does shopping only when he has spare time to do that. All these effectively communicate that while Teppo is a modern man with awareness of clothing trends, he is not overly fussy about the clothes, does not spend a lot of time and money for clothes and, accordingly, has a reasonable and manly attitude towards dress. Although Teppo expresses his awareness of clothing trends, his ideas regarding clothing come close to what van der Laan and Velthuis (2016, p. 28) found in interviewing 20–30-year-old Dutch urban men. For these men, getting dressed was not determined by their attempts to highlight their individuality but by routine and practical considerations, such as weather conditions, accompanied with an aim to maintain 'authenticity' and coherence in their clothing styles.

The working-aged middle-class men's relative interest in and knowledge of clothing trends is largely explained by their work. As they work in business and expert organisations, they are aware of the importance of physical appearance in their work, particularly in contacts with customers (cf. Pajunen, Chapter 5). On a more abstract level, knowledge of trends is also an important sign of a person's ability to keep up with the times (Twigg, 2020). Most middle-class men (both retired and those still working) expressed ideas of certain clothing styles required at work and that these styles have to be followed, even if they were not in line with a person's own taste. For example, 56-year-old Tero says that he doesn't 'like to wear a suit at all, but there is no other choice' in his work. In a similar vein, Ilmari (retired, 74 years) concluded that, 'I don't wear a tie unless I really have to because I wore it enough at one time'.

As discussed above, working-class and older interviewees often expressed active disinterest in clothing, appearance-related consumption and fashion as they had often interpreted this as the feminine life spheres. However, sometimes men's inexperience in buying clothes was not dependent on cultural norms, but rather caused by the gendered division of reproduction within families. Hannes's wife suffers from memory disorders. As her illness has progressed, she has become increasingly possessive of Hannes, and would not let him leave the house. Therefore, Hannes has started two new hobbies that provide him with regular opportunities to spend a few hours away from home. His wife's inability to buy him clothes has opened up new opportunities for Hannes.

Excerpt 4

> Interviewer: Well, when you go to a clothing store so what do you usually buy there?
>
> Hannes (72 years): Yes, that's a good question because for me-, when I lived at home [in adolescence] my mother bought my clothes and when I got married the wife bought the clothes. I could really say that, was it half a year ago when I decided to start buying my own clothes. And I've bought these jeans. And then I bought blue corduroys because they were on sale. And then, when I was leaving for Lapland, I bought [mentioning trademark] hiking trousers. These are the clothes [laughing] that I have bought myself.
>
> Interviewer: OK, how was that experience [to buy the clothes]?
>
> Hannes: Listen, it was very nice, very nice. And I certainly decided that from now on I buy all the clothes I need, though there's not much I really need. But in my whole life I've not – I was 72 when I started to buy clothes [short laughter].

Hannes's interview was an exception among the older participants in that he expressed sharp-eyed and nuanced comments on his peers' clothing and appearance. However, in line with his generation's gendered practices, he has not bought his own clothes as that task has belonged to his mother and wife. Quite ironically, his wife's illness has introduced him to new opportunities to feel himself agentic in a manner that gendered norms and generational habitus have blocked earlier in his life. This highlights that while norms related to age, gender, generation and normative life courses may prevent men from getting engaged in certain activities for most of their lives, sudden life changes may provide an individual with access to new life spheres.

Conclusion

A running thread in research on appearance-related consumption is that by consuming products and services, people engage in appearance work aimed at making distinctions. In particular, men are thought to base their consumption, and generally their appearance work, on attempts to distance themselves from women and practices considered feminine, a notion highlighted in several previous studies (Calasanti et al., 2018; Hurd Clarke, Currie, & Bennett, 2020; Ojala et al., 2016). Our analysis additionally shows how hesitant men are to attach any aesthetic motives to their choices, independently of whether the appearance work relates to skin care, hair, physical exercise, diet or clothing. However, it is important to bear in mind that alongside gender-based distinctions, appearance work also includes age and class-based distinction makings.

In an ageist society, being old is a marginalised position. Therefore, a crucial element of appearance work for middle-aged and older people is to avoid being seen as old by other people. On the other hand, Simpson (2015, p. 40) has pointed out that people more generally aim to avoid 'age-inappropriate' forms of self-presentation. While maintaining youthful looks is essential not to be seen as old, one also should not look 'too youthful', for instance by wearing clothes that young people wear, as that might signal a denial of one's inevitable ageing. As van der Laan and Velthuis (2016) pointed out, an important norm in terms of clothing is to maintain 'authenticity'. We argue that an important constituent of this authenticity is people's awareness of 'generational habitus' (Simpson, 2015) that embodies the codes of appropriate clothing and other aspects of appearance for each generation. While wearing blue jeans is a daily practice for middle-aged and older people today, this was not so in the 1970s when jeans were strongly associated with younger generations' clothing styles. Generations similarly have different views on other dimensions of appearance work regarding, among others, use of cosmetics or dyeing of hair. Consequently, what in any historical moment appears to be age-appropriate appearance has more to do with generation rather than chronological age.

Despite generations having their own 'collective consciousness' regarding appearance (Simpson, 2015), it would be an oversimplification to interpret generational habitus to be a coherent set of norms uniformly characterising preferences of various cohorts. Other intersecting differences, such as class, also play a role in people's appearance work. Generational habitus intersects with class-based habitus, by which various aspects of appearance (clothing, hair, etc.) are important factors for individuals in gaining class-based 'respectability' (Skeggs, 2004). Our analysis also shows that occupational status sets rules for appropriate appearance as various jobs demand certain looks (cf. Pajunen, Chapter 5). In our interviews, the middle-class men were particularly aware of these demands and articulated the rules for clothing in their work. Gaining appearance-related capital, as one form of cultural capital, certainly yields symbolic value for people in various life spheres. However, it is important to note that aesthetic capital and respectable appearance also bear more concrete exchange value, such as (sexualised) attraction in the coupling market. This demonstrates that even for aged men, appearance may be viewed as a distinct form of capital.

In discussions of 'appearance-obsessed Western society', it is often assumed that the increasing valuation of appearance primarily concerns younger and working-aged people, whereas it has minor effects on older people's lives. We argue that appearance has a vital importance for ageing people in fighting against marginalisation caused by old age. Therefore, even men, who often are considered less receptive of appearance-related cultural demands than women, recognise the 'rules' of how appearance signals successful ageing. Awareness of appearance as a sign of a person's moral worth and gendered limits of bodywork are central elements of ageing capital in contemporary Western societies.

References

Atkinson, M. (2008). Exploring male femininity in the 'crisis'. Men and cosmetic surgery. *Body and Society*, *14*(1), 67–87. https://doi.org/10.1177/1357034X07087531

Bourdieu, P. (1986). The forms of capital. In J. G. Richardson (Ed.), *Handbook of theory and research for the sociology of education* (pp. 241–258). Greenwood Press.

Calasanti, T., & King, N. (2018). The dynamic nature of gender and aging bodies. *Journal of Aging Studies*, *45*, 11–17. https://doi.org/10.1016/j.jaging.2018.01.002

Calasanti, T., King, N., Pietilä, I., & Ojala, H. (2018). Rationales for anti-aging activities in middle age. Aging, health, or appearance? *The Gerontologist*, *58*(2), 233–241. https://doi.org/10.1093/geront/gnw111

Featherstone, M. (1982). The body in consumer culture. *Theory, Culture and Society*, *1*(2), 18–33. https://doi.org/10.1177/026327648200100203

Gill, R., Henwood, K., & McLean, C. (2005). Body projects and the regulation of normative masculinity. *Body and Society*, *11*(1), 37–62. https://doi.org/10.1177/1357034X05049849

Higgs, P., Leontowitsch, M., Stevenson, F., & Rees Jones, I. (2009). Not just old and sick. The 'will to health' in later life. *Ageing and Society*, *29*(5), 687–707. https://doi.org/10.1017/s0144686x08008271

Hurd Clarke, L., Currie, L., & Bennet, E. V. (2020). 'I don't want to be, feel old'. Older Canadian men's perceptions and experiences of physical activity. *Ageing and Society*, *40*(1), 126–143. https://doi.org/10.1017/S0144686X18000788

Hurd Clarke, L., & Griffin, M. (2007). The body natural and the body unnatural. Beauty work and aging. *Journal of Aging Studies*, *21*(3), 187–201. https://doi.org/10.1016/j.jaging.2006.11.001

Hurd Clarke, L., & Griffin, M. (2008). Visible and invisible ageing. Beauty work as a response to ageism. *Ageing and Society*, *28*(5), 653–674. https://doi.org/10.1017/s0144686x07007003

Hurd Clarke, L., & Korotchenko, A. (2011). Aging and the body. A review. *Canadian Journal on Aging*, *30*(3), 495–510. https://doi.org/10.1017/s0714980811000274

Hurd Clarke, L., & Lefkowich, M. (2018). 'I don't really have any issue with masculinity'. Older Canadian men's perceptions and experiences of embodied masculinity. *Journal of Aging Studies*, *45*, 18–24. https://doi.org/10.1016/j.jaging.2018.01.003

Hurd Clarke, L., Repta, R., & Griffin, M. (2007). Non-surgical cosmetic procedures. Older women's perceptions and experiences. *Journal of Women and Aging*, *19*(3–4), 69–87. https://doi.org/10.1300/J074v19n03_06

Hurd, L., & Mahal, R. (2019). "I'm pleased with my body". Older men's perceptions and experiences of their aging bodies. *Men and Masculinities*. https://doi.org/10.1177/1097184X19879188

van der Laan, E., & Velthuis, O. (2016). Inconspicuous dressing. A critique of the construction- through-consumption paradigm in the sociology of clothing. *Journal of Consumer Culture*, *16*(1), 22–42. https://doi.org/10.1177/1469540513505609

Lodge, A. C., & Umberson, D. (2013). Age and embodied masculinities. Midlife gay and heterosexual men talk about their bodies. *Journal of Aging Studies, 27*(3), 225–232. https://doi.org/10.1016/j.jaging.2013.03.004

Ojala, H., Calasanti, T., King, N., & Pietilä, I. (2016). Natural(ly) men. Masculinity and gendered anti-ageing practices in Finland and the USA. *Ageing and Society, 36*(2), 356–375. https://doi.org/10.1017/S0144686X14001196

Sarpila, O., & Erola, J. (2016). Physical attractiveness. Who believes it is a ticket to success? *Research on Finnish Society, 9*, 5–14.

Sarpila, O., Koivula, A., Kukkonen, I., Åberg, E., & Pajunen, T. (2020). Double standards in the accumulation and utilization of 'aesthetic capital'. *Poetics.* https://doi.org/10.1016/j.poetic.2020.101447

Shilling, C. (2011). *The body and social theory* (2nd ed.). Sage.

Simpson, P. (2015). *Middle-aged gay men, ageing and ageism. Over the rainbow?* Palgrave Macmillan.

Simpson, P. (2016). The resources of ageing? Middle-aged gay men's accounts of Manchester's gay voluntary organizations. *The Sociological Review, 64*(2), 366–383. https://doi.org/10.1111/1467-954X.12363

Skeggs, B. (2004). *Class, self, culture.* Routledge.

Tulle, E. (2007). Running to run. Embodiment, structure and agency amongst veteran elite runners. *Sociology, 41*(2), 329–346. https://doi.org/10.1177/0038038507074978

Twigg, J. (2013). *Fashion and age. Dress, the body and later life.* Bloomsbury.

Twigg, J. (2020). Dress, gender and the embodiment of age. Men and masculinities. *Ageing and Society, 40*(1), 105–125. https://doi.org/10.1017/S0144686X18000892

Part II
Contested Conversions – Everyday
(Re)workings of Aesthetic Capital

Chapter 5

Too Smart-looking for a Waiter? – Scripting Appearance Norms at the Theatre of Working Life

Tero Pajunen

Introduction

People dress for work. They do it for many reasons; it may be for protection or for symbolical purposes. However, these reasons do not explain why, for example, salespersons wear black straight trousers more often than any other kind of pants, or why a sweater is more commonly seen on a youth worker than, for example, on a lawyer. Some could say that they are *normal* outfits for those persons. This chapter will examine how these 'normal outfits' are constituted and maintained in everyday working life.

To put it in more sociological form, this chapter will be an examination of aesthetic norms in working life and more particularly the process in which norms are created and maintained. In other words, the aim is not to describe the appearance norms of particular occupations, but to focus on the dynamics of these everyday norms: how they are created, maintained, enacted or challenged. I study the everyday encounters that employees have with other people at their work, and how these relations shape situational appearance norms.

I interpret the norms in this chapter through the Goffmanian theatre metaphor, which sees social life as a theatrical play and people as actors (Goffman, 1959). Norms can be seen as the scripts of the play that guide the role performances of the actors. However, the actors may improvise and interpret the scripts in their own ways and thus change the way the play turns out. Moreover, there is no single 'scriptwriter' in the theatre of social life nor a single script, but the script itself is a product of interactions between the actors. The focus in this chapter is on those interaction dynamics among different actors, employees' relations to their supervisors, colleagues, customers, clients or other people they encounter in

Appearance as Capital, 87–101

doi:10.1108/978-1-80043-708-120210006

their work. The analysis shows that the aesthetic norms employees face are often the sum of many (sometimes contradictory) expectations rather than 'coming from the top' or being solidly established.

The aim of this examination is, first, to describe the dilemmas employees face in interactions with other people in their work, when they are trying to figure out the right way to look. I focus more on the costumes rather than their physical characteristics, such as body size, sex or symmetricity. However, the main interest is not in the actual looks of the employees, but in the meanings they represent. I analyse these meanings in terms of impression management, in which employees battle to match their outfit with the situational expectations of multiple actors (or audiences). This empirical analysis of employees' everyday appearance dilemmas informs us about the situational logics of aesthetic norms. As explicated in the introduction and in the first chapter by Kukkonen in this book, aesthetic norms are at the core of defining how aesthetic capital works and produces social differences.

Theoretical Framework: Impression Management with Work Costumes

> Appearances are at the very core of how we structure social life and interact with each other.
>
> (Shulman, 2016, p. 1)

For Erving Goffman, a classical sociological thinker, social life is fundamentally structured as a play in a theatre (Goffman, 1959). In short, for Goffman, we are characters who act in different roles and follow certain scripts in our everyday life. The audience consists of the other people with whom we are interacting, and we are, in turn, their audience. An audience can give different sanctions based on the performances of the actors. In a successful scene, actors play along with the script seamlessly, performing their tasks and sustaining their roles. These performances reproduce a certain social structure, patterning how everyday life is structured. Our everyday interactions and relations rely on the success of these performances. The appearance of an actor is an important part of the performance. Appearances are full of visual symbols that create the impression of the actor for the audience (i.e. the role s/he may be playing, his/her motives, aims etc.) and thus inform how the audience should relate to that person. On some level, we all know this, although we may not necessarily be conscious of it, as we change the way we look depending on the situation. We try to manage the impressions we convey for the sake of successful performances and interactions, 'to grease the wheels of social interaction' (Reyers & Matusitz, 2012, p. 143).

Managing impressions is not only an act of an individual presenting oneself but also a way to define, at the same time, the situation and its rules – it tells others how the current situation should be interpreted:

> The doctor wears a white coat, the magician waves a wand, and the accomplished chef has a wide assortment of culinary

accoutrement displayed in the kitchen. Similarly, professors typically hand out syllabi, meet with students in classrooms, and stand at the front of the room near the board. These symbols of meaning help people key into expected role performances and thus aid in establishing the definition of the situation. Drawing on these symbols of meaning that convey commonly held associations enables us to define a working consensus for successful social interactions.

(Preves & Stephenson, 2009, p. 246)

Impression management aims at credibly performing certain social roles. Conveying a credible impression necessitates an audience who determines the credibility of the performance (Grayson & Shulman, 2000, p. 56). The audience determines whether actors' appearance-based impressions are credible and based on that, it credits or discredits the actor. In sociological terms, crediting and discrediting is akin to sanctioning. Social sanctions (positive and negative) may be formal (explicit) or informal rules that can be expressed in various ways, verbally or nonverbally. Altogether, sanctions are a key mechanism maintaining social norms (Encyclopædia Britannica; Lapinski & Rimal, 2005). At the same time, social sanctions bring out the current social norms, whereas norm-conforming performances are more often ignored, as they are in harmony with expectations. Norms are thus simultaneously produced, maintained, negotiated and challenged. Who is to blame, however, for establishing this script of our everyday show? Everyone in the situation is. Although the power among people is unevenly distributed, all actors contribute to the situational norms that are a result of collective action. People play the roles of an actor and of their audience, often at the same time (Bendor & Swistak, 2001; Claridge, 2020).

From the perspective of an employee and his/her everyday working context, who is responsible for creating, maintaining and monitoring the appearance code of his/her role (costume)? It varies for different occupations, but basically, there are three key audiences that most employees in occupations including human contacts encounter at some point: employers (or superiors and other higher status representatives in the occupation), their workmates (colleagues) and other people employees encounter in their work (customers, clients, employees of other workplaces) (Grayson & Shulman, 2000, pp. 56–57). These categories include a large spectrum of different actors, but altogether, these can be seen as the main audiences receiving and reviewing the credibility of employees at their work.

As mentioned above, actors are not equal when it comes to determining the looks of an employee. As a result, the employees may sometimes need to adhere to norms of which they do not approve or that are even harmful for them. This question has been addressed more in the research on emotional and aesthetic labour (Warhurst & Nickson, 2009; Witz et al., 2003). Studies on emotional and aesthetic labour emphasise that employers demand certain kinds of looks and behaviour more and more from their employees, in other words, requiring more acting skills from the workers (Bryman, 2004, pp. 122–127). These forced norms increase the workload of the employees and may cause, for example, emotional exhaustion, if the employees do not feel comfortable with the roles they have to play (Reyers & Matusitz, 2012). In these cases, employees are depicted to have little chance to determine their appearances and the script of their play is already established. However, few occupations are comprehensive in their aesthetic demands of their employees. Instead, the scripts for aesthetic norms at workplaces are more often written in the dynamics of multiple actors, which are shown in the analysis of this chapter.

Data and Method

As I was interested in the everyday importance of appearance, which often goes unnoticed, in contrast to more obviously appearance-centred situations and occupations (such as actors, models etc.), we contacted with our research group employees from several different occupations that include some kind of service work with people. We aimed to map out the role of appearance more generally in everyday working life, which touches on the experience of many. Hence, we included occupations that require higher and lower education, that are male- and female-dominated and those that are not clearly gendered. We gathered the employees of the same occupations to groups (one to three groups per occupation) and arranged a total of 12 focus group interviews, which each included two to five occupational colleagues and that lasted about two hours each and they were conducted in 2017 and 2018. The occupations were as follows:

- Lawyers and judges
  - One group of 5 women.
- University lecturers
  - Three groups: (a) 4 men, (b) 4 women, (c) 3 women and 2 men.
- Youth workers
  - Two groups: (a) 2 men and 2 women, (b) 3 women and 2 men.
- Car and electronics salesmen
  - Two groups: (a) 2 men, (b) 4 men.
- Nurses
  - Two groups: (a) 4 women, (b) 4 women.
- Bar and restaurant workers
  - Two groups: (a) a man and a woman, (b) 3 women.

I applied an interpretation of Goffman's dramaturgy and the idea of impression management while performing a content analysis of the interviews. I coded all parts in which the interviewees spoke about the appearance norm in their work. I classified these scenes by the audience that was present in the moments the interviewees described. These audience categories consisted of employees' relation to their (a) employer or supervisor, (b) colleagues and (c) outsiders of the workplace (customers, clients, patients, students or other non-colleagues or supervisors). The categories were not mutually exclusive. Instead, in some situations, all of them were present at the same time. This was the case, for example, when a salesman at an electronics store served a customer, while his colleagues and supervisor observed him from a distance, which included three different audiences at once.

Group interviews are unusual data with which to employ Goffman-inspired methodology, especially when the main emphasis is on the content of the interviews rather than on the interviewing situation itself. Whereas Goffmanian analyses usually concentrate on observing the actions of a present moment, in the interview data, the analysed situations are filtered through the interviewees' talk. Thus, the observations are limited to the interviewees' formulations of those situations, which in the group interviews reflect the dynamics and discourses of the groups and their collectively created meanings (Pietilä, 2010). Some aspects of the situations may be left untold and others may be exaggerated, which applies to direct observations as well, but in group interviews, there is another layer that shapes the nature of the data at hand.

Despite its limits, focus group interviews offer excellent data for studying the subject. Different things are said aloud in a group than would be said alone with the interviewer or in a different group. Some of the interviewees knew each other, which also shaped the dynamics of talk. In a group, there is always a certain pressure guiding the conversation and framing the rules that defines what is being said and how. This creates a space that itself reflects the shared norms of the particular group, which is in this case the group of colleagues. In contrast to individual interviews, group interviews produce talk that better illuminates the shared values and perceptions in the group rather than their personal relations to the subject matter (e.g. Frey & Fontana, 1991; Pietilä, 2010, p. 215). For the sake of brevity, all interviewed occupations are not explicitly addressed. Instead, only the most expressive examples that illuminate the dynamics of norm negotiation are discussed in more detail in the analysis.

The focus in the analysis is on the general patterns of how role costumes (i.e. aesthetic norms) are scripted in everyday working life. Group interviews of the selected occupations from Finnish working life function here as a case example. However, it should be noted that, in every occupation, the specific aesthetic norms and appearances of the employees signified different meanings as the employees acted in different roles. For example, a judge acts as a specialist and a neutral representative of the legal system, a waiter acts as a servant of the customers, and a youth worker acts in the role of a reliable adult. In some occupations, there were more formal and explicitly dictated working costumes (such as for nurses, car and electronics salesmen and restaurant workers), whereas other occupations allowed employees to choose their work suits more freely (such as youth workers and university teachers). Moreover, there were occupations (for example, lawyers) that did not have many explicit appearance norms but neither were the employees free to choose their outfit, as their colleagues and other people they encountered actively guarded employees' conformity with the norm. These particular differences among occupations should be acknowledged, although they are not the main interest in the analysis.

Analysis

Impressing the Employer

People pay particular attention to their looks when they have their first encounter with the organisation at which they are looking for a job. They thus try to manage the impressions they convey to serve their interests (e.g. to get hired) by using their looks as a means. Impression management leans heavily on appearances.

Job applicants try to give a good impression of themselves, to show that they are a good fit for the job and represent what is probably a slightly better version of themselves than they usually are. In other words, job candidates manage the impressions they give by means of their appearances, the main audience of which is the prospective employer. Besides their skills, candidates need to impress the employers with their appearance to show that they are suitable to enter the position they pursue. In this respect, employers are in a dominant position in relation to employees' appearance, as they can set the rules and norms governing proper looks for workers.

In the following example, Lasse, a restaurant worker with an academic background, tells about a contradiction he caused, when he wore different glasses in a job interview for a waiter's position than he wore later when he started the job. The supervisor commented on his appearance on his first day of work by saying: 'we didn't hire you looking like that'.

> Lasse: The glasses were like too 'woke', maybe too conscious-looking and a appearance of an academic. And you can't of course, I don't know what it was, but you can't really show off there. [–] It was the supervisor of the kitchen who commented it, but I did notice that the head of the restaurant was like, 'yeah I noticed your new glasses...' [laughter] I should have been looking like more boyish or so...
>
> Interviewer: But you kept the glasses anyway?
>
> Lasse: ... yeah I yet kept them anyway.
>
> I: So you can't look too smart there?
>
> Lasse: Maybe not too smart though.

This quotation contains several interesting points. First, presumably there were no explicit remarks made about the glasses in the job interview, but nevertheless, the employer had noticed them and later had interpreted that the employee had somewhat misled him/her by not wearing the same glasses at the workplace. The representative of the job interpreted that Lasse had fabricated a certain image of himself that had led the employer to act in a favourable manner and hire the candidate. Although Lasse had not misled employer on purpose, but just happened to need new glasses at that time, the employer felt cheated. This shows that the appearance of a job candidate in the job interview represents a certain promise of what the employer will get. Although job candidates often present somewhat polished versions of themselves in the interviews, their appearance should not differ too much from their normal looks. Otherwise, their act in the interview may be interpreted as misleading and fabricated.

The second point worth highlighting concerns fields and their different norms. The job position in question was for a certain nightclub restaurant with a particular image, style and pool of customers. That means that there are specific scripts for appropriate looks for the employers as well, as they represent the image of the company (see also Warhurst et al., 2000). These codes are seldom explicit, but still remarkably recognisable, due to socialisation, environmental cues and nonverbal signals of others (Grayson & Shulman, 2000, p. 53). Lasse diverged from the script the restaurant provided with his new glasses and was immediately sanctioned in his supervisor's comments. His glasses looked 'too smart' for the restaurant, implying that the customers would interpret him in a somehow unfavourable light in relation to the restaurant's image. In other restaurants with other kinds of customers, Lasse's glasses may well have passed.

Appearance codes for employees come as much from the expectations of the employer as from the customers. Expectations of an employer reflect his/her thoughts, how customers will act – will they trust the firm and use its services or take their money to some other place? This shows the extent to which the interconnectedness of all of these actors (employer, employee and customer) determines how the employer should look at that specific situation.

Most aesthetic norms in working life are implicit and informal, as in Lasse's case. They become apparent on certain occasions, when someone diverges from them and is sanctioned. However, companies and employers also manage their employees' appearances with explicit and formal instructions. Most obviously, these appear in workplaces that require a certain work suit or uniform for their employees, for example, in hospitals and many restaurants. In these cases, the appearance of an employee is predetermined by the employer, and there is little space for employees' personal expression or individuality (cf. Tyler & Abbott, 1998). Yet, the employer never has total control over the looks of their employees. Employees practice a so-called 'secondary adjustment' in which they manipulate and interpret the given rules to their own ends to perform better at their job (Shulman, 2016, pp. 96–97). This often transcends the limits of an employer's official appearance codes, and shows how the manifested appearances are a sum of relations of different actions. For example, in our interviews, youth workers stated that they did not have many official rules for their appearance at their work, except for one: they were advised to avoid wearing any kind of provocative symbols (i.e. religious or otherwise). The experience of the youth workers, how-ever, was the opposite. They found that having somewhat provocative elements in their outfit (for example, prints on their t-shirts or noticeable earrings) was a great way to make the first contact with the youth (see also Sillanpää, 2009).

The employees broke the official rules to better connect with their clients than they would have if they had literally obeyed the employer's instructions. In other words, they stretched the norm for the purpose of doing their job better (Sillanpää, 2009).

Employees' Relation to the Outsiders

The interviewees described two kinds of strategies to affect outsiders' impressions in their work. The first was a strategy mainly utilised in occupations that are institutionalised professions, for example, nurses and lawyers. Some of them were profit-seeking companies and others non-profit organisations, such as public hospitals and legal aid lawyers. These professions have a rather straightforwardly (but not necessarily explicitly) determined appearance code, a role suit, for the employees. The employee is, first and foremost, a representative of that particular organization rather than an individual. The second strategy to affect outsiders' impressions was a more personal kind that was practiced especially by the youth workers and those waiters of a more 'casual' or 'relaxed' bar. Their employers controlled minimally the looks of their employees with explicit norms, and thus they needed to work more with their personalities and individual looks. They needed to create the appearance for their role and to get clients/customers convinced by themselves, not by relying on the existing brand of the organisation.

Altogether, the purpose of both strategies was the same: to convince outsiders of the workplace to trust that the employee could act his/her role credibly to get the job done. Thus, the result of an accomplished impression management was a sense of trust between the actors. A successful act resulted in a shared understanding of the current situation and its rules between the actors. However, if the act failed and the client interpreted the employee to act totally improperly for his/her role, for example a lawyer wearing a too sexy skirt, it caused questions and the actor appeared as suspicious. A successful impression instead creates a sense of a shared interpretation of the situation, its codes, goals and roles for actors. Those shared interpretations that we make based on each other's appearances are kind of scripts, the social structure that guide our lives. At the same time, it is a way to communicate with each other and to determine each other's characteristics that tell how to cooperate and play along in the same scene.

Next, I give two examples from our interviews of the consequences of failed impression management. The first example is from the youth workers, reflecting their appearance norm in relation to the youth they work with.

They provided two perspectives, when asked about the role of looks in their job to make contact with young people. First, they highlighted the importance of employees' similarity with the youth – that one should not give an impression that one is from a different reality than the young people by looking too adult. Hence, youth workers more often preferred hoodies over suits. As the conversation continued, it was pointed out that an elementary thing in youth workers' appearance is to not exactly mimic the appearances of their clients. The interviewees stated that the youth would easily spot it if the worker tried to be someone other than s/he is, in other words, trying to fabricate the impression s/he is giving, and then not placing any worth (trust) in them. Or as Mikko put it:

> ...grown-ups are in any case from a different world so it doesn't matter what cool clothes you wear so basically you make a clown of yourself when you're trying to be 'MC Cool McDude'.

Their role as a youth worker required acting in the role of an adult mentor who works as a kind of a role model at the same time, teaching how life is to be lived. Thus, rather than trying to look like their youths, they more often promoted individuality and difference with their appearance. They valued authenticity and acceptance in one's looks highly, as they said that it is important to look like the person one really is, whether it is against the norm or not. They did not necessarily teach these views to the youth verbally, but by acting and showing an example of how to be 'real' to oneself and to accept that for others as well. This type of acting has been called authentic self-presentation, self-projection or deep acting (Grayson & Shulman, 2000, p. 59).

The second example of failed impression management comes from the lawyers' interview. Here, the audience is a person from another profession who has an encounter with the lawyer, who works as a legal aid lawyer and is used to dressing less formally to be more approachable to her more penurious clients.

> I haven't had jackets before like particularly for example to go to trial, and I had this new long leather jacket. So my client was charged with drug offence, nothing mild but rather a bigger case but it was like, the client was wearing sneakers and some jacket and, there wasn't security checks back then like in airports. So they checked me thoroughly, they went through my tampons and such, took them from my purse and for my client they did nothing. [laughing] So like I was very irritated, first of all I lost money, you can't use those tampons after that. And well, after that came quickly the, the gate for the court of appeal and then gate for the lawyers, but I went and bought myself a more conservative jacket right after.
>
> (Mirja, legal aid lawyer)

In this case, the audience of the lawyer's act was not her client, boss or colleagues but the security person(s) of the courthouse. They misinterpreted the lawyer's role, as she wore an atypical jacket for a lawyer at the courthouse. The security person(s) acted based on that false image by inspecting the lawyer instead of her client. It appeared that the lawyer had not given much thought to the impression she would give to others before that incident. The appearance norm became apparent, as her act failed and her role was misidentified, resulting in an embarrassing situation that made her buy a more accurate role costume.

In addition, the dimension of trust appears in the former incident very concretely. However, the trust is different and a more generalised sort than it was in the case of youth workers, for whom the trust was primarily personal. Here, the security person(s) evaluated trust connected to certain roles, positions and groups of people. If a person gives an impression that s/he is a lawyer, then s/he can pass through the building without inspection. The appearance norm or role costume of a lawyer communicates a certain kind of more generalised trust that is shared by all people in the particular category, a trust related to a profession.

The above example illustrates that these more general images of the looks of certain professions and occupations, as well as brands, may appear through the sanctions of other people outside of the workplace. The appearance norms need not be explicit and literal to be real. As the norms manifest in sanctions that are given in interactions between actors, it means that the norms are also in constant flux, varying according to the relationships between the actors and audience.

Colleagues Monitoring Each Other's Performances

The third audience category not yet addressed is that of colleagues and co-workers of the employees. They vastly participate in the formation and negotiation of appearance norms and role costumes at work (Vonk, 2020). First, the script is expressed nonverbally in the outfits of other employees that give the newcomer a hint of the aesthetic norm of the workplace. However, other employees may also comment aloud about the appearances, making the norm explicit.

For example, the group of lawyers came up with several cases in which their colleagues had somehow violated the appearance norm, and to which they had normatively reacted. In one of these cases, a lawyer wore shiny sneakers with an otherwise appropriate black suit to a courtroom, which the interviewee thought an inappropriate look for a lawyer and which she saw putting the lawyers' professional credibility in question. 'A lawyer should not shock with one's appearance', the interviewee added. The official etiquette for lawyers advised avoiding bright colours in their clothes and endorsed neutrality. Our interviewees showed that they keep guard of this norm, although they did not say whether they had expressed their disapproval to the subject and sanctioned her somehow more concretely than just discussing it afterwards. Altogether, they had recognized a certain dramaturgical script for a lawyer and interpreted that the lawyer with shiny shoes somewhat 'ruined the show' with inappropriate role costume. This kind of norm violation may be seen as disloyalty towards the dramaturgical order (Shulman, 2016, p. 85).

The group of lawyers also admired certain appearances of their colleagues, and hence affected the appearance norm of their workplace. They, for example, described noticing the small differences in their seemingly uniform costumes, and being able to spot whether some wore more expensive or higher quality clothes than others. They admired each other's appearances, but at the same time changed their own appearances based on those observations.

Two typical examples of verbal sanctioning among colleagues reoccurred in the group interviews: the 'are you ok?' and the 'so, what's the special event?' talks. In the following discussion, three female nurses in the group interview recognise the 'are you ok?' talk when one of the interviewees brings it up, and they mimic it together:

> Laura: I remember once I came to work, like I usually put on make-up for work, but this once I came to work without make-up, and one ward clerk was like – hey Laura, are you like ill or something – and I was like nooo, [laughter]...
>
> Anna: I've had the same thing happen to me, like are you, are you ill...
>
> Laura: (–) like horrible-looking or something...
>
> Anna: ...do you have a flu or something...
>
> Laura: ...yeah yeah...
>
> Anna: ...did you not have a good sleep...
>
> Laura: ...yeah like, have you been crying...
>
> Anna: ...yeah.
>
> Maria: I've also encountered that.

In a sense, the 'are you ok?' talk marks the lower boundary of acceptable appearance. As one nurse's comment suggests, the 'are you ok?' talk is interpreted as a sign that one is not looking good ('like horrible-looking or something...'). It may thus be regarded as a verbal sanction for not doing enough to live up to the workplace norm (see also Dellinger & Williams, 1997). In contrast, the second reoccurring trope, i.e. 'so what's the special event?' talk, can be interpreted as a verbal sanction for doing 'too much' or looking 'too good' to live up to the workplace norm:

> Laura: (Well just today) one, like one of my work mates came in and she had like really done her hair really nicely and the rest, and I was like ooh, like, like, are you going somewhere after work? Well, she wasn't, but, well, it's like... If they are someone who doesn't usually like wear make-up, and then she comes in with her face and hair all made up, then, well, I'm not like judging, but I'm like, ok I wonder what she's doing after work... [laughter] Yeah.

The nurses in this interview agree that colleagues, rather than customers or patients, pay most attention to their looks. Yet, they do not necessarily see these discourses as problematic, but appear to regard even appearance-related comments that sound quite harsh (e.g. comments Essi received upon colouring her previously blonde hair pink: 'why did you do that to your hair?', 'did you drop a can of paint on your head... quickly go was that off') as light banter between colleagues.

Conclusions

Here, I have analysed how the role costumes of employees are scripted in workplaces in the relations between employees and the people they encounter at work. I did this by employing a Goffmanian framework, which sees social life as a theatrical dramaturgy and people as actors who exercise impression management while playing different roles. The analysis informed us in many respects on the questions mentioned.

First, it described how aesthetic norms at workplaces are a result of multiple relations. Bosses, customers, students, patients, clients and workmates have certain expectations about how an employee should look; they make interpretations of his or her looks and sometimes express the norm by giving the employee (positive or negative) sanctions. These actors may give contradictory sanctions to the employees, as their expectations are different from each other's: colleagues may admire, whereas the boss may say it is bad for the brand. However, employees do not necessarily change their looks in accordance with the sanctions they get, but they may in some cases challenge the norms or interpret them in their own ways, which eventually puts norms in motion.

Norms are constantly battled, which turns the attention into power relations. Whose sanctions have power over employees' looks? Why are some employees allowed to break appearance norms more than others? Who is the main 'scriptwriter' in each situation? Based on my analysis, the answer to these questions is more complex than the space of this chapter allows to explore. It can be said, at least, that there are multiple scriptwriters in each situation. They are the actors and the spectators of the play, giving impressions and interpreting others' impressions at the same time. Some of them, however, are equipped with more status, stronger character, same-minded people or other forms of power that make their sanctions more powerful than those of the others, which ultimately determines in whose play we are acting. A lawyer may be constrained by the general conceptions of professional appearances, which his or her clients, colleagues and other people interpret and guard, for example.

Second, the analysis informed us about the consequences and purposes of impression management: what ends does the norm-conformance serve? The interviewees talked about several occasions on which their appearance had somehow shaped the situations in desirable ways: for some, it helped to get hired, build a trustful relation with another, give credibility or professionalism to one's appearance, 'grease the wheels of economy' by pleasing and attracting the customers, or it helped to get the work done in other ways. These positive consequences of impression management became particularly apparent in cases in which impression management failed and appearance norms were broken. These resulted in interpersonal misunderstandings, feelings of shame, contempt, mistrust and inability to make a contact, for example.

From a more sociological perspective, the analysis informed us about mechanisms of how appearance is used in everyday working life to maintain social order. The Goffmanian framework of impression management highlights that we order social life by constructing 'scenes', in which we act in certain roles. The scripts of the scenes that set the rules (and norms) for the actors and give meaning to the situation are socially (together) negotiated. Diverging from the script violates the norm, it shakes the social order and as a result, the violator may be sanctioned. Appearance norms sometimes have no purpose other than to be a symbol of a certain social role. For example, why does an electronics salesman have to wear black trousers? Why it is not suitable for a lawyer to wear shiny silver shoes? What purpose do they serve? They are hardly more practical than any other colours for the job, but instead, they are collectively regarded as symbolising these occupations. Shiny silver shoes in a courtroom may be seen as a seed of chaos in the social order of a litigation. It disrupts the expectations of the situation and the sense of known order by drawing the attention: something that does not fit in the picture. At the same time, it opens a door for social change: the audience needs to decide whether or how the act should be sanctioned, which determines whether the social norm is maintained or somehow changed.

Third, it showed that employees may break appearance norms if they find it somehow beneficial for them in their job. Then, they need to struggle between different aesthetic expectations of different audiences and choose which to follow. For example, the more provocative outfit of a youth worker or the less formal jacket of a legal aid lawyer are norm violations, but both render them more approachable in the eyes of their clients and thus helped them in their work. The lawyer changed her outfit after she confronted the security guard, whereas the youth worker continued to rebel against the employer's appearance guidelines. This substantiates the point made in recent studies on aesthetic labour: getting the right looks for a job requires extra unpaid work and resources from the employees (e.g. Donaghue, 2017; Vonk, 2020). Employees often must navigate within the pressure of conflicting expectations, pondering the right choice, what to wear and in whose play to act. This highlights the main argument of this chapter, which is that aesthetic norms are situationally and relationally negotiated and created. In terms of aesthetic capital, that means that when there are multiple audiences with different expectations, it becomes difficult for an employee to predict how his or her appearance will be sanctioned. This makes the exchangeability of aesthetic capital unpredictable and prone to situational codes and norms. It thus necessitates that employees also have the right kind of cultural capital and that they are able to embody it in their physical expressions at work. To conclude, there is no one way appearances act as capital in working life as the conception of the 'right looks' is inseparably tied to situational norms and actors with different resources and capabilities.

Acknowledgements

I would like to thank Antti Maunu and commentators in the PhD seminar of the Unit of Economic Sociology Turku in the fall 2020 for precious notes and support for this study, and Anna Grahn for her help in translating excerpts from the interviews.

References

Bendor, J., & Swistak, P. (2001). The evolution of norms. *American Journal of Sociology, 106*(6), 1493–1545. https://doi.org/10.1086/321298

Bryman, A. (2004). *The disneyization of society.* Sage.

Claridge, T. (2020, February 12). Social sanctions – overview, meaning, examples, types and importance. *Social Capital - Research & Training.* https://www.socialcapitalresearch.com/social-sanctions/

Dellinger, K., & Williams, C. L. (1997). Makeup at work: Negotiating appearance rules in the workplace. *Gender & Society, 11*(2), 151–177. https://doi.org/10.1177/089124397011002002

Donaghue, N. (2017). Seriously stylish: Academic femininities and the politics of feminism and fashion in academia. In A. Elias, R. Gill, & C. Scharff (Eds.), *Aesthetic labour. Dynamics of virtual work* (pp. 231–246). Palgrave Macmillan. https://doi.org/10.1057/978-1-137-47765-1_13

Encyclopædia Britannica. (n.d.). *Sanction.* Retrieved from https://www.britannica.com/topic/sanction. Accessed on September 23, 2020.

Frey, J. H., & Fontana, A. (1991). The group interview in social research. *The Social Science Journal, 28*(2), 175–187. https://doi.org/10.1016/0362-3319(91)90003-M

Goffman, E. (1959). *The presentation of self in everyday life.* Anchor Books.

Grayson, K., & Shulman, D. (2000). Impression management in services marketing. In T. Swartz & D. Iacobucci (Eds.), *Handbook of services marketing and management* (pp. 1–67). Sage.

Lapinski, M. K., & Rimal, R. N. (2005). An explication of social norms. *Communication Theory, 15*(2), 127–147. https://doi.org/10.1111/j.1468-2885.2005.tb00329.x

Pietilä, I. (2010). Ryhmä-ja yksilöhaastattelun diskursiivinen analyysi. Kaksi aineistoa erilaisina vuorovaikutuksen kenttinä. In J. Ruusuvuori, P. Nikander, & M. Hyvärinen (Eds.), *Haastattelun analyysi* (pp. 212–243). Vastapaino.

Preves, S., & Stephenson, D. (2009). The classroom as stage. *Teaching Sociology, 37*(3), 245–256. https://doi.org/10.1177/0092055x0903700303

Reyers, A., & Matusitz, J. (2012). Emotional regulation at Walt Disney World: An impression management view. *Journal of Workplace Behavioral Health, 27*(3), 139–159. https://doi.org/10.1080/15555240.2012.701167

Shulman, D. (2016). *The presentation of self in contemporary social life.* Sage Publications.

Sillanpää, T. (2019). *Ulkonäkö osana nuorisotyöntekijän ammatillisuutta: Ammattilaisten näkemyksiä ulkonäön merkityksestä työssä.* Thesis, Seinäjoki University of Applied Sciences. http://urn.fi/URN:NBN:fi:amk-2019053113716

Tyler, M., & Abbott, P. (1998). Chocs away: Weight watching in the contemporary airline industry. *Sociology, 32*(3), 433–450. https://doi.org/10.1177/0038038598032003002

Vonk, L. (2020). Peer feedback in aesthetic labour: Forms, logics and responses. *Cultural Sociology, 15*(2), 213–232. https://doi.org/10.1177/17499755209623

Warhurst, C., & Nickson, D. (2009). 'Who's got the look?' Emotional, aesthetic and sexualized labour in interactive services. *Gender, Work and Organization, 16*(3), 385–404. https://doi.org/10.1111/j.1468-0432.2009.00450.x

Warhurst, C., Nickson, D., Witz, A., & Marie Cullen, A. (2000). Aesthetic labour in interactive service work: Some case study evidence from the 'new' Glasgow. *Service Industries Journal, 20*(3), 1–18. https://doi.org/10.1080/02642060000000029

Witz, A., Warhurst, C., & Nickson, D. (2003). The labour of aesthetics and the aesthetics of organization. *Organization, 10*(1), 33–54. https://doi.org/10.1177/1350508 403010001375

Chapter 6

Generating Aesthetic Capital: Prospects from Autobiographical Narratives

Tero Pajunen

The sociological conception of aesthetic capital refers to relations of physical appearance and its sanctions that appear at the level of society. In other words, certain forms of physical appearance are systematically valued and sanctioned in certain ways, which makes such appearances function as social currencies or capital (see Kukkonen, Chapter 1). From large-scale statistical data, we can detect the macro-level powers of that capital: how different aspects of appearance (for example, attractiveness, symmetry or fatness) are related to unequal outcomes in many aspects as well as they show how our relationships to appearance reflect social (class) structures in many ways (e.g., Vandebroeck, 2016). However, it is also important to look on the level of lived lives to better understand how these differencing mechanisms appear in actual experiences and how appearances and capital are interrelated.

In this chapter, I will approach aesthetic capital without predetermined measurements and turn the examination on the subjective level – perceptions and narrations of how appearance has affected the lives of individuals. I focus on the individual narratives and explanations of the consequences of physical appearance in narrators' lives in the autobiographical appearance narratives. The aim is to open up the process of appearance turning into capital by shifting the focus onto individual perspectives and to ponder whether these perspectives could broaden the understanding of how appearance-related inequalities are generated on the larger scale.

Background for the Study

Physical appearance has a major role in shaping societal dynamics in many ways. Studies report its consequences on economic and social rewards, such as higher income (e.g., Anýžová & Matějů, 2018; Biddle & Hamermesh, 1998; Cawley,

Appearance as Capital, 103–115

doi:10.1108/978-1-80043-708-120210007

2004; Johnston, 2010; Kanazawa & Still, 2018), better hiring opportunities and career advancements (e.g., Baert & Decuypere, 2014; Hamermesh, 2011; Hamermesh & Abrevaya, 2013; Hosoda et al., 2003; Ruffle & Shtudiner, 2014; Wolbring & Riordan, 2016), electoral success (e.g., Berggren et al., 2010; Jäckle & Metz, 2017), partner selection (e.g., Mathes & Kozak, 2008; McClintock, 2014) and socioeconomic status (Jæger, 2011). Hence, it has been argued that physical appearance should be conceptualised as a form of capital (Anderson et al., 2010; Holla & Kuipers, 2015; Mears, 2015; Shilling, 2004; cf. Bourdieu, 1984; this book). The measurements of physical appearance vary in these studies. Very commonly, physical appearance has been approached as attractiveness or beauty, but size and shape of body, facial symmetry and aspects of femininity and masculinity have also largely been used as measurements. Altogether, the variables in such studies are always predetermined. These studies produce information about the magnitudes of different measurements that are prechosen by the researchers. The empirical justification to use the concept of aesthetic capital comes from these studies, as they aim to find generalisable logics in how physical appearance causes systematic inequalities. However, these approaches do not provide data to develop explanations and understanding of aesthetic capital further, as they just calculate the volumes of already-presumed variables and outcomes. Explanations for the different effects of appearance are construed from previously made hypotheses that could be either confirmed or supported (Timmermans & Tavory, 2012; see for example Maestripieri et al., 2017; Wolbring & Riordan, 2016).

Novel meanings and outcomes of appearance, in contrast, could be brought out in studies that employ data that are less structured by the researchers in the first hand, allowing more spontaneity to appear. Examples of these are ethnographically oriented studies that observe appearance-related questions of certain groups (e.g., Balogun, 2020; Mears, 2015; Weinberg & Williams, 2014), interview studies that are open to meanings the participants create (e.g., van der Laan & Velthuis, 2016; Ojala & Pietilä, Chapter 4; Pajunen, Chapter 6), observations based on the Internet and social media (see Puhakka, Chapter 8; Åberg & Salonen, Chapter 9) and studies employing expressive literary data, such as autobiographical writings (e.g., Innola, 2020). The theoretical understanding of aesthetic capital could be expanded from the results of these kind of studies. They provoke new questions about the impacts of appearance, illuminate more precisely the logics of accumulation and conversion in different fields and show how people relate to appearance-related issues and *how* they are meaningful for them. In addition, these approaches have a potential to inform about the processes of how appearance may turn into capital. In turn, they rarely provide information about the scale of those phenomena or formulate suggestions on how their findings could be operationalised to study them on a larger scale.

Both of these strains of research (generalisation-reaching statistical analyses and theory-broadening qualitative analyses) are important in themselves and increase the general knowledge of the impacts of appearance in our everyday life and society. Yet there are fewer attempts to make a framework that synthesises the findings and makes room for a more comprehensive understanding of appearance-related issues. The concept of aesthetic capital, however, bears a potential to combine these quantitative and qualitative perspectives (see e.g., Kuipers, 2015).

Bourdieu's theory of the forms of capital itself is built on various kinds of data that Bourdieu had adopted and which he developed into a more or less uniform description of how society works. It is widely applied in empirical research, which means that many find it to meaningfully explain empirical phenomena. However, Bourdieu's original formulation of the theory was not particularly clear or conclusive. Hence, it was interpreted and complemented in many ways afterwards in the research, and there is not one theory of capital but many formulations and interpretations (see Kukkonen, Chapter 1). This chapter's relation to capital theories is essentially an explorative one by spectating on the movements of capital from the perspectives of individuals. Although capital per se refers to macro-level phenomena, it consists of actions of individuals. However, the perspectives of individuals are never fundamentally unique and subjective but are thoroughly embedded in cultural ways of understanding. In brief, these different levels are thus fundamentally inseparable and co-constitutive, meaning that the macro-level inequalities are produced in the actions of individuals, whose actions are guided by cultural frameworks (e.g., Lamont et al., 2014).

In Bourdieu's terms, those frameworks that guide action are habitus – a person's internalised and embodied history – as structuring structures (Bourdieu, 1990, p. 56). However, the concept of habitus has been criticised for putting too much emphasis on habituality and continuality of action while acknowledging to a lesser extent individuals' potential to change the 'cultural script' they are acting in. Shilling (2004, pp. 478–479) suggests that the concept of habitus should be replaced with a pragmatism-based concept of situated action. In short, while the concept of habitus highlights how the actions of individuals are determined by their backgrounds and environments, pragmatism sees individuals as being in a constant dialogical relation to their surroundings. Actions of individuals are sometimes unpredictable because individuals have a potential to reflect on their actions and act differently than is expected (Ibid., p. 480). Reluctance to adopt the norms of thinness or hairlessness (see Puhakka, Chapter 8; Åberg & Salonen, Chapter 9) by being proud about something that one should be ashamed of are examples of the kind of dialogical relations that may eventually change norms (which are a constituent of a cultural framework) and thus affect the logics of aesthetic capital. From the perspective of situated action, individuals' relation to the cultural framework (including aesthetic norms) guiding their action could be habitual (they rather unreflectively reproduce the norms), they could end up in crisis with the norms or they could find new ways to act beyond a previous framework (Shilling, 2004, pp. 481–482).

I understand aesthetic capital as a macro-level term that reflects the systematic 'doings' of individuals whose actions are guided by (meso-level) cultural frameworks, and these frameworks are changed by the (micro-level) reflective actions of individuals. In order to broaden the understanding of how appearance can turn into capital, focus should be turned to the relations between micro- and meso-levels (Lamont et al., 2014, p. 24). That means examining how individuals interact with the cultural framework provided, which in this case is how they relate to aesthetic expectations (i.e., aesthetic norms). This is about studying the processes of how appearance turns into capital, which in turn reflects how appearances are related to social inequalities.

In contrast to studying the mechanisms of aesthetic capital, which aim at explaining the causal relationship between two variables (certain cause and effect), a process-oriented approach does not necessarily presume any predetermined causes and outcomes (Lamont et al., 2014, p. 26; cf.; Wolbring & Riordan, 2016). In other words, the aim is not to explain why, for example, attractive people are more often favoured in recruitments than less attractive people, but to study the generative process that ends up producing inequalities – for example, how classifications and links between things are made in practice.

Here I will focus on how individuals understand the outcomes of appearance. The definition of appearance is left open for individual interpretations by enabling one to understand it, referring either very particularly to a certain trait or to the totality of one's outward appearance. Additionally, the outcomes are here treated as an open-ended question that emphasises the 'effects' individuals themselves identify as relevant. I will thus ask how the process of appearance turning into inequalities-producing capital appears from individuals' perspectives and how individuals define the outcomes when their appearance either fits or fails to fit prevailing aesthetic norms. In addition, I will ponder whether this prospect could broaden the understanding about the process of how appearance functions as capital.

Data, Methods and Research Questions

I employ data from autobiographical appearance narratives of Finns. The data consist of 40 textual narratives that were sent in response to data collection conducted by the Unit of Economic Sociology in Turku on 2016. The participants were instructed to write an autobiography in which they reflect on the role of appearance throughout their lives. Participants were provided with a few prompts to guide their writing; they were asked to reflect on the meanings and importance of appearances in different stages of life and invited to discuss the possible beneficial or disadvantageous effects that appearance has had in their lives. In this chapter, I will focus on the latter aspect – the descriptions of the effects of appearance in the narratives.

The analysis is a product of thought that has developed over three years of being in touch with the data. I have read and coded the data on multiple occasions in a longer period of time from different perspectives and interpreted it from different angles. I have, for example, examined what usual situations of appearance-related outcomes are mentioned in appearance biographies, how appearance is affected in those situations and how the meaning of appearance changes and develops through life in the narratives. These are all relevant aspects in terms of how aesthetic capital manifests on an individual level, but at the same time they require more space for their analysis than the length of this chapter provides. Here, I focus only on the narrated outcomes of appearance in the writings.

The qualitative variation of the narratives is large, and they vary greatly in their length and level of detail. Those aspects set certain limits as well as open some opportunities for interpreting the data. The limitation is that the variety of styles and discussed themes in the narratives makes comparisons between texts difficult in some cases. The advantage of the variation is that novel perspectives may more likely arise. Although the participants had some guidelines for writing, there was more heterogeneity in the data than was present in more researcher-controlled settings, such as structured interviews. Here, the participants wrote about various kinds of appearance-related advantages and disadvantages that they had faced.

I employed content analysis and multiple-time coding on the data. After coding the outcomes the narrators mentioned, I analysed their contents and further categorised them by the main themes that were presented in the analysis. With this method, I aimed to discern how appearance issues appear at the individual level, when researchers have not predetermined outcomes, and to ponder what that reveals about the process of appearance turning into inequalities-producing capital.

This leads me to ask the following questions:

What kinds of descriptions do narrators give about the appearance-related outcomes?
Do they widen the understanding of how aesthetic capital is constructed, and how do appearances matter in society?

Appearance-related Outcomes in the Biographies

In the following analysis, I will examine what kinds of appearance-related consequences the narrators perceived as relevant in their life stories. These fell under three larger themes: (1) appearance as a symbol of making an impression, (2) appearance as a medium of social inclusion and exclusion and (3) the relation of appearance and psychological well-being. The themes are not ultimately separate from each other. Rather, they are different dimensions in the process of appearance turning into capital.

Appearance as Symbol of Making an Impression

Very common to our basic knowledge is that the first impression we get of people is largely based on their looks. Appearance is a symbol that communicates nonverbally certain meanings that, either truthfully or not, tell something about the carrying person as well (cf. Burgoon et al., 2016, pp. 95–124; Knapp et al., 2014, pp. 153–196). Thus, it was no wonder that appearance-mediated impressions were often brought up in the biographies as well. Although impressions are to a large extent subjective and context-dependent, they certainly could be seen as socially relevant outcomes of physical appearance. Next, I elaborate how these appearance-related impressions appeared in the narratives.

> Being uncertain of my physical appearance has influenced my
> career choices to some extent. I dreamed of a career as physical
> training master, but I discarded those dreams because I felt that
> my appearance was not enough to be credible in that job.
>
> (Elli, female, 26)

In the above citation, there was not even an actualised situation – only a fearful belief of the narrator that she could not make a right impression with her physical appearance to pass for a physical training master. Yet the narrator's concern in the citation of being disqualified on the basis of her outward looks argues for the meaningfulness of appearance as an impression-giving symbol for individuals.

However, impressions per se are not tangible but rather abstract images in respondents' consciousness. One cannot see straightforwardly what kind of impression any appearance gives to someone else, but impressions often precede (re)actions. Then, we can look at how people treat each other on the basis of their appearances and deduce something about the impressions made. There is a vast amount of research on that subject. For example, most 'CV studies' that examine the callback rates in CVs of different-looking persons could be seen as studying impression-based reactions to appearances (e.g., Maurer-Fazio & Lei, 2015; Patacchini et al., 2015; Ruffle & Shtudiner, 2014). Also, studies examining how attractiveness of a person affects different aspects of how they are treated by other people inform us about the same phenomenon. Narrators in this study thus brought few novel outcomes to the appearance research. In line with previous research (e.g., Hamermesh, 2011), there were stories about, for example, how attractiveness had helped participants to get a job or a spouse as well as how participants had been discriminated against due to their body size. In the narrators' texts, making a right impression with physical appearance was important in many contexts, including being a customer in a store, seeking a job, trying to impress a potential spouse, being an employee and a representative of a job, etc. (cf. Warhurst & Nickson, 2001). The right impressions opened doors, while diverging from the norm closed them.

What is noteworthy is that the impressions given and others' interpretations of them were described in situational terms in the narratives. Unexpected parts of participants' appearances had affected the impressions of others, and their appearances were interpreted and treated differently depending on the situation and context. In other words, in their depictions, any kind of appearance, such as beauty or attractiveness, that worked in every situation was absent. Instead, narrators described how changing the environment and people with whom they interacted affected what kinds of impressions were created. For example, one narrator was living in a bad relationship in which her husband mocked her physical appearance, as he did not like his impression of the narrator. She described that divorce and finding a new partner who adored her appearance improved her quality of life and general well-being. Beauty was in the eye of the beholder in cases such as this.

The main finding here was not that people make impressions of each other based on their appearance and that those impressions have social relevance. The key point, instead, was to show how the narrators described the relation between appearance and the impressions it 'caused'. The result was that visual cues rarely give similar impressions in every situation and for everyone. Physical appearance is a symbol that is interpreted always by someone in some context, which causes variation in the impressions made. This should be taken as a prerequisite for any research studying the outcomes of physical appearance.

Appearance as a Medium for Inclusion and Exclusion

One main theme in the biographies that described the process of how appearance may turn into capital was the narrators' explicit testimonies on how they had experienced that appearance acts as a mediator that determines who are to be included and excluded from various social circles and groups. In those cases, appearance either helped the narrators to get acceptance from others or prevented them from it. The dynamics of inclusion and exclusion were said to happen in different levels of social life, both in personal relationships between two or more people and on a larger scale as a profound feeling of being accepted by other people in the society. Next, I will show how these dimensions of acceptance were described in the narratives.

Firstly, a rather common theme was romantic relationships, on which the narrators wrote that their appearance had played a central role in arousing initial interest and getting to know another person. Relations between two people are the smallest form of social inclusion and exclusion. In the case of romantic relationships, judgements on whether to include or exclude were described as matters of personal taste or mutual attraction and were described to have at least some degree of 'biological' or 'natural' justification. But the logics of inclusion and exclusion applied also on levels that involved more people and thus reflected preferences not just of an individual but of a group of people and their culture, as in the following example:

> [When I was at high school,] we went on a holiday trip to Vyborg [with my family]. They bought me pirated Levi's jeans and buttoned Adidas sweatpants from there. [–] Buttoned sweatpants were in fashion, and now I've got those. I didn't feel like I was selling myself to the mass fashion, because at least I had chosen the pirated version. Companies that trick people with commercials to buy their products didn't get any profit off those. Yet I was able to fit in, to be part of the mainstream crowd and not an outsider. On one hand, I tried to be unique and different from the others, but on the other hand, I wanted to be like everyone else – not too different.
>
> (Reima, male, 37)

Reima's appearance reflected here the norms of his peer group (not any individual person), which in turn reflected the current fashion. His desired outcome was to be accepted by a certain group of people but at the same time to be slightly different from them to accentuate his individuality. Reima used his appearance as a means to get a certain social acceptance, but he utilised it rather consciously by taking a distance from the masses and multinational companies. Altogether, he conveyed that appearance had a central role in the dynamics of fitting in and gaining acceptance in certain social circles, because otherwise there was a threat of being excluded.

Reima's citation reflected the importance of appearance, especially in adolescence, identity construction and friend relationships. However, similar logics of inclusion and exclusion appeared also in the narratives in later stages of life. The most commonly discussed context in the narratives was working life and its various fields. Appearance helped or hindered narrators, both in entering working life and while being employed and acting in everyday work. The previous citation of Elli, who dreamed of a career as a physical training master, exemplifies the exclusion of people by their appearance in certain occupations by preventing them from entering the job in the first hand. Some other narrators instead described their experiences of being more easily employed because they felt they had had a suitable appearance for the job. In other words, appearance was depicted as a mediator to control entering working life in the narratives as well. This phenomenon has also been widely documented by previous research (e.g., Paustian-Underdahl & Walker, 2016; Rooth, 2009; Ruffle & Shtudiner, 2014).

Besides the recruitment situations, the importance of looks in everyday working life was also discussed in the narratives (see also Pajunen, Chapter 5). The narrators were rather vague in their descriptions on how appearance controlled the dynamics of inclusion and exclusion in everyday work. They wrote, for example, that it was important to 'dress accordingly' and 'correct[ly]', 'be well-groomed' and 'give a good impression' while at work, which was described as 'advantageous' behaviour in work. Kerttu said, 'My job allowed for dressing up and even encouraged it; without my job, things would not have been quite like that. I think it is important to present and represent oneself'. It was thus clear that appearance mediated how well the narrators could perform in their jobs, but they did not elaborate the details of how exactly it did. Chapter 7 by Åberg and Koivula could also be read as complementing this question.

Lastly, appearance was described as mediating the sense of belongingness in a more extensive sense in relation to the whole society – a sense of being fundamentally different and excluded from other people. There was not any single act of being excluded or included, but multiple experiences of being treated as different by others had shaped narrators' conception of their 'compatibleness' with society. The most illuminating example of this was the narrative of Säde, a young transgender person. She vividly described her experiences, how appearance (gender, clothing, hair, body size) is determined, how one gets friends, acceptance, relationships and employment and, more generally, how people treat each other. If one does not meet the standards of 'the audience', one gets bullied and receives nasty comments from others, and if one does not conform, one is excluded from the social circle in question. She highlights how diverging from appearance norms is a constant struggle that requires a lot of courage from individuals. At the moment of her writing, she was in the middle of the process of a surgical sex change. Writing about experiences of exclusion, she gave a rationalisation of the need for the surgical operation. The cross-sectional theme in her narrative is to show that when one does not meet appearance standards, it is possible to see and sense how central appearance actually is to controlling one's sense of belonging and hence to affecting one's identity and self-worth.

The Relation of Appearance to Psychological Well-being

As may have already become apparent from this analysis, the so-called 'inner consequences' of appearance went hand in hand with the more 'objective' or 'tangible' outcomes (such as economic or social outcomes). In many cases, these psychological consequences were the most predominant topics in the narratives. These 'outcomes' are in the first place subjectively observed mental states, and they do not necessarily cause any 'objective' outcomes that others could detect. However, a person's psychological well-being determines to a large extent that person's ability to act in the world. Hence, while the appearance-related psychological consequences could not be taken straightforwardly as outcomes that reflect movements of capital, they at least could be defined as a mediating factor in the process of how appearance generates inequalities (e.g., Mobius & Rosenblat, 2006).

These outcomes appeared in many forms in the narratives, and appearance was depicted to influence one's well-being in both positive and negative ways. For example, narrators described how positive comments from a spouse, their own reflections in the mirror or daily practices of getting groomed for work raised their spirit and conferred self-confidence. For many, though, their own appearance caused anxiety, lowered self-assurance, made them feel isolated from others, caused depression and led to eating disorders.

> When I was younger, physical appearance was a source of issues and strain. I was a chubby child, and I guess I was told so too. When I was in my twenties, I developed bulimia, which I suffered from for about four years. In those days, I was having very bad fights with my mum, and I was dating a man who was into bodybuilding. At that time, one had to be slender yet curvy. I could say that my self-esteem was very low, and I could not respect myself.
>
> (Reetta, female, 44)

The negative effects of appearance on psychological well-being were often described as being rather long term and not necessarily materialised immediately. A single negative appearance-related comment may have felt bad instantly, but they also built a more profound sense of self and thus affected longer-term well-being and self-respect.

The sources, which were described to affect one's psychological well-being, varied from direct comments from others to a more abstract sense of appearance norms or what is required to meet appearance standards. For example, in Reetta's citation, she had a sense that 'one had to be slender yet curvy'. In these cases, narrators compared themselves to the prevailing norms, and divergence from those caused mental issues for some. Weight-related norms were the most often mentioned issues in the narratives, but height, clothing, skin, hair and other body parts were also mentioned as negatively affecting narrators' well-being if they found such features to diverge from the norm.

On the other hand, some found that appearance was a means for them to enhance their well-being. Some discussed, for example, that their body made them feel good, but more often, the positive effects of appearance were due to putting on makeup or wearing 'sharp' clothes. Time and effort (for example, exercising or grooming – i.e., *aesthetic* or *appearance work*) were thus often required to gain these positive effects, which could be seen as accomplishments to meet with appearance norms (cf. Kukkonen, Chapter 2).

It appeared as an unquestionable fact that appearance issues were seen to affect narrators' psychological well-being to a large extent. From a sociological perspective, these psychological effects could also be seen as consequences of appearance-related social norms in those contexts. They may manifest as sanctioning by other people, or they may be internalised and guide individuals' behaviour as an 'inner voice', as in the case of Elli. Altogether, prevailing (appearance) norms reflect individuals' psychological health and alter it in various ways and degrees.

Conclusions

The first aim of this chapter was to explore how the effects of physical appearance appear in subjective narratives in comparison to the macro-level findings on aesthetic capital. The answer is that the narratives provided supplementary rather than contradictory details to the whole understanding of how aesthetic capital affects people and society. This analysis provided two key points to this discussion.

Firstly, the relations of appearance and its outcomes were depicted as more diverse than beauty and ugliness. Appearance was described as a means to create impressions and as a mediator of social inclusion and exclusion. The interpretations of appearances were always tied with certain situations, contexts and interpersonal dynamics. Hence, the same appearances were not valued and treated similarly in every situation by every individual. Instead, there were always field-specific logics that controlled how different traits of appearance were treated (see also Green, 2014). Furthermore, some of the narrators also had experiences of economic-related outcomes of physical appearance, for example, in a recruitment situation, yet such outcomes could be interpreted as a particular example of more general logics of physical appearance as a mediator of social inclusion and exclusion. The conclusive recommendation for future research based on these findings is that the context and field in which appearance is being evaluated should always be taken into account when analysing appearance-related outcomes. Different fields have different appearance norms and thus they differ in their logics of inclusion and exclusion.

The second aim of this chapter was to broaden the understanding of the outcomes of aesthetic capital. The main contribution thereby was to link appearance-related psychological and mental health issues with appearance norms. There is still little multidisciplinary discussion that links appearance-related mental issues to macro-level social inequalities. The link of mental illnesses and social structure (including the compositions of capital) seems to intersect with various appearance-related issues, which future investigations should better take into account. The relation between appearance or different traits of appearance and capital is rarely straightforward (e.g., attractive individuals are paid more). Instead, the relation is more often less direct and a result of multiple different level interactions that include different actors, their actions and interpretations and situational social norms. For example, appearance-related bullying is firstly an act of social exclusion and affects one's social capital, but it also may have an effect on one's self-esteem, which further affects one's future choices and social stance. Thus, the whole process of how appearance may turn into capital should be scrutinised in order to understand and solve the inequality-producing mechanisms of physical appearance.

I have discussed here how the different consequences of appearance appear on the individual level and how they could complement the understanding of aesthetic capital. On the basis of the narrators' subjective perspectives on this matter, I suggest that further research on aesthetic capital should attempt to combine and adopt a more multidimensional interpretation framework that addresses the impact of appearance on economic, social and psychological levels to understand more fully how appearance is linked to social inequalities.

References

Anderson, T. L., Grunert, C., Katz, A., & Lovascio, S. (2010). Aesthetic capital: A research review on beauty perks and penalties. *Sociology Compass*, *4*(8), 564–575. https://doi.org/10.1111/j.1751-9020.2010.00312.x

Anýžová, P., & Matějů, P. (2018). Beauty still matters: The role of attractiveness in labour market outcomes. *International Sociology*, *33*(3), 269–291. https://doi.org/10.1177/0268580918760431

Baert, S., & Decuypere, L. (2014). Better sexy than flexy? A lab experiment assessing the impact of perceived attractiveness and personality traits on hiring decisions. *Applied Economics Letters*, *21*(9), 597–601. https://doi.org/10.1080/13504851.2013.877564

Balogun, O. M. (2020). *Beauty diplomacy: Embodying an emerging nation*. Stanford University Press.

Berggren, N., Jordahl, H., & Poutvaara, P. (2010). The looks of a winner: Beauty and electoral success. *Journal of Public Economics*, *94*(1–2), 8–15. https://doi.org/10.1016/j.jpubeco.2009.11.002

Biddle, J. E., & Hamermesh, D. S. (1998). Beauty, productivity, and discrimination: Lawyers' looks and lucre. *Journal of Labor Economics*, *16*(1), 172–201. https://doi.org/10.1086/209886

Bourdieu, P. (1984). *Distinction. A social critique of the judgement of taste*. Routledge.

Bourdieu, P. (1990). *The logic of practice*. Stanford University Press.

Burgoon, J. K., Guerrero, L. K., & Manusov, V. (2016). *Nonverbal communication*. Routledge.

Cawley, J. (2004). The impact of obesity on wages. *Journal of Human Resources, 39*(2), 451–474. https://doi.org/10.3368/jhr.XXXIX.2.451

Green, A. I. (2014). The sexual fields framework. In A. I. Green (Ed.), *Sexual fields: Toward a sociology of collective sexual life* (pp. 25–56). University of Chicago Press.

Hamermesh, D. S. (2011). *Beauty pays: Why attractive people are more successful*. Princeton University Press.

Hamermesh, D. S., & Abrevaya, J. (2013). Beauty is the promise of happiness? *European Economic Review, 64*, 351–368. https://doi.org/10.1016/j.euroecorev.2013.09.005

Holla, S., & Kuipers, G. (2015). Aesthetic capital. In L. Hanquinet & M. Savage (Eds.), *Routledge international handbook of the sociology of art and culture* (pp. 290–303). Routledge.

Hosoda, M., Stone-Romero, E. F., & Coats, G. (2003). The effects of physical attractiveness on job-related outcomes: A meta-analysis of experimental studies. *Personnel Psychology, 56*(2), 431–462. https://doi.org/10.1111/j.1744-6570.2003.tb00157.x

Innola, T. (2020). Sukupuolen intensiteetit ja materiaalisuuden toiminta ulkonäkökokemuksen affektikokoumassa. *Sukupuolentutkimus*, No. 3.

Jäckle, S., & Metz, T. (2017). Beauty contest revisited: The effects of perceived attractiveness, competence, and likability on the electoral success of German MPs. *Politics & Policy, 45*(4), 495–534. https://doi.org/10.1111/polp.12209

Jæger, M. M. (2011). "A thing of beauty is a joy forever"? Returns to physical attractiveness over the life course. *Social Forces, 89*(3), 983–1003. https://doi.org/10.1093/sf/89.3.983

Johnston, D. W. (2010). Physical appearance and wages: Do blondes have more fun? *Economics Letters, 108*(1), 10–12. https://doi.org/10.1016/j.econlet.2010.03.015

Kanazawa, S., & Still, M. C. (2018). Is there really a beauty premium or an ugliness penalty on earnings? *Journal of Business and Psychology, 33*(2), 249–262. https://doi.org/10.1007/s10869-017-9489-6

Knapp, M. L., Hall, J. A., & Horgan, T. G. (2014). *Nonverbal communication in human interaction*. Wadsworth Cengage Learning.

Kuipers, G. (2015). Beauty and distinction? The evaluation of appearance and cultural capital in five European countries. *Poetics, 53*, 38–51. https://doi.org/10.1016/j.poetic.2015.10.001

van der Laan, E., & Velthuis, O. (2016). Inconspicuous dressing: A critique of the construction-through-consumption paradigm in the sociology of clothing. *Journal of Consumer Culture, 16*(1), 22–42. https://doi.org10.1177/1469540513505609

Lamont, M., Beljean, S., & Clair, M. (2014). What is missing? Cultural processes and causal pathways to inequality. *Socio-Economic Review, 12*(3), 573–608. https://doi.org10.1093/ser/mwu011

Maestripieri, D., Henry, A., & Nickels, N. (2017). Explaining financial and prosocial biases in favor of attractive people: Interdisciplinary perspectives from economics, social psychology, and evolutionary psychology. *Behavioral and Brain Sciences, 40*, e19. https://doi.org/10.1017/S0140525X16000340

Mathes, E. W., & Kozak, G. (2008). The exchange of physical attractiveness for resource potential and commitment. *Journal of Evolutionary Psychology*, *6*(1), 43–56. https://doi.org/10.1556/jep.2008.1004

Maurer-Fazio, M., & Lei, L. (2015). "As rare as a panda" How facial attractiveness, gender, and occupation affect interview callbacks at Chinese firms. *International Journal of Manpower*, *36*(1), 68–85.

McClintock, E. A. (2014). Beauty and status: The illusion of exchange in partner selection? *American Sociological Review*, *79*(4), 575–604. https://doi.org/10.1177/0003122414536391

Mears, A. (2015). Girls as elite distinction: The appropriation of bodily capital. *Poetics*, *53*, 22–37. https://doi.org10.1016/j.poetic.2015.08.004

Mobius, M. M., & Rosenblat, T. S. (2006). Why beauty matters. *The American Economic Review*, *96*(1), 222–235. https://doi.org/10.1257/000282806776157515

Patacchini, E., Ragusa, G., & Zenou, Y. (2015). Unexplored dimensions of discrimination in Europe: Homosexuality and physical appearance. *Journal of Population Economics*, *28*(4), 1045–1073. https://doi.org/10.1007/s00148-014-0533-9

Paustian-Underdahl, S. C., & Walker, L. S. (2016). Revisiting the beauty is beastly effect: Examining when and why sex and attractiveness impact hiring judgments. *International Journal of Human Resource Management*, *27*(10), 1034–1058. https://doi.org/10.1080/09585192.2015.1053963

Rooth, D. O. (2009). Obesity, attractiveness, and differential treatment in hiring a field experiment. *Journal of Human Resources*, *44*(3), 710–735. https://doi.org/10.3368/jhr.44.3.710

Ruffle, B. J., & Shtudiner, Z. E. (2014). Are good-looking people more employable? *Management Science*, *61*(8), 1760–1776. https://doi.org/10.1287/mnsc.2014.1927

Shilling, C. (2004). Physical capital and situated action: A new direction for corporeal sociology. *British Journal of Sociology of Education*, *25*(4), 473–487. https://doi.org/10.1080/0142569042000236961

Timmermans, S., & Tavory, I. (2012). Theory construction in qualitative research: From grounded theory to abductive analysis. *Sociological Theory*, *30*(3), 167–186. https://doi.org/10.1177/0735275112457914

Vandebroeck, D. (2016). *Distinctions in the flesh: Social class and the embodiment of inequality*. Routledge.

Warhurst, C., & Nickson, D. (2001). *Looking good, sounding right*. Industrial Society.

Weinberg, M. S., & Williams, C. J. (2014). Sexual field, erotic habitus, and embodiment at a transgender bar. In A. I. Green (Ed.), *Sexual fields: Toward a sociology of collective sexual life* (pp. 57–70). University of Chicago Press.

Wolbring, T., & Riordan, P. (2016). How beauty works. Theoretical mechanisms and two empirical applications on students' evaluation of teaching. *Social Science Research*, *57*, 253–272. https://doi.org/10.1016/j.ssresearch.2015.12.009

Chapter 7

The Ouroboros of Seeking Validation? Exploring the Interconnection of Appearance (Dis)satisfaction and Content Creation on Social Media

Erica Åberg and Aki Koivula

Ouroboros is an ancient Egyptian symbol depicting a serpent or dragon devouring its tail. The origin of this motif is ancient Egyptian iconography, and it is often interpreted as a symbol of eternal cyclic renewal or a cycle of life, death and rebirth. The earliest, first known example of the true Ouroboros icon is on the second gold shrine of Tutankhamun, where they are seen surrounding a large mummiform figure, a representation of the unified reborn Re-Osiris (Reemes, 2015). The connection between ancient Egypt and social media may seem a bit distant at first glance. However, a snake devouring its tail is a concept that captures the intention of this chapter: to elaborate the possible motives for people to create content on social media, yearning for comments and likes to be reborn, but also becoming accustomed to receiving positive feedback. This eternal cycle may be essential to describe individuals in an appearance-oriented society, creating content on social media, seeking validation and multiplying the audiences of their aesthetic performances.

In this chapter, we use the concept of aesthetic capital to illustrate how appearance-related assets are displayed and controlled, but also accumulated and utilised on social media platforms. Social media offers its users endless possibilities to fulfil the desires of the 'performing self' (Featherstone, 1982), a person preoccupied with a stylised presentation, impression management and versatile self-expression. The visual and textual expressions on social networking sites intend to give off impressions about the self, as well as advance particular narratives about one's life and identity for a particular audience, most often for peers (boyd, 2008; Dobson, 2016). Regardless of the 'mediated public' (boyd, 2008), the

Appearance as Capital, 117–134
Copyright © 2022 Erica Åberg and Aki Koivula
Published by Emerald Publishing Limited. These works are published under the Creative Commons Attribution (CC BY 4.0) licence. Anyone may reproduce, distribute, translate and create derivative works of these works (for both commercial and non-commercial purposes), subject to full attribution to the original publication and authors. The full terms of this licence may be seen at http://creativecommons.org/licences/by/4.0/legalcode
doi:10.1108/978-1-80043-708-120210008

performance of appropriately presenting oneself to one's audience in daily life remains similar to that of offline, that is, through clothing, speech and embodiment.

However, despite being offered various modes of presentation, platforms and audiences, that appearance performer may remain unfulfilled in terms of attention, gratification and accumulating appearance-related resources in consumer society. Previous literature has indeed established that social media use predominantly leads to negative individual-level outcomes: increased appearance pressures (e.g. Åberg, Koivula, & Kukkonen, 2020), body image concerns and disordered eating (for a systematic review, see Holland & Tiggemann, 2016). However, these findings do not apply similarly to all social media users, as the propensity to report social media as a source of appearance-related strains is higher especially for younger women (e.g. Fardouly et al., 2015; Tiggemann & Miller, 2010; Tiggemann & Slater, 2013). More recent studies have identified these concerns as being specifically more prevalent among the female users of Instagram (e.g. Tiggemann et al., 2020b; Åberg, Koivula, & Kukkonen, 2020).

Despite well-documented negative outcomes, other scholars have stressed the positive sides of social media, emphasising its possibilities for empowerment (Barnard, 2016; Kedzior et al., 2016; Tiidenberg & Gómez Cruz, 2015, see also Åberg & Salonen in this book) and gratification for people who might otherwise suffer from low self-esteem. Pounders et al. (2016) claimed that improving one's self-esteem is simultaneously a motivator for as well as the outcome of the practice of selfie-posting. Previous studies have stated that positive feedback is especially important for female millennials (Pounders et al., 2016).

This chapter aims to elaborate on this 'online Ouroboros', by focusing on whether appearance dissatisfaction leads to an increased tendency to post content on social media and seek gratification from one's peers. We reverse the previous assumptions that social media is a one-sided source of appearance concerns by approaching it from the viewpoint of the outcome (that is, for example, appearance dissatisfaction) being the motivator for downloading content. Previous research has identified the gendered differences in the consumption of social media content (e.g. Koiranen et al., 2019) as well as the gendered effects of social media on psychological well-being (e.g. Mills et al., 2018; Tiggemann & Barbato, 2018). Still, relatively little is known about how appearance satisfaction is related to the creation of social media content. Moreover, we do not know whether appearance dissatisfaction is associated with an increased or decreased propensity to create content on social media to firstly test, but also verify the value of one's capitals. To address these gaps in research, this study offers insights into the discussion on the relationship between physical appearance and social media use.

We analysed overall appearance satisfaction, and the effects of facial and body satisfaction separately, to determine whether they result differently in employing social media affordances. Additionally, previous research has generally been conducted through experimental designs with small and unrepresentative samples, and there is (to our knowledge) no previous research that can be explicitly generalised to broader populations. The novelty value of our study hence lies in turning previous research designs the other way around: assessing appearance satisfaction as a predictor of content creation, as well as using nationally representative data.

This study draws mainly from two perspectives that have been used predominantly to explain the effects of social media on female body image: social comparison theory (Festinger, 1954) and objectification theory (Fredrickson & Roberts, 1997). The former refers to women comparing themselves with unrealistic and idealised media images that result in body and appearance dissatisfaction (Levine & Murnen, 2009; Want, 2009). The latter refers to socialising women to internalise an observer's perspective on themselves and come to view themselves in objectified terms (for a review, see Tiggemann, 2011).

This chapter elaborates on these previous claims further, first, by assessing how appearance satisfaction predicts content creation on social media. Second, we examine the differences between Facebook and Instagram users on how appearance satisfaction affects content creation. Last, we ask about the extent to which the detected associations are gendered. Before turning to the empirical analysis, we formulate the hypotheses for these research questions based on previous theoretical literature and research findings. We then present our data and methods. Finally, we discuss whether content creation has an impact on appearance (dis)satisfaction and feeds the online Ouroboros of appearance society, rather than offers a release from it. Additionally, we discuss the role of different social networking platforms, as well as gender differences in appearance-induced inequality on social media.

Hypotheses Development

Appearance Satisfaction and Content Creation

Previous empirical studies on content creation are focused mainly on selfies and their relation to self-esteem. In a study by Pounders et al. (2016), participants revealed that, rather than striving to appear authentic and real, the informants indicated a desire to portray themselves as living happy lives and displaying positive physical self-images, regardless of their internal feelings. The initial motivator for posting selfies was impression management, and informants disclosed posting both genuine and non-genuine posts to manage the impression of happiness and physical appearance. Findings also showed that self-esteem plays an integral role in understanding selfie-posting, and the number of 'likes' can positively or negatively affect the person's self-esteem.

In other words, taking and posting happy selfies can provide a self-esteem boost, regardless of the initial mindset of the person posting them (Kedzior et al., 2016), pointing to the empowering potential of social media and selfies. As networked technologies allow for capturing and sharing embodied experience (Tiidenberg & Gómez Cruz, 2015), social media can empower its users. Moreover, taking and sharing selfies offers groups that have previously been objectified and denied agency possibilities to challenge their public portrayal (Barnard, 2016). However, the very same studies have also suggested that such empowerment includes a threat to self-esteem, as it requires constant validation from others in the form of likes, retweets and comments. This conditional provision of validation may start to arouse the need to perform in specific ways to meet the audience's expectations to receive the aforementioned comments and likes (Tiidenberg & Gómez Cruz, 2015). Seeking validation from peers and its effect on self-esteem can be seen as a perfect illustration of what is described in Fredrickson and Roberts's (1997) objectification theory. The theory claims that the pervasiveness of sexual objectification gradually socialises women and girls to internalise an observer's perspective of their bodies and view themselves as an object to be looked at and evaluated based on appearance.

Despite the possibilities for self-presentation, as well as empowerment and broader appearance ideals, the online presentations of other people in general predominantly promote such attributes as youthfulness and thinness. Fulfilling these appearance ideals is impossible to achieve for most women, who are said to be vulnerable to body dissatisfaction, particularly concerning body shape and weight (Groesz et al., 2002; Tiggemann & Slater, 2013). The most often used and generally accepted framework for understanding the prevailing body dissatisfaction of women is the sociocultural theory, which claims that contemporary beauty ideals are reinforced and sustained by sociocultural influences, most notably parents, peers and media (e.g. Thompson et al., 1999). These sociocultural ideals are hard to overcome individually: if the source is flawed, it cannot be fixed by retouching one's photos. A study by Shome et al. (2020) established that the opportunity to retake and modify selfies before posting them on social media predicted a decrease in the participant's social anxiety. However, other negative outcomes, like decreased feelings of self-confidence and the desire to undergo cosmetic surgery, were higher among the participants who had an option to retouch their selfies. These findings were partly consistent with the conclusion of Mills et al. (2018), who correspondingly observed that taking and uploading selfies resulted in negative feelings: decreased confidence and feelings of anxiety, irrespective of the opportunity to edit the selfie.

The above-cited studies focus on selfie-related behaviours and appearance concerns but speak in terms of general appearance. Other studies have distinguished between facial and body dissatisfaction, and claim that individuals who have greater body satisfaction are, to begin with, more likely to engage in posting selfies (Ridgway & Clayton, 2016). Cohen et al. (2018) found similar associations in their study. However, as selfies predominantly include portrait photos rather than full-bodied images, it may be that the relationships between appearance concerns and selfie-related behaviours may contribute more to facial appearance dissatisfaction than to body dissatisfaction. Moreover, it has been stated that taking and editing of selfies leads to experiences of more negative mood and resulted especially in facial dissatisfaction (Tiggemann et al., 2020b). Similarly, viewing idealised selfies with makeup on social media specifically influenced women's face appearance concerns, rather than concerns about their overall physical appearance (Fardouly & Rapee, 2019). A more extensive approach was found in Wang et al. (2019), establishing a reciprocal relationship among selfie-related behaviours, associating them with self-objectification and appearance concerns among adolescents. Their results indicate that selfie-editing, but not selfie-posting, predicted an increase in adolescents' self-objectification and appearance concerns (both body and face) over time. However, selfie-viewing predicted increases in self-objectification and facial dissatisfaction, but not body dissatisfaction, over time. Moreover, participants' facial dissatisfaction positively predicted selfie-viewing and selfie-editing, whereas body dissatisfaction did not influence subsequent selfie-related behaviours.

To our knowledge, only a few studies (e.g. Ridgway & Clayton, 2016; Wang et al., 2019) have explicitly examined the interconnection of distinguished appearance dissatisfaction and selfie practices. However, despite stressing the central role of appearance dissatisfaction in selfie-related behaviour, only bodily dissatisfaction has been associated with an increased tendency for selfie-posting in these studies. Thus, we use our data to investigate whether body dissatisfaction or facial dissatisfaction predicts content creation in overall, not just selfies, differently on social media.

With this previous research and their findings in mind, we assume that social media increases self-objectification and social comparison that results in appearance (dis)satisfaction, which predicts content creation. Thus, we propose the following hypotheses: *People who are less satisfied with their facial appearances create more content on social media than those who are satisfied with their facial appearances* (H1.1). Second, *people who are less satisfied with their bodily appearances create more content on social media, compared to those who are satisfied with their bodily appearances* (H1.2).

Appearance Satisfaction and Content Creation on Different Social Media Platforms

Previous research has found several differences among social networking sites, in terms of the method of interaction, self-presentation and importantly, the types of social ties that those different platforms allow. As social media platforms have been designed for specific user purposes and are structured in varied ways, their user profiles differ accordingly. Like other countries, in Finland, active social media use and content generation are more common among women and young people (Ertiö et al., 2018). Young people on Instagram are highly focused on self-presentation through visual means and aim to control how others receive them or their tastes (Sheldon & Bryant, 2016).

When it comes to platform-specific features, Instagram, compared to other social media sites, is based on embodying one's identity. 'Selfies', i.e. photographs people take of themselves, are abundant on Instagram (Ridgway & Clayton, 2016). Based on its visuality, studies have found negative consequences for engaging in the appearance-related features of social media. For example, a meta-analysis by Mingoia et al. (2017) found that internalisation of sociocultural ideals, such as thinness, is mainly associated with posting and viewing images on social media.

Moreover, social media platforms are also distinguished by their social nature. Facebook is based more on social interaction, which focuses on reciprocity between individuals, as well as consent to social bonding. Facebook is more like an extension of social life outside the Internet, as its users form social ties with people who they typically have known from real life (Manzi et al., 2018). Social interaction on the platform is also more social and reciprocal: on Facebook, people belong to groups with like-minded people or those who are interested in the same things. Moreover, Facebook has become increasingly popular as a market platform for peer-to-peer trade with other users, peers, on Facebook. (Lee et al., 2014).

In contrast to Facebook, on Instagram, a profile can be public and thus, not requiring approval from the person followed. Hence, Instagram invites being followed by and, in particular, following of strangers, including celebrities (cf. Lup et al., 2015.). As a result, increasing the size of different networks, as well as increased visibility, is easier on Instagram Phua et al. (2017). However, the quality of networks may be different on Instagram, where one-sided following is more likely to occur, which also means that information flows in only one direction. Instagram is also more performative than Facebook; it is not based on information-sharing or other social reciprocity in the same way as Facebook. Given its visual nature, it can be seen as focusing more specifically on selective self-presentation and performative identities (e.g. boyd, 2008; Dobson, 2016), as well as more niched performances, such as 'doing pregnancy' (Tiidenberg & Baym, 2017). Moreover, the content can also be tagged and thus made available to the so-called 'attention economy' (Marwick, 2015, see also Åberg & Salonen in this book) prominent on social media. Besides tagging one's content, tagging, but also sharing publicly available content, for example, cute animals or funny memes, can be seen as a type of performance in and of itself (e.g. Tiidenberg & Baym, 2017).

As previous studies have indicated, Instagram allows for a selective self-presentation, more performative use and, potentially, a more extensive network. Thus, we hypothesise that *the relationship between appearance (dis)satisfaction and content creation is more prominent among Instagram users when compared to the users of other social media platforms* (H2).

Appearance Satisfaction, Content Creation, Social Media Platforms and Gender

Most of the previously presented findings are consistent with the prediction of Fredrickson and Roberts's objectification theory (1997) that engaging in a self-objectifying activity (like selfie posting) results in worsened body image outcomes for women. This theory claims that sexual objectification in contemporary society socialises girls and women to treat themselves as objects to be looked upon and evaluated based upon bodily appearance, leading to four negative subjective experiences: body shame, appearance anxiety, diminished peak motivational status and reduced connection with one's internal bodily states (Fredrickson & Roberts, 1997). In addition to self-objectification, body image disturbances and appearance concerns of women are often approached with social comparison theory (Festinger, 1954). According to social comparison theory, people seek to compare their appearances with prevailing social standards, including the appearance standards presented in the media. Making evaluative comparisons between their appearance and the idealised and artificially created appearance of women in the media, most women are likely to feel they need to meet that standard. Due to that shortage, female viewers typically end up feeling dissatisfied with their appearance.

From subjective experiences, Terán et al. (2019) identified body shame and appearance anxiety as the most relevant to the potential consequences of selfies for women. Similarly, Tiggemann and Barbato (2018) claimed that objectification theory may be particularly relevant in the context of a photographic social media site like Instagram, with its primary function being posting photos of oneself for others to look and comment. According to their study, women's body dissatisfaction increased in response to viewing images and posted comments on Instagram. In addition to self-objectification, it has been established that social networking sites are associated with upward social comparison and lowered feelings for women (e.g. Fox & Vendemia, 2016). Moreover, contemporary body ideals on social media have become even more unattainable for most women: relatively thin, but also toned and strong (Tiggemann & Zaccardo, 2018). Although most of these previous studies have focused on women, social media has an impact on men also, reproducing stereotypical norms of masculinity in the form of embodying strength and power (Fox & Vendemia, 2016), and it forces men to increasingly rely on their bodies for personal value creation (Hakim, 2015, see also Sarpila in this book).

Moreover, men and women differ in their social media practices. Whereas women typically use social media more actively and are more likely to use social media to view others' photos (Smith, 2014), as well as compare themselves with others, men are more likely to use social media to find or contact friends (Haferkamp et al., 2012). Social networking sites allow for self-conspicuousness, and young women, in particular, present idealised images of themselves on social media (Dhir et al., 2016). Consequently, other young women see these idealised images of their peers and compare themselves with them, causing appearance-related distress (e.g. Holland & Tiggemann, 2016). A recent study found that active social media usage with attractive peers on appearance-based social media resulted in worsened body image for young adult women, whereas interacting with members of the family did not affect body image (Hogue & Mills, 2019).

Moreover, living up to prevailing appearance norms is effectively ensured on social media, where followers, 'likes' and positive appearance comments on uploaded content can be seen as rewarding appearance ideals. Prior research reveals a tendency for women to both receive and give compliments on appearance (Åberg, Koivula, Kukkonen, Sarpila, & Pajunen, 2020; Holmes, 1998) and well as place a higher premium on receiving those comments. These gendered commenting norms tend to reinforce the norm of placing even more emphasis on and directing the viewer's focus to women's appearances.

Following these strands of literature, we formulate the next hypotheses: *Women who are less satisfied with their appearances create more content on Instagram than equally satisfied men* (H3.1). Second, *appearance (dis)satisfaction is not associated with men's content creation on social media* (H3.2).

This Study

In sum, this study aims to investigate the effect of facial and body satisfaction on social media content creation. Based on previous research, we predict that appearance (dis)satisfaction drives the creation of more content. Moreover, we assume that the relationship between appearance dissatisfaction and content creation is more salient among women, and especially prominent on Instagram. Next, we proceed to our data and present our analysis strategy before unpacking the results of the analysis.

Participants

Our data were derived from the survey 'Finland in the digital age' (Sivonen et al., 2018), that included a total of 3,724 respondents. The survey data were collected in two parts, using two different sampling methods. First, the survey reached a total of 2,470 participants aged 18–74 years, who were from the initial group of 8,000 Finnish-speakers sampled randomly from the Finnish census. Additionally, the data were improved with 1,254 participants (also aged 18–74 years) from a nationally representative online panel of volunteer respondents administrated by a market research company.

Although the total share represents relatively well the share of the Finnish population, older users were slightly overrepresented. Consequently, the data were post-stratified in terms of age and gender distribution to correspond with the official population distribution in Finland according to the Official Statistics of Finland.

In this study, the analyses were based on social media users, totalling 2,761 respondents who comprise 74 % of the total data. Our final study sample included 1, 319 women (47%) and the mean age was 47.7 (SD = 15.8).

Measures

The applied measures are shown in Table 1. The dependent variable measured how often respondents shared their own created content on social media. The item was a part of a question battery in which we asked a total of 14 sub-questions, with a question: 'How often do you do the following?'. The responses and their distribution were 1 'Never' (22.9%), 2 'Less than weekly' (51.4%), 3 'Weekly' (22.5%) and 4 'Daily' (3.2%). Only 0.7% of the answers were missing. In the analysis, we focused on predicting active content creation. We dichotomised the variable into a binary, in which 1 differentiates those who created content at least weekly (25.7%) from those who created content less than weekly (74.3%).

The main predictor variables were satisfaction with bodily appearance and satisfaction with facial appearance. The dimensions were explored separately with the same main question, namely, 'How satisfied are you with (a) your face (b) your body?' The responses were scored with a 5-point interval scale, in which 1 was labelled as 'Not content at all' and 5 was 'Very content'.

Table 7.1. Descriptive Statistics of Applied Variables.

Variable	Obs	Mean/%	Std. Dev.
Content creation	2,726		
No		0.74	0.44
Yes		0.26	0.44
Body satisfaction	2,748	3.30	0.99
Facial satisfaction	2,749	3.63	0.87
Social network site	2,761		
Other		0.17	0.38
Only Facebook		0.41	0.49
Instagram		0.42	0.49
Gender	2,753		
Male		0.48	0.50
Female		0.52	0.50

The moderating variables were the preferred social network site (SNS) and gender. Initially, gender was queried via three categories. However, we had just one observation from individuals other than men or women social media users, and consequently, we excluded the 'other' category from further analyses. In terms of SNS, we paid especially attention to differences between the users of Facebook and Instagram by differentiating the respondents who used both Facebook and Instagram or just Instagram, from those who only used Facebook. We also filtered those who did not use Facebook or Instagram at all but use some other platform(s) into the category 'Else'. Accordingly, the final variable labelled as 'The preferred SNS' had three categories, namely, 1 'Only Facebook', 2 'Instagram', 3 'Else'.

Analysis Strategy

The analysis was performed with Stata 16. First, we conducted logit models to predict the probability of creating content on social media at least weekly, according to satisfaction with facial and body appearance. Next, we focused on the moderating effect of the preferred SNS. We added an interaction term 'the preferred SNS × appearance satisfaction' into the base model. Finally, we continued the procedure and added the interaction term 'the preferred SNS × appearance satisfaction × gender' to determine whether the effect of appearance satisfaction is potentially gendered.

Instead of presenting odds ratios from the logit models, we estimated the predicted probabilities that describe the adjusted percentage point estimates of the differences in the outcome variables, according to the different levels of predicting variables (Muller & MacLehose, 2014). We illustrated the predicted probabilities into the figures by utilising the user-written coefplot-package (Jann, 2014). In each figure, the y-axis describes the probability of content creation at the different levels of appearance satisfaction indicated at the x-axis. The results of interaction analyses were presented by plotting the relationship between appearance satisfaction and content creation for each moderating variable.

Results

We began an analysis by examining how appearance satisfaction predicts the likelihood of creating content on social media. Our main expectation was that those users who were less satisfied with their appearance create more content on social media. By considering recent studies (e.g. Cohen et al., 2018; Ridgway & Clayton, 2016), we also distinguished facial and body appearance. To find mechanisms that explain active behaviour on social media, we targeted our model to estimate how likely it is that users create content at least weekly.

The results of analysis partly confirmed our hypotheses. First, people who were dissatisfied with their bodily appearance had a higher probability of creating content, as we expected. The predicted probabilities shown in Fig. 7.1 indicate that the probability of content creation may decrease by 15 percentage points between dissatisfied and satisfied. Against our expectations and literature emphasising the emergence of facial dissatisfaction due to selfie-related practices,

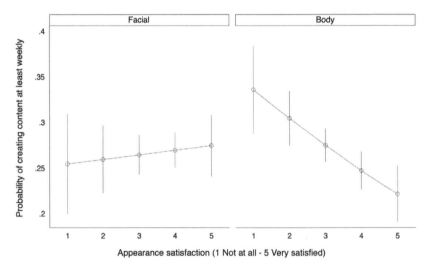

Fig. 7.1.   The Likelihood of Creating Content on Social Media According to Appearance Satisfaction. Predicted probabilities with confidence intervals (95%). The y-axis describes the probability of content creation and the x-axis describes facial and body satisfaction.

we could not find that satisfaction with facial appearance is associated with the probability of creating and sharing content on social media.

Next, we continued the analysis to determine whether the effect of appearance satisfaction is dependent on the social network site users prefer. We assumed that the effect or interconnection of appearance dissatisfaction and content creation is more prominent on Instagram, which is the most visual platform in this comparison. We focused solely on the effect of body satisfaction revealed as significant in the first analysis. The results presented in Fig. 7.2 confirmed our assumption and indicated that the effect of appearance satisfaction is particularly strong on content creation on Instagram. Those users who were less satisfied with their appearance were more likely to create content. To underline our expectations, we did not observe effects of body satisfaction on content creation among Facebook users. Among the users of other platforms, the effect of appearance satisfaction was almost positive, i.e. the opposite of that on Instagram.

The third part of the analysis concentrates on the gendered patterns of Instagram users. We proposed two separate hypotheses: First, we assumed that women who are less satisfied with their appearances create more content on social media. Second, we expected that appearance concerns do not drive men to create content on social media. The results partly confirmed our hypotheses. Fig. 7.3 indicates that those women who were not satisfied with their body appearance were more likely to create content on social media than equally satisfied men. In contrast to our hypothesis, we could not find a significant interaction effect of

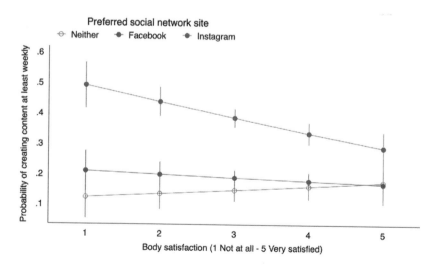

Fig. 7.2.   The Relationship between Creating Content and Body Satisfaction According to the Preferred Social Network Site. Predicted probabilities with confidence intervals (95%). The y-axis describes the probability of content creation and the x-axis describes body satisfaction.

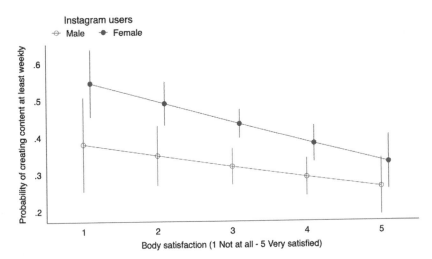

Fig. 7.3.   The Relationship between Creating Content and Body Satisfaction According to Gender among Instagram Users. Predicted probabilities with confidence intervals (95%). The y-axis describes the probability of content creation and the x-axis describes body satisfaction.

gender, as the effect of body satisfaction was also, although not significant, negative among men.

Discussion

This study elaborated on how appearance satisfaction predicts content creation on social media, and how aesthetic capital is negotiated on those platforms. We also examined the differences between different platforms and finally assessed whether the detected associations are gendered.

The results of a representative survey partly confirmed our first hypotheses. We found that content creation is related to body satisfaction of social media users, but not to facial satisfaction. This finding was consistent with Ridgway and Clayton's (2016) findings, but inconsistent with those of Wang et al. (2019), who posited that participants' facial dissatisfaction predicted selfie-viewing and selfie-editing but not selfie-posting over time, whereas body dissatisfaction did not influence subsequent selfie-related behaviours.

We assume that, despite not being in line with previous studies, our results indicate that especially visual social media platforms, such as Instagram, allow for more facial diversity, but are still evolving on bodily variance. In light of objectification theory (Fredrickson & Roberts, 1997), as well as social comparison theory (Festinger, 1954; Fardouly et al., 2015), our findings can be interpreted as an indication of bodies being different from faces. They are theoretically more 'manageable' and thus, offer more possibilities from which to experience pressures. Furthermore, unsatisfying bodies are easier to cover up with complementary clothing, or in the context of social media, possibly smoothed with filters. Moreover, as previous research has mainly concentrated on selfies, it seems noteworthy too that selfies seldom include full-body images. Thus, selfie-related behaviours and appearance concerns may contribute more to facial appearance concerns (see Cohen et al., 2018), rather than eliciting concerns about overall physical appearance (Fardouly & Rapee, 2019).

The second analysis confirmed our hypothesis that the relationship between appearance satisfaction and content creation is prominent among Instagram users. As an image-based and visual platform, Instagram provides a favourable base for appearance-driven content creation (Ridgway & Clayton, 2016). We also suggest that algorithms may influence the emergence of appearance pressures on Instagram. Instagram may suggest content that is visually similar to those previously watched or created, even though the user is capable of blocking pressuring content (Cotter, 2019), making the platform more unpredictable and manageable for social media users.

Finally, in terms of our third hypothesis, the results suggested that women's activity on social media is more likely to be associated with appearance satisfaction compared to activity among male users. This outcome is in line with Fredrickson and Roberts's objectification theory (1997), which claims that sexual objectification in contemporary society socialises girls and women to treat themselves as objects to be looked upon and evaluated based upon bodily appearance. Thus, any self-objectifying activity, such as selfie-posting, results in worsened body image, appearance dissatisfaction, shame and anxiety (ibid., see also Terán et al., 2019; Tiggemann & Barbato, 2018). We can conclude that these feelings are associated with sharing content, and they encourage women to seek validation from their online community. However, instead of experiencing personal empowerment, they may end up feeding the Ouroboros of appearance-oriented society that is forcing them to create more, better and different content than other people.

Overall, our results are in line with theories that associate social media with the heightened tendency for social comparisons and upward appraisals (Leahey et al., 2007; McMullin & Cairney, 2004) that reinforce the socially constructed, normative ideals of beauty. Elaborating this in light of the overall topic of this book, social media is an accelerator of appearance-oriented society. Moreover, prior research has revealed a tendency for women to both receive and give compliments on appearance (Åberg, Koivula, Kukkonen, Sarpila, & Pajunen, 2020; Holmes, 1998), as well as place a higher premium on receiving such comments. These gendered commenting norms contribute to the gendered differences, emphasising women's appearances, making them feel even more on display and pressured to look good. There have been occasional attempts to contest the objectifying nature of social media by, for example, adding self-compassion statements (Lonergan et al., 2019). However, Tiggemann et al. (2020a) suggested that presenting a more diverse array of women's bodies on social media is likely a more effective way to foster body satisfaction and appreciation than textual contestation of prevailing appearance norms that place more emphasis on looks.

Finally, we present two separate but overlapping directions for future research. First, future research should consider how appearance concerns may result in a different kind of disordered behaviour on social media. Previous research has already found that active social media use with body image concerns is related to disordered offline behaviour, such as disordered eating (e.g. Holland & Tiggemann, 2016). In this respect, it is also possible that frequent content creation driven by appearance dissatisfaction is related to problematic use of social media. Moreover, previous research has found conflicting results for online self-compassion statements (Lonergan et al., 2019) and body-positive captions (Tiggemann et al., 2020a) on visual imagery and their relationship to body dissatisfaction. This discrepancy should be studied more: Which contributes more potently to appearance dissatisfaction, the idealised image or the textual content? Acknowledging the discrepancy may help to solve the perpetual motion machine or the online Ouroboros that encourages individuals, first, to create content, but also to seek gratification, on social media. Moreover, it could help understanding the ways of, but also motivations for, accumulating different capitals online, and how those ways are related to existing inequalities.

Naturally, our study has limitations. First, according to our dependent variable, we could not interpret what kind of content creation was associated with appearance satisfaction. Our measure covered all the activities that users have engaged in on social media, even though previous studies have generally focused solely on the production and sharing of selfies (e.g. Pounders et al., 2016). In this respect, future studies should use more accurate measures of social media behaviour to determine outcomes of appearance satisfaction. Second, it is important to acknowledge that we used cross-sectional data that did not enable causal inferences. Therefore, we suggest that future studies should use longitudinal data sets to investigate whether appearance satisfaction predicts content creation over time.

References

Barnard, S. R. (2016). Spectacles of self (ie) empowerment? Networked individualism and the logic of the (post) feminist selfie. In *Communication and information technologies annual*. Emerald Publishing Limited. https://doi.org/10.1108/S2050-206020160000011014

boyd, D. (2008). Why youth (heart) social network sites: The role of networked publics in teenage social life. In D. Buckingham (Ed.), *Youth, identity, and digital media. The John D. and Catherine T. MacArthur foundation series on digital media and learning*. The MIT Press, 2007–2016.

Cohen, R., Newton-John, T., & Slater, A. (2018). 'Selfie'-objectification: The role of selfies in self-objectification and disordered eating in young women. *Computers in Human Behavior, 79*, 68–74. https://doi.org/10.1016/j.chb.2017.10.027

Cotter, K. (2019). Playing the visibility game: How digital influencers and algorithms negotiate influence on Instagram. *New Media & Society*, *21*(4), 895–913. https://doi.org/10.1177/1461444818815684

Dhir, A., Pallesen, S., Torsheim, T., & Andreassen, C. S. (2016). Do age and gender differences exist in selfie-related behaviours?. *Computers in Human Behavior*, *63*, 549–555. https://doi.org/10.1016/j.chb.2016.05.053

Dobson, A. S. (2016). *Postfeminist digital cultures: Femininity, social media, and self-representation*. Springer.

Ertiö, T., Kukkonen, I., & Räsänen, P. (2018). Social media activities in Finland: A population-level comparison. *Convergence*, *26*(1), 193–209. https://doi.org/10.1177/1354856518780463

Fardouly, J., Diedrichs, P. C., Vartanian, L. R., & Halliwell, E. (2015). Social comparisons on social media: The impact of Facebook on young women's body image concerns and mood. *Body Image*, *13*, 38–45. https://doi.org/10.1016/j.bodyim.2014.12.002

Fardouly, J., & Rapee, R. M. (2019). The impact of no-makeup selfies on young women's body image. *Body Image*, *28*, 128–134. https://doi.org/10.1016/j.bodyim.2019.01.006

Featherstone, M. (1982). The body in consumer culture. *Theory, Culture & Society*, *1*(2), 18–33. https://doi.org/10.1177/026327648200100203

Festinger, L. (1954). A theory of social comparison processes. *Human relations*, *7*(2), 117–140. https://doi.org/10.1177/001872675400700202

Fox, J., & Vendemia, M. A. (2016). Selective self-presentation and social comparison through photographs on social networking sites. *Cyberpsychology, Behavior, and Social Networking*, *19*(10), 593–600. https://doi.org/10.1089/cyber.2016.0248

Fredrickson, B. L., & Roberts, T. A. (1997). Objectification theory: Toward understanding women's lived experiences and mental health risks. *Psychology of Women Quarterly*, *21*(2), 173–206. https://doi.org/10.1111/j.1471-6402.1997.tb00108.x

Groesz, L. M., Levine, M. P., & Murnen, S. K. (2002). The effect of experimental presentation of thin media images on body satisfaction: A meta-analytic review. *International Journal of Eating Disorders*, *31*(1), 1–16. https://doi.org/10.1002/eat.10005

Haferkamp, N., Eimler, S. C., Papadakis, A. M., & Kruck, J. V. (2012). Men are from mars, women are from venus? Examining gender differences in self-presentation on social networking sites. *Cyberpsychology, Behavior, and Social Networking*, *15*(2), 91–98. https://doi.org/10.1089/cyber.2011.0151

Hakim, J. (2015). 'Fit is the new rich': Male embodiment in the age of austerity. *Soundings*, *61*(61), 84–94. https://doi.org/10.3898/136266215816772197

Hogue, J. V., & Mills, J. S. (2019). The effects of active social media engagement with peers on body image in young women. *Body Image*, *28*, 1–5. https://doi.org/10.1016/j.bodyim.2018.11.002

Holland, G., & Tiggemann, M. (2016). A systematic review of the impact of the use of social networking sites on body image and disordered eating outcomes. *Body Image*, *17*, 100–110. https://doi.org/10.1016/j.bodyim.2016.02.008

Holmes, J. (1998). Complimenting: A positive politeness strategy. In J. Coates (Ed.), *Language and gender: A reader* (pp. 100–120). Blackwell Publisher Ltd.

Jann, B. (2014). Plotting regression coefficients and other estimates. *The Stata Journal*, *14*(4), 708–737. https://doi.org/10.1177/1536867X1401400402

Kedzior, R., Allen, D. E., & Schroeder, J. (2016). The selfie phenomenon–consumer identities in the social media marketplace. *European Journal of Marketing*, *50*(9/10), 1767–1772. https://doi.org/10.1108/EJM-06-2016-0363

Koiranen, I., Keipi, T., Koivula, A., & Räsänen, P. (2019). Changing patterns of social media use? A population-level study of Finland. *Universal Access in the Information Society*, 1–15. https://doi.org/10.1007/s10209-019-00654-1

Leahey, T. M., Crowther, J. H., & Mickelson, K. D. (2007). The frequency, nature, and effects of naturally occurring appearance-focused social comparisons. *Behavior Therapy*, *38*(2), 132–143. https://doi.org/10.1016/j.beth.2006.06.004

Lee, M. R., Yen, D. C., & Hsiao, C. Y. (2014). Understanding the perceived community value of Facebook users. *Computers in Human Behavior*, *35*, 350–358. https://doi.org/10.1016/j.chb.2014.03.018

Levine, M. P., & Murnen, S. K. (2009). "Everybody knows that mass media are/are not [pick one] a cause of eating disorders": A critical review of evidence for a causal link between media, negative body image, and disordered eating in females. *Journal of Social and Clinical Psychology*, *28*(1), 9–42. https://doi.org/10.1521/jscp.2009.28.1.9

Lonergan, A. R., Bussey, K., Mond, J., Brown, O., Griffiths, S., Murray, S. B., & Mitchison, D. (2019). Me, my selfie, and I: The relationship between editing and posting selfies and body dissatisfaction in men and women. *Body Image*, *28*, 39–43. https://doi.org/10.1016/j.bodyim.2018.12.001

Lup, K., Trub, L., & Rosenthal, L. (2015). Instagram# instasad?: Exploring associations among instagram use, depressive symptoms, negative social comparison, and strangers followed. *Cyberpsychology, Behavior, and Social Networking*, *18*(5), 247–252. https://doi.org/10.1089/cyber.2014.0560

Manzi, C., Coen, S., Regalia, C., Yévenes, A. M., Giuliani, C., & Vignoles, V. L. (2018). Being in the social: A cross-cultural and cross-generational study on identity processes related to Facebook use. *Computers in Human Behaviour*, *80*, 81–87. https://doi.org/10.1016/j.chb.2017.10.046

Marwick, A. E. (2015). Instafame: Luxury selfies in the attention economy. *Public Culture*, *27*(1–75), 137–160. https://doi.org/10.1215/08992363-2798379

McMullin, J. A., & Cairney, J. (2004). Self-esteem and the intersection of age, class, and gender. *Journal of Aging Studies*, *18*(1), 75–90. https://doi.org/10.1016/j.jaging.2003.09.006

Mills, J. S., Musto, S., Williams, L., & Tiggemann, M. (2018). "Selfie" harm: Effects on mood and body image in young women. *Body Image*, *27*, 86–92. https://doi.org/10.1016/j.bodyim.2018.08.007

Mingoia, J., Hutchinson, A. D., Wilson, C., & Gleaves, D. H. (2017). The relationship between social networking site use and the internalisation of a thin ideal in females: A meta-analytic review. *Frontiers in Psychology*, *8*, 1351. https://doi.org/10.3389/fpsyg.2017.01351

Muller, C. J., & MacLehose, R. F. (2014). Estimating predicted probabilities from logistic regression: Different methods correspond to different target populations. *International Journal of Epidemiology*, *43*(3), 962–970. https://doi.org/10.1093/ije/dyu029

Phua, J., Jin, S. V., & Kim, J. J. (2017). Uses and gratifications of social networking sites for bridging and bonding social capital: A comparison of Facebook, Twitter, Instagram, and Snapchat. *Computers in Human Behaviour*, *72*, 115–122. https://doi.org/10.1016/j.chb.2017.02.041

Pounders, K., Kowalczyk, C. M., & Stowers, K. (2016). Insight into the motivation of selfie postings: Impression management and self-esteem. *European Journal of Marketing*, *50*(9/10), 1879–1892. https://doi.org/10.1108/EJM-07-2015-0502

Reemes, D. M. (2015). *The Egyptian Ouroboros: An iconological and theological study*. Doctoral dissertation, UCLA.

Ridgway, J. L., & Clayton, R. B. (2016). Instagram unfiltered: Exploring associations of body image satisfaction, Instagram# selfie posting, and negative romantic relationship outcomes. *Cyberpsychology, Behavior, and Social Networking*, *19*(1), 2–7. https://doi.org/10.1089/cyber.2015.0433

Sheldon, P., & Bryant, K. (2016). Instagram: Motives for its use and relationship to narcissism and contextual age. *Computers in Human Behavior*, *58*, 89–97. https://doi.org/10.1016/j.chb.2015.12.059

Shome, D., Vadera, S., Male, S. R., & Kapoor, R. (2020). Does taking selfies lead to increased desire to undergo cosmetic surgery. *Journal of Cosmetic Dermatology*, *19*(8), 2025–2032. https://doi.org/10.1111/jocd.13267

Sivonen, J., Koivula, A., Saarinen, A., & Keipi, T. (2018). *Working papers in economic sociology: Research report on the Finland in the digital age-survey*. Working Papers in Economic Sociology. University of Turku.

Smith, A. (2014). *What people like and dislike about Facebook*. Pew Research Center, 3.

Terán, L., Yan, K., & Aubrey, J. S. (2019). "But first let me take a selfie": US adolescent girls' selfie activities, self-objectification, imaginary audience beliefs, and appearance concerns. *Journal of Children and Media*, *14*(3), 343–360. https://doi.org/10.1080/17482798.2019.1697319

Thompson, J. K., Heinberg, L. J., Altabe, M., & Tantleff-Dunn, S. (1999). Sociocultural theory: The media and society. In *Exacting beauty: Theory, assessment, and treatment of body image disturbance* (pp. 85–124). American Psychological Association. https://doi.org/10.1037/10312-003

Tiggemann, M. (2011). Mental health risks of self-objectification: A review of the empirical evidence for disordered eating, depressed mood, and sexual dysfunction. In R. M. Calogero, S. Tantleff-Dunn, & J. K. Thompson (Eds.), *Self-objectification in women: Causes, consequences, and counteractions* (pp. 139–159). American Psychological Association. https://doi.org/10.1037/12304-007

Tiggemann, M., Anderberg, I., & Brown, Z. (2020a). # Loveyourbody: The effect of body positive Instagram captions on women's body image. *Body Image*, *33*, 129–136. https://doi.org/10.1016/j.bodyim.2020.02.015

Tiggemann, M., Anderberg, I., & Brown, Z. (2020b). Uploading your best self: Selfie editing and body dissatisfaction. *Body Image*, *33*, 175–182. https://doi.org/10.1016/j.bodyim.2020.03.002

Tiggemann, M., & Barbato, I. (2018). "You look great!": The effect of viewing appearance-related Instagram comments on women's body image. *Body Image*, *27*, 61–66. https://doi.org/10.1016/j.bodyim.2018.08.009

Tiggemann, M., & Miller, J. (2010). The Internet and adolescent girls' weight satisfaction and drive for thinness. *Sex Roles*, *63*(1–2), 79–90. https://doi.org/10.1007/s11199-010-9789-z

134   *Erica Åberg and Aki Koivula*

Tiggemann, M., & Slater, A. (2013). NetGirls: The Internet, Facebook, and body image concern in adolescent girls. *International Journal of Eating Disorders*, *46*(6), 630–633. https://doi.org/10.1002/eat.22141

Tiggemann, M., & Zaccardo, M. (2018). 'Strong is the new skinny': A content analysis of# fitspiration images on instagram. *Journal of Health Psychology*, *23*(8), 1003–1011. https://doi.org/10.1177/1359105316639436

Tiidenberg, K., & Baym, N. K. (2017). Learn it, buy it, work it: Intensive pregnancy on Instagram. *Social Media + Society*, *3*(1), 1–13. https://doi.org/10.1177/2056305116685108

Tiidenberg, K., & Gómez Cruz, E. (2015). Selfies, image and the re-making of the body. *Body & Society*, *21*(4), 77–102. https://doi.org/10.1177/1357034x15592465

Wang, Y., Xie, X., Fardouly, J., Vartanian, L. R., & Lei, L. (2019). The longitudinal and reciprocal relationships between selfie-related behaviors and self-objectification and appearance concerns among adolescents. *New Media & Society*, *23*(1), 1461444819894346. https://doi.org/10.1177/1461444819894346

Want, S. C. (2009). Meta-analytic moderators of experimental exposure to media portrayals of women on female appearance satisfaction: Social comparisons as automatic processes. *Body Image*, *6*(4), 257–269. https://doi.org/10.1016/j.bodyim.2009.07.008

Åberg, E., Koivula, A., & Kukkonen, I. (2020a). A feminine burden of perfection? Appearance-related pressures on social networking sites. *Telematics and Informatics*, *46*, 101319. https://doi.org/10.1016/j.tele.2019.101319

Åberg, E., Koivula, A., Kukkonen, I., Sarpila, O., & Pajunen, T. (2020b). Compliment rules or compliments rule? A population-level study of appearance commenting norms on social media. In *International conference on human-computer interaction* (pp. 16–28). Springer. https://doi.org/10.1007/978-3-030-49576-3_2

Chapter 8

Sofie's World: Resistance toward the Thin Ideal in Sofie Hagen's Fat Activist Online Content

Anna Puhakka

Introduction

One of the core elements of the Western beauty ideal is the thinness norm. The normative body – a body that is not fat – is associated with normality and desirability (Brewis, 2017, p. 5), whereas the norm-breaking fat body presents its polar opposite. In this way, norms regulate, to a large extent (although specific contexts, or fields, always do have a role to play), which bodies possess aesthetic capital, itself exchangeable for other forms of capital. In today's day and age, a thin body equals aesthetic capital and thus potential for upward mobility or socioeconomic advantage, while a fat body equals the opposite – the reversal of existing opportunities (Brewis, 2017, p. 6; Puhl & Brownell, 2001). There-fore, aesthetic capital is a useful way to conceptualize the power that norms hold.

Fat activism, with its 50+ years of history, has risen as a response to discrimi-nation against fat people. With the advent of the World Wide Web and, more recently, social media, this movement for social justice, 'always growing and refining itself' (Cooper, 2008), has spread throughout the Internet environment. In response, I explore stand-up comedian Sofie Hagen's fat activist online content in this chapter. I am interested in how social media activism can be used as an avenue, first, to deconstruct norms related to physical appearance and, second, to show appreciation and recognition for bodies that do not confirm to those norms. I ask: In which ways does Sofie Hagen challenge appearance-based norms via her online fat activism?

Three distinct themes arise out of Hagen's public timeline photo captions on her Facebook business page, which I analyse qualitatively with the help of dia-logic thematic analysis (Koski, 2020): offensive resistance, doing fatness wrong

Appearance as Capital, 135–148

doi:10.1108/978-1-80043-708-120210009

and ambivalence. Further, an additional motif, encompassing the other themes, presents itself – namely, non-communication, or Hagen's perceived reluctance to engage in dialogue on social media. I argue that, taken together, these four elements institute a strategy through which Hagen is able to break the prevailing physical appearance norm that thinner is always better.[1]

My impression is that Sofie Hagen's intended audience is comprised mainly of two separate groups: those already sympathetic to the fat activist cause and those critical of it. These groups do not necessarily follow any particular demographics, although the majority of body positivity advocates, for instance, tend to be young (and white) cis females. That women in particular would be drawn to these thematics is corroborated by research showing that gender plays a central role in how body size is experienced and interpreted: Expectations vis-à-vis embodiment differ among genders, as do their consequences, which tend to be more negative for women than for men (Gailey, 2014; Harjunen, 2009).

This chapter is structured as follows. I first discuss the theoretical underpinnings of the study and then introduce the text's central concepts and some methodological considerations. Next, I lay out an analysis of the study's data before presenting the conclusions and suggestions for further research.

Theoretical Underpinnings: Appearance Norms, Fat Stigma, Fatphobia and the Good Fatty

To understand weight discrimination and fatphobia, it is imperative to be cognisant of the prevailing appearance-related norms that give rise to these phenomena. In this study, the focus is on norms related to size and weight of the body in particular. The overall parameters of what constitutes a 'normal' or acceptable body are narrow indeed: one must not be too thin, muscular, short or tall. The most prevailing appearance norm in the Western world today, however, dictates that the body – especially the female one (e.g. Harjunen, 2020) – must, first and foremost, not be fat.

This norm is upheld by many core societal institutions, such as school, science (particularly medicine) and the media (Harjunen, 2009). It is maintained and perpetuated through diverse practices and discourses; one example of such a norm-sustaining discourse is that of the obesity epidemic (Harjunen, 2020). Here, fat people are seen to pose a threat to the advancement of the society, including the economy and even the environment. With these types of discourses circulating widely, it is not surprising that fatness is a heavily stigmatised trait, labelling fat people with such qualities as lazy, dirty and even immoral (Brewis, 2017, p. 2; Jutel, 2005; Pausé, 2017).

Fat stigma, in turn, leads to weight discrimination and fatphobia (e.g. Farrell, 2011). I interpret weight discrimination and fatphobia as sanctions for breaking social norms; they can be seen as penalties for exceeding the body weight or size generally deemed 'normal' and acceptable. As a term, 'weight discrimination' includes all those who are marginalised because, for one reason or another, they do not fit in the 'normal' category – in addition to fat bodies, 'underweight' bodies may face weight discrimination. 'Fatphobia', for its part, denotes the widespread fat-hating and fat-fearing culture as well as its concrete ramifications, to which fat people are subjected every day (Harjunen & Kyrölä, 2007, pp. 305–307).

The consequences of fatphobia include negative attitudes, mistreatment, lack of services and outright discrimination (Harjunen, 2020). Studies show that fatness is socially sanctioned in many life areas of central importance, such as education (Weinstock & Krehbiel, 2009), working life (Härkönen & Räsänen, 2008; Kauppinen & Anttila, 2005) and healthcare (Puhl & Heuer, 2011; Sabin et al., 2012). In addition, weight discrimination has adverse consequences for fat people's physical and mental health, along with an increased mortality risk (Schvey et al., 2014; Sutin et al., 2015).

One attempt to manage fat stigma is to become a so-called good fatty, or 'the fatty that people will tolerate' (Stryker, 2016; see also: Chastain, 2014). A good fatty actively aspires to become not fat or at least subscribes to the idea that thinner is better (Bias, 2014). Deliberately trying to distance oneself from a fat identity and framing fatness as unwanted can be called 'doing fatness right'; such actions might include losing weight on purpose and/or weight loss talk (Harjunen et al., 2007, p. 288) as well as displaying healthy eating and daily exercise (Southard Ospina, 2017).

Adopting a good fatty's behaviours and ways of speaking might alleviate the stigma for the individual engaging in these practices, but it does not question the underlying fatphobic culture (Chastain, 2016). Instead of managing fat stigma, fat activism's *raison d'être* is to challenge it and, ultimately, break appearance-based norms. To remind the reader of the confrontational nature of (Hagen's) fat activism, I call it 'oppositional' (see Pausé, 2015a, p. 2) on occasion.

Studying Sofie Hagen's Online Fat Activism

As a general starting point, I take activism to mean concrete actions with an established end goal. The ultimate objective of fat activism is to end the marginalisation of fat people, and to reach that target involves 'many sites and interests' (Cooper, 2016, p. 2). In this chapter, I define online fat activism as intentional activity intended to inform and influence others in matters related to fatness, in the soci(et)al sphere in particular, and carried out via digital content on the Internet.

Sofie Hagen is a stand-up comedian, activist, podcaster and author (Hagen, 2019). She is a Dane based in the United Kingdom who writes and performs in English. Hagen is active on several social media platforms – as of April 2020, she had 48,348 followers on Facebook. As an activist, she has been vocal about issues related to discrimination against fat people; one such instance was criticising Cancer Research UK's advertising as fat shaming (e.g. Therrien, 2018). In addition to fatness, she discusses other human-rights-related questions, such as class, race and gender (she describes herself as non-binary; I refer to Hagen as 'she', since she has indicated that her preferred pronoun usage is 'she/he/they' [11 July 2020], thus indicating that pronouns are unimportant to her).[2]

Although Sofie Hagen has a larger audience and perhaps more activity on Instagram and Twitter, I opted for Facebook as a data source for this chapter because all of her posts are preserved there, making it a more reliable text repository than the two other social media sites. I selected data from among the 537 timeline photos on Hagen's Facebook business page with the criterion that photo captions be written in English. Such captions began appearing consistently in early 2015, with the last one included in this chapter posted on 24 April 2020. Since the focus is on captions, I comment on pictures only where appropriate.

There is no need to be logged in to Facebook to access Sofie Hagen's posts. I interpret this to be a conscious choice to allow as many individuals as possible to access her content. In addition to fat activism, Hagen writes regularly on several other themes, such as social anxiety, politics and numerous lighter topics – nevertheless, in accordance with my research task, the analysis is limited to her fat-activism-related writings.

Categories of Analysis

To analyse the data, I used Leena Koski's (2020) dialogic thematic analysis. The method is comprised of three stages; in this work, they were implemented as follows. First, I acquainted myself with theories related to aesthetic capital, which helped to form the preliminary research question. This theoretical framework then served as the point of departure from which I studied the entire data set. Second, after having read through the data, and keeping the theoretical framework and research question in mind, I formulated some initial content categories (not yet themes per se) – the so-called thick excerpts (Koski, 2020, p. 163) found in the captions were particularly useful here. Finally, I proceeded from categories to proper themes, again, by a constant dialogue between theory and data (hence the method's name).

With dialogic thematic analysis as my interpretative tool, I distinguished four main themes in the data: non-communication with the audience, offensive resistance, doing fatness wrong and ambivalence. Non-communication was the only category of analysis not supported by a prior theoretical backbone; it arose entirely from the data set. In the future, and potentially drawing on a grounded-theory-inspired approach, it would be interesting to apply this theme to activism research more generally. Unfortunately, due to space constraints, I am not able to develop this viewpoint further here.

Another lens through which I analyse Sofie Hagen's activism is that of offensive resistance. According to Caitlin Cawley (2015, p. 2), offensive resistance is first and foremost a rhetorical strategy; in other words, her definition emphasizes the central role of language. For that reason, I will employ offensive resistance as a heuristic aid to distil meaning from the data, especially in terms of the language used in Hagen's activist content. In addition, still following Cawley's (2015, p. 4) lead, I understand the word 'offensive' both as an adjective and a noun. When used as an adjective – as in 'offensive resistance' – it is synonymous to aggressive and obnoxious, among others (Merriam-Webster, n.d.a.). The noun form of 'offensive', on the other hand, signifies attack (Merriam-Webster, n.d.a.).

A third theme found in Sofie Hagen's oppositional online fat activism is what Cat Pausé (2015b) has called 'doing fatness wrong'. In fact, for Pausé, doing fatness wrong has to do primarily with rejecting neoliberalism (Pausé, 2015b). This is certainly one part of Hagen's activism, since on many occasions, she criticises capitalism vehemently – as well as diet culture as one of its many guises. However, Hagen 'does fatness wrong' in numerous ways, and not all of them are necessarily tied to this neoliberal ideal; for instance, non-communication is a non-neoliberal way to do fatness wrong (cf. previous subsection).

For this reason, I will also be using the concept of 'flaunting'. This term comes originally from Kenji Yoshino (2006, in Saguy & Ward, 2011, p. 57), who sees flaunting as the non-acceptance to hide, which has the consequence of drawing attention to a visible stigma – in this case, fatness. By using the notions 'flaunting' and 'doing fatness wrong' interchangeably, I want to emphasise that whereas the theme of offensive resistance is chiefly tied to language use, this theme concerns itself with behaviours. Often, flaunting one's fat entails engaging in activities that are considered entirely neutral for non-fat bodies, but off limits for fat ones. Indeed, Jeannine A. Gailey (2014, p. 143) has noted that

> ...the fat woman who wears tight clothing [is] perceived as flaunting because [she is] marginalized ... From the perspective of the flaunters, they are simply engaging in behaviors that those who are socially unobtrusive engage in all the time without criticism.

Such behaviours include eating something deemed 'bad' in public, wearing a bikini and getting up on stage to perform (Read, 2011).

The fourth category of analysis is that of ambivalence. Ambivalence – or simultaneous and contradictory attitudes or feelings (Merriam-Webster, n.d.b.) – in fat activism has been discussed by many in academia (Cooper, 2016; Maor, 2013; McMichael, 2010; Meleo-Erwin, 2011; Murray, 2010, 2008, 2005). The consensus seems to be that in societies infused with fatphobia, it is very difficult to accept (one's) fat embodiment at all times. Thankfully, this need not be the case for oppositional fat activism to continue to function; resistance can coexist simultaneously with more socially conforming thoughts (Maor, 2012, p. 19).

Sofie's World: Features of Sofie Hagen's Oppositional Fat Activism

Non-communication with the Audience

As I mentioned at the beginning of this chapter, Sofie Hagen's interaction with her Facebook followers is very limited. Hagen openly admits to not seeing all the messages she receives (11 March 2018), and not responding to comments (4 June 2017). This strategy does not adhere to the commonly held assumption that one should display reciprocal behaviour on social media platforms. Indeed, Hagen deliberately chooses non-communication:

> I'm not reading comments because I'm too busy being beautiful and awesome to read sad man-boys weeping.
>
> (1 October 2017)

Fat activists are frequently exposed to online hate speech (Cooper, 2018; Kinzel, 2016; Read, 2013, 2018), including fatphobic antagonism (Bolden, 2018). I would therefore suggest that the unwillingness to engage in reciprocal communication points to Hagen wanting to protect herself from being silenced (the reference to 'sad man-boys weeping'). In other words, by maintaining non-communication on Facebook, Hagen 'negotiate[s] the risk of interference from perceived outsiders' (Bolden, n.d.). According to my interpretation, this allows her to continue her fat activist role while reaching an ample number of people via the largest social networking site in the world.

At the same time, Sofie Hagen acknowledges that she receives contact from those members of the audience who are sympathetic to her cause:

> I don't see everything you guys message or email me, so I rarely answer, but I truly appreciate that you reach out.
>
> (11 March 2018)

This passage, then, suggests that Hagen values contact from her audience but is not often able to reply – one of the reasons being that she does not read the messages, anticipating that many contain hate speech (cf. the preceding quote). Indeed, as indicated, to continue producing thought-provoking content without self-censorship, activists such as Hagen may avoid reading the messages and comments they receive. Consequently, they have less opportunity to communicate with those who could be open or curious about the fat activist cause. This can have a stifling effect on fat activism in the long run, particularly because a significant part of it happens online. What is more, prospective fat activists might be repelled from the movement upon learning of the frequency of receiving online hate.

Offensive Resistance

Of the forms Sofie Hagen's oppositional fat activism takes, offensive resistance is perhaps the one that would be most intuitively associated with opposition. As mentioned above, I employ offensive resistance as an aid for analysis, notably in terms of language use; I interpret content that includes swearing and/or insults as offensive. The following excerpt serves as an example:

> This is a big day. I am on the front cover of Politiken with one of my best friends and idols, Andrea Storgaard Brok, because of our

newly started movement, FedFront – an obesity-glorifying and anti-capitalist movement. We are trying to create a network for fat people. And we are trying to kick social structure in the dick. Front page, motherfucker. Front page.

(7 February 2017)

Some of Sofie Hagen's fat-activist messaging is directed towards marginalising societal structures, as in the passage above. Her text not only celebrates the visibility of her non-normative body on the cover of Denmark's biggest paid newspaper (also related to the next theme, doing fatness wrong); in addition, it vigorously opposes structures that promote capitalism and discrimination on the basis of body size. According to media scholars, the virtual space becomes more competitive by the day, and provocation is seen to be more effective than moderation in growing one's follower base (Maasilta, 2012, p. 51) – Hagen's colourful language use could be suggestive of this phenomenon.

In addition to criticising society at large, at other times, Hagen's communication is aimed at those harbouring negative opinions about fat people:

The post I made a few days ago has naturally meant that a lot of people have commented with either extreme ignorance (dieting advice or pretending to be concerned about my health – in which case, go fuck yourself) or with vile and abusive comments.

(26 September 2017)

According to my analysis, a significant part of the captions I categorised as offensive resistance directly address a simultaneously singular and collective 'you'. Here, the previous emphasis on abstract societal elements is switched to individuals. This shift makes it transparent that in the end, prejudices are always held and acted upon by human beings.

Offensive resistance and non-communication with the audience can be seen to intersect in three ways. First, by not responding to comments and messages and thus not 'playing by the rules', i.e. that social media usage should be based on interaction, Sofie Hagen breaks the social media platforms' rules, which in itself can be interpreted as offensive. Second, by not responding and by being offensive, Hagen violates the gender norm that females should be courteous and considerate of others. Third, she breaks the norm dictating that fat folks must act in an obedient manner, almost to the point of rendering themselves invisible. Interestingly, the demands of the two latter norms converge quite a bit.

Doing Fatness Wrong

Earlier in the chapter, I outlined some characteristics of 'doing fatness right', such as living a healthy lifestyle. I then turned to its opposite – doing fatness wrong – and its sub-category, flaunting, which include actions like eating and drinking without restraint. This exact activity is present in the excerpt below, which, moreover, contains a hallmark element of offensive resistance: swearing.

I have decided to just fucking eat and drink and love myself. I'm not going to eat kale and be a miserable prick so that I can live even longer and eat even more kale. Kale begets kale. So nah, fuck that. I know it bothers you that I am fat and I have no shame about it. ... #KaleBegetsKale (22 March 2018).

Of particular interest here is the 'mock' hashtag #KaleBegetsKale, used as an ironic counterpoint (Weller, 2011, p. 70). In addition to the caption above, which discusses neither eating nor being fat as shameful, several of the photos picture Sofie Hagen eating in public (either in restaurants or at home settings with other people; Zdrodowski, 1996). As Saguy and Ward (2011, p. 70) stated,

> ...when fat-identified women affirm their difference, whether in a bikini or in a restaurant, [they are often doing it] ... to challenge social norms in order to gain social inclusion.

Speaking of bikinis, another way that Sofie Hagen does fatness wrong – or flaunts her fat – is by donning a swimsuit in public and writing about it. Here, Hagen's refusal to cover (to apply Yoshino's definition of flaunting) happens both literally and metaphorically. Not only does the swimsuit expose her bare skin, but by posting about the photo shoot, with a picture included, she also renounces the societal preference for fat folks to remain invisible and not stand out:

> Oh hi, this is a photo of me taken from a swimsuit photo shoot in Dubai for a women's magazine. Objectively speaking, I look fucking hot as shit.
>
> (26 September 2017)

In addition, Sofie Hagen exposes her stomach in more than a dozen photos. To underline that she is comfortable in her own skin, a sympathetic face is often drawn on her midsection. Such a picture is also the cover photo of her book (although not in all language versions – something worthwhile to explore in itself). I interpret Hagen flaunting her fat body as a conscious choice to break the norms and to question the prevailing beauty standards, all while pointing out how they have been thoroughly fabricated and upheld by the current system.

While Sofie Hagen's fat body does not constitute aesthetic capital in the society at large in this day and age – quite the contrary – it is important to note that it might in some smaller circles. If the general societal ethos revolves around dieting, exercise and weight loss attempts, those norms are not accepted in Hagen's 'world'. Suddenly, fatness and the exposure thereof, so abhorred elsewhere, become the 'currency' through which one can express independent critical thinking, heightened awareness of social justice issues and empowerment (cf. Åberg, 2019). Ergo, although a body's size might not accommodate mainstream norms, physical appearance is still being used to make a statement about oneself.[3]

Ambivalence

I have discussed how Sofie Hagen challenges appearance-based norms through her activism. Up to now, and besides the theme of non-communication, I have analysed this opposition through the concepts of offensive resistance and doing fatness wrong/flaunting, which both rest on a solid fat identity. In order for these strategies to be carried out successfully, there can be no 'wavering' in (one's) fat corporeality and the messaging about it: if oppositional activism is to be efficient, the fat identity needs to be wholly endorsed. Still, this does not seem to hold true entirely for Hagen's content. In some captions, albeit admittedly few and far between, she acknowledges the ambivalence she feels towards her body:

> I want to say something about this photo. My initial reaction was 'I look big'. And not in a cheerful-hurrah-YAY-I-LOOK-BIG way, but in a 'Why didn't I wear a belt; I look bigger than I am, I could have looked smaller if I had worn something else' [way].
>
> (28 November 2016)

In the following passage, in turn, Sofie Hagen draws the audience's attention to the oft-repeated mistaken idea that the work of a fat activist would and/or should be grounded on them loving their body:

> … one of the questions I got asked the most … was about how OFTEN I loved my body. If I had bad days. And the answer is, yes I am human. Of course I have bad days. But I can honestly not remember the last one. It's been months. I either like my body, or I don't think about it. It's neutral. … (Not that it's easy to change the way you think and feel. It's taken me 5–6 years. Lots of therapy and unlearning and educating myself. But – the feeling is forever. 95% of diets fail. So you might as well put your eggs in the brain-basket).
>
> (17 January 2020)

Of note here is that Hagen speaks of either 'liking' her body or considering it neutral. Although the original questions are about 'loving' one's body, she does not use that word herself (thus, perhaps, instantiating yet another aspect of non-communication by formulating the answers in a way that she herself sees fit?). She is aware that, to a certain extent, the ambivalence regarding (her) fatness might be a permanent feature in her thinking but also that loving one's body uncondi-tionally is not required to engage in fat activism (see also Omaheimo & Särmä, 2017). According to Hagen, it is possible for her readers, too, to acquire this sense of body neutrality – by '[putting their] eggs in the brain-basket'.

Unavoidably, what I present above is a limited selection of the central findings; for example, Sofie Hagen's reservations about the body positivity movement would certainly warrant further analysis. As one indication of the data's richness, multiple themes at times can be found within a single caption; due to space constraints, I have not been able to include the captions in their entirety. Readers are encouraged to seek out the posts in question to get a deeper sense of their context (the attached dates should be of help). In addition, the boundaries between the themes are porous. In this chapter, I have presented the four themes as distinct for clarity, but they do share common traits – for instance, swearing is often present in both offensive resistance and doing fatness wrong, and non-communication intersects with all three.

Conclusions

In this chapter, I set out to enquire about how Sofie Hagen challenges appearance-based norms via her online fat activism. The analysis revealed that Hagen resists the real-life ramifications of aesthetic capital for fat people through four main avenues: non-communication with the audience, offensive resistance, doing fatness wrong and ambivalence.

Non-communication with the audience turned out to be a cross-cutting theme, intersecting with the other three strategies. I interpret this reluctance or unwillingness to engage in reciprocal interaction as being rooted – at least partially – in the fatphobic climate currently rampant in some online fora. In an effort not to expose herself to hate speech, Sofie Hagen ended up inadvertently missing many of the messages meant to encourage her and show support to the movement.

Offensive resistance is first and foremost a linguistic strategy, containing swearing and directed towards oppressive societal structures and prejudiced individuals alike. Doing fatness wrong, in turn, focuses on describing resistant behaviours that affirm the fat body's agency by 'flaunting', i.e. refusing to cover or hide it. Finally, reflecting on ambivalence (conflicting emotions regarding fatness) becomes yet another route by which to challenge body privilege, by showing that activism is possible without a perfectly solid (fat) identity. Taken together, these tactics institute a strategy through which Sofie Hagen can break the prevailing physical appearance norms and question the thinness norm as a widespread form of aesthetic capital.

Of these four elements, some potential paths for especially regarding flaunting now will be proposed for future research. More specifically, academic enquiry would do well to look more closely at the so-called bravery discourse circulating on several social media platforms. The whole idea of flaunting rests on the presumption that when fat bodies do certain things in public, frequently related to eating or dressing – and in so doing often draw negative attention – such actions can be revolutionary because they break the norms regarding what fat folks can or cannot do. Indeed, donning a bikini or eating a hamburger *can* be interpreted as bravery precisely because these behaviours are socially sanctioned, especially for fat women.

However, by emphasising how brave someone is, for e.g. wearing a swimsuit in public (as Gailey (2014) pointed out, flaunting might not be considered as such from the *flaunters'* point of view; on the contrary, they feel they are just engaging in regular activities that nobody would even notice were their bodies norm-accommodating), not only are the activists reduced to their physicality, with their verbal and/or written messaging overlooked, but the bravery discourse also ends up unintentionally reinforcing the very norms it is intended to challenge. After all, there is nothing brave about looking like the societally preferred norm, whereas the 'So brave!' exclamations serve to underline those instances in which the commented-upon bodies are in some way lacking.

This chapter has shown that Sofie Hagen's activism addresses and questions the thinness norm in a multitude of ways. While fat activists' work is to be applauded, I don't think that ridding the world of fatphobia should be the responsibility of only a few individuals. Because discrimination against fat people is a societal and a cultural phenomenon, it must be tackled on the same level. For example, taking legislative measures to prohibit weight discrimination (see, e.g. Puhl et al., 2015) would be one step in the right direction. Assuredly, fat activism – online and off – is making a dent in the appearance-centredness of society, but allies are needed to eradicate structural injustices.

Acknowledgements

The work by this author was partially supported by the University of Jyväskylä Department of Social Sciences and Philosophy.

Notes

1. Throughout this chapter, I use the term 'fat' instead of 'overweight' or 'obese'. 'Overweight' alludes to a normative idea of excess weight, whereas 'obese' has been used in the medical context – particularly in the West – with a firm emphasis on quantification, measuring and BMI charts (Lupton, 2018). Choosing the word 'fat' over 'obese' and 'overweight' is a way for activists to take it back by deflating the associated derogatory connotations (e.g. Harjunen, 2009, pp. 21–22).
2. The dates indicate the point in time when Sofie Hagen published said post.
3. In fact, one could argue that, as someone who is white, young and able-bodied, being fat is one of the few ways in which Sofie Hagen does not conform. This, in turn, raises a question on the kinds of fat activism that are actually welcomed or acknowledged – especially in the social media sphere. Or conversely: is it possible to do *fat activism* 'wrong'? For instance, will the visually oriented audience on Instagram be able to recognise fat activism if the activists choose to no longer follow the platform-specific, established and aestheticised conventions of (re)presenting fat bodies?

References

Bias, S. (2014). 12 good fatty archetypes. http://stacybias.net/2014/06/12-good-fatty-archetypes/

Bolden, S. E. (2018). *Unsettling boundaries: (Pre-)digital fat activism, fatphobia, and enclave ambivalence.* https://surface.syr.edu/cgi/viewcontent.cgi?article=1200&context=thesis

Bolden, S. E. (n.d.). *Sarah E. Bolden.* https://ischool.syr.edu/people/directories/view/sebolden/

Brewis, A. (2017). Introduction: Making sense of the new global body norms. In E. P. Anderson-Fye & A. Brewis (Eds.), *Fat planet: Obesity, culture, and symbolic body capital* (pp. 1–13). School for Advanced Research Press.

Cawley, C. (2015). Offensive resistance: Vulnerability, agency, and the political performance of radical fatness. https://www.academia.edu/12630682/Offensive_Resistance_Vulnerability_Agency_and_the_Political_Performance_of_Radical_Fatness

Chastain, R. (2014). There are two kinds of fat people. https://danceswithfat.org/2014/04/01/there-are-two-kinds-of-fat-people/

Chastain, R. (2016). Good fatty bad fatty BS. https://danceswithfat.org/2016/03/15/good-fatty-bad-fatty-bs/

Cooper, C. (2008). What's fat activism?. https://ulsites.ul.ie/sociology/sites/default/files//Whats%20Fat%20Activism.pdf

Cooper, C. (2016). *Fat activism: A radical social movement.* HammerOn Press.

Cooper, C. (2018). Last post...for now. http://obesitytimebomb.blogspot.com/2018/01/last-postfor-now.html

Farrell, A. E. (2011). *Fat shame: Stigma and the fat body in American culture.* New York University Press.

Gailey, J. A. (2014). *The hyper(in)visible fat woman: Weight and gender discourse in contemporary society.* Palgrave Macmillan. https://doi.org/10.1057/9781137407177

Hagen, S. (2019). *Happy fat: Taking up space in a world that wants to shrink you.* HarperCollins.

Harjunen, H. (2009). *Women and fat: Approaches to the social study of fatness.* University of Jyväskylä.

Harjunen, H. (2020). Ruumiin kokoon liittyvä sukupuolittunut syrjintä. In M. Mattila (Ed.), *Eriarvoisuuden tila Suomessa 2020* (pp. 215–238). Kalevi Sorsa -säätiö.

Harjunen, H., Hämäläinen, A., & Kyrölä, K. (2007). Oikeus olla oman kokoinen. In K. Kyrölä & H. Harjunen (Eds.), *Koolla on väliä! Lihavuus, ruumisnormit ja sukupuoli* (pp. 277–295). Like.

Harjunen, H., & Kyrölä, K. (2007). Sanoilla on väliä. Pieni lihavuussanakirja. In K. Kyrölä & H. Harjunen (Eds.), *Koolla on väliä! Lihavuus, ruumisnormit ja sukupuoli* (pp. 297–313). Like.

Härkönen, J., & Räsänen, P. (2008). Liikalihavuus, työttömyys ja ansiotaso. *Työelämän tutkimus – Arbetslivsforskning, 6*(1), 3–16.

Jutel, A. (2005). Weighing health: The moral burden of obesity. *Social Semiotics, 15*(2), 113–125. https://doi.org/10.1080/10350330500154717

Kauppinen, K., & Anttila, E. (2005). Onko painolla väliä? Hoikat, lihavat ja normaalipainoiset naiset työelämän murroksessa. *Työ ja ihminen: Työympäristötutkimuksen Aikakauskirja, 19*(2), 239–256.

Kinzel, L. (2016). Falling out of fatshion: How I lost my appetite for writing about fat politics. http://www.lesleykinzel.com/how-i-lost-my-appetite-for-fat-politics/

Koski, L. (2020). Teksteistä teemoiksi – dialoginen tematisointi. In A. Puusa & P. Juuti (Eds.), *Laadullisen tutkimuksen näkökulmat ja menetelmät* (pp. 157–172). Gaudeamus.

Lupton, D. (2018). *Fat.* Routledge. https://doi.org/10.4324/9781351029025

Maasilta, M. (2012). Perinteinen ja sosiaalinen media ruokkivat toinen toisiaan. In M. Maasilta (Ed.), *Maahanmuutto, media ja eduskuntavaalit* (pp. 23–51). Tampere University Press.

Maor, M. (2012). The body that does not diminish itself: Fat acceptance in Israel's lesbian queer communities. *Journal of Lesbian Studies, 16*(2), 177–198. https://doi.org/10.1080/10894160.2011.597660

Maor, M. (2013). Becoming the subject of your own story: Creating fat-positive representations. *Interdisciplinary Humanities, 30*(3), 7–22.

McMichael, M. R. (2010). *The dynamics of fat acceptance: Rhetoric and resistance to the obesity epidemic.* Texas Tech University.

Meleo-Erwin, Z. (2011). 'A beautiful show of strength': Weight loss and the fat activist self. *Health, 15*(2), 188–205. https://doi.org/10.1177/1363459310361601

Merriam-Webster. (n.d.a). Offensive. https://www.merriam-webster.com/dictionary/offensive

Merriam-Webster. (n.d.b). Ambivalence. https://www.merriam-webster.com/dictionary/ambivalence

Murray, S. (2005). (Un/be)coming out? Rethinking fat politics. *Social Semiotics, 15*(2), 153–163. https://doi.org/10.1080/10350330500154667

Murray, S. (2008). *The 'fat' female body.* Palgrave Macmillan. https://doi.org/10.1057/9780230584419

Murray, S. (2010). Doing politics or selling out? Living the fat body. *Women's Studies, 34*(3–4), 265–277. https://doi.org/10.1080/00497870590964165

Omaheimo, R., & Särmä, S. (2017). Kuuma läskikeskustelu. https://hairikot.voima.fi/artikkeli/kuuma-laskikeskustelu/

Pausé, C. (2015a). Express yourself: Fat activism in the web 2.0 age. In R. Chastain (Ed.), *The politics of size: Vol. 1. Perspectives from the fat acceptance movement* (pp. 1–8). Praeger.

Pausé, C. (2015b). Rebel heart: Performing fatness wrong online. *M/C Journal, 18*(3). http://www.journal.media-culture.org.au/index.php/mcjournal/article/view/977

Pausé, C. (2017). Borderline: The ethics of fat stigma in public health. *Journal of Law, Medicine & Ethics, 45*(4), 510–517. https://doi.org/10.1177/1073110517750585

Puhl, R., & Brownell, K. D. (2001). Bias, discrimination, and obesity. *Obesity Research, 9*(12), 788–805. https://doi.org/10.1038/oby.2001.108

Puhl, R. M., & Heuer, C. A. (2011). Obesity stigma: Important considerations for public health. *American Journal of Public Health, 100*(6), 1019–1028. https://doi.org/10.2105/AJPH.2009.159491

Puhl, R. M., Latner, J. D., O'Brien, K. S., Luedicke, J., Danielsdottir, S., & Ramos Salas, X. (2015). Potential policies and laws to prohibit weight discrimination: Public views from 4 countries. *The Milbank Quarterly, 93*(4), 691–731. https://doi.org/10.1111/1468-0009.12162

Read, K. (2011). Flaunting our fat. https://fatheffalump.wordpress.com/2011/10/30/flaunting-our-fat/

Read, K. (2013). Why I don't take any shit from anyone in my online spaces. https://fatheffalump.wordpress.com/2013/05/28/why-i-take-no-shit-from-anyone-in-my-online-spaces/

Read, K. (2018). Why I don't blog any more. https://fatheffalump.wordpress.com/2018/05/05/why-i-dont-blog-any-more/

Sabin, J. A., Marini, M., & Nosek, B. A. (2012). Implicit and explicit anti-fat bias among a large sample of medical doctors by BMI, race/ethnicity and gender. *PLoS One*, *7*(11). e48448. https://doi.org/10.1371/journal.pone.0048448

Saguy, A. C., & Ward, A. (2011). Coming out as fat: Rethinking stigma. *Social Psychology Quarterly*, *74*(1), 53–75. https://doi.org/10.1177/0190272511398190

Schvey, N. A., Puhl, R. M., & Brownell, K. D. (2014). The stress of stigma: Exploring the effect of weight stigma on cortisol reactivity. *Psychosomatic Medicine*, *76*(2), 156–162. https://doi.org/10.1097/PSY.0000000000000031

Southard Ospina, M. (2017). 9 ways to defy the 'good fatty' trope. https://everydayfeminism.com/2017/02/9-ways-defy-the-good-fatty-trope/

Stryker, K. (2016). 6 ways I was taught to be a good fatty (and why I stopped). https://everydayfeminism.com/2016/04/taught-to-be-good-fatty/

Sutin, A. R., Stephan, Y., & Terracciano, A. (2015). Weight discrimination and risk of mortality. *Psychological Science*, *26*(11), 1803–1811. https://doi.org/10.1177/0956797615601103

Therrien, A. (2018). Is it wrong to be blunt about obesity?. https://www.bbc.com/news/health-43240986

Weinstock, J., & Krehbiel, M. (2009). Fat youth as common targets for bullying. In E. Rothblum & S. Solovay (Eds.), *The fat studies reader* (pp. 120–126). New York University Press.

Weller, M. (2011). *The digital scholar: How technology is transforming scholarly practice*. Bloomsbury Academic.

Yoshino, K. (2006). *Covering: The hidden assault on our civil rights*. Random House.

Zdrodowski, D. (1996). Eating out: The experience of eating in public for the "overweight" woman. *Women's Studies International Forum*, *19*(6), 655–664. https://doi.org/10.1016/S0277-5395(96)00086-6

Åberg, E. (2019). Näkökulma: Karvainen pääoma?. In I. Kukkonen, T. Pajunen, O. Sarpila, & E. Åberg (Eds.), *Ulkonäköyhteiskunta. Ulkoinen olemus pääomana 2000-luvun Suomessa* (pp. 119–121). Into Kustannus Oy.

Chapter 9

Well-beshaved Women Rarely Make History – Exploring the Contestation of the Hairless Beauty Ideal with Case #Januhairy

Erica Åberg and Laura Salonen

Introduction

Close your eyes and imagine the sound of an accelerating motorcycle continued with Princess Nokia's assertive lyrics: 'Who that is, ho? That girl is a tomboy' (Nokia & Ramirez, 2017). The forceful vocals are accompanied with feminine soft pastel aesthetics: pink fuzzy slippers, women looking at you with bedroom eyes, stroking their bristly legs and underarm hair with content. Does this sound like a feminist utopia, where women can sport their unibrows freely and decide what to do with their hairy legs, bushy bikini lines, woolly underarms or downy bellies for themselves? Not quite. It illustrates a commercial for the company Billie that sells products for body hair removal by saying 'Whatever you decide to do with your body hair, we're here'. There are also other examples of brands (again, razors) using feminist discourses on their commodities, stressing the optionality of something that is often connected tightly with feminists' appearances: body hair. However, this time the removal of body hair is associated with self-love, and branding the products as pain-free, vegan or environmentally friendly to make them appealing to a particular niche: cool consumers with a feminist orientation. Similarly, what is called the 'hairless beauty ideal' or the 'hairlessness norm' is now contested in social media campaigns by posting aestheticised pictures of hairy female bodies. How did something that used to be 'dreaded otherness' become a hot and sexy trend?

This chapter approaches the contradictory nature of female body hair with the scholarship of the hairlessness norm. We expand it to the theory of aesthetic

Appearance as Capital, 149–164

capital, which in this chapter can be understood as context-dependent physical appearance, which also has ideological significance. Even though body hair bears a negative value in broader society, it can help accruing assets that are appreciated in a certain field, among social media activists. Appropriately manifesting this local cultural capital can be used to gain, for example, social capital (friends, followers and likes), but also turned into economic capital (paid collaborations, representing certain brands). We investigate how the hairlessness norm is challenged by studying participants and commentators who took part in the Januhairy movement. Using content analysis, we elaborate the images and captions under the #januhairy posted on Instagram during 2019 and 2020, and the comments these posts received. This chapter aims to explore, first, how the hairlessness norm is contested in an online context, and second, how the commentators respond to this contestation.

We will start by presenting theoretical literature on the norms related to female body hair. We move on to describe how activism in general takes form in social media platforms and how it is related to commodity feminism. Next, we introduce our research questions, data and methods, results and finally, a discussion and our conclusions.

Background

The (Un)hairy Female Body

Women's unruly bodies have been normatively governed by beauty ideals throughout the ages. One example of these gendered beauty ideals is the 'hairlessness norm' (e.g. Basow, 1991; Tiggemann & Kenyon, 1998; Tiggemann & Lewis, 2004; see also Widdows, 2018). This norm demands women to remove the hair on, for example, their legs and underarms to appear feminine and aesthetically appealing, and thus, avoid the social stigma of 'dreaded otherness' (Fahs, 2011), followed by others' shame and disgust. In this approach, making oneself attractive by body hair removal is not just a choice but also a mandate, one communicated by not only women's parents and friends but also strangers, coworkers and friends of friends.

The norms regarding body hair have been addressed since the 1960s. Since those times, it has been considered the 'last taboo' (Lesnik-Oberstein, 2006; Smelik, 2015), something that is not discussed openly and needs to be challenged. By far, the majority of women in Western countries follow this practice (Herzig, 2015; Lesnik-Oberstein, 2006). This results in seeing body hair removal as commonplace and everyday behaviour for most women, who do not question its origin or necessity. However, the extent of removal has increased in time: nearly complete hair removal is becoming more common for younger women (e.g. Tiggemann & Hodgson, 2008), and simultaneously, associated with cleanliness and respect for sexual partners (e.g. Basow, 1991; Fahs, 2011).

It is important to keep in mind that despite hair growing all over the body, only some zones of hair bear social significance and raise popular interest. Hair has gendered and ideological significance as it represents the 'oppositeness' of the sexes. For example, while long hair represents ultimate ideal beauty on female bodies, on male bodies it represents the opposite (Synnott, 1987). Moreover, as unshaved legs or bikini lines are considered 'excessive' and thus unfeminine and repulsive, the very same hair represents ultimate masculinity on men's bodies. Following this, common reasons for removing body hair include the willingness to appear sexually attractive and desirable (e.g. Tiggemann & Hodgson, 2008; Tiggemann & Lewis, 2004). For example, women internalise ideas about their bodies as central to 'proper' femininity and become other-directed, concerned about the male gaze and oriented toward the heterosexual dating market. As the hairlessness norm is so pervasive, deviations from the norms are extremely powerful. Hairy legs, unplucked eyebrows and axillary hair are symbols of feminism and egalitarian ideology. Similarly, removing this hair is seen as a symbol of traditional gender roles. Synnott (1987) concluded that a woman's body hair signifies one's commitment to feminism, which makes the hair a political statement. Therefore, the body (with or without hair) is not only a political symbol but also political in itself.

The unquestionability of body hair removal can be linked to capitalist patriarchy and how this 'last taboo' is silenced still today. This injustice could be overcome by showing body hair exists and using the feminist critical practice as a deconstructive strategy by exposing the reasons behind these practices (Lesnik-Oberstein, 2006). In her writing, Lesnik-Oberstein (2006) also refers to the female body as something that is described as 'lacking' in patriarchal societies: lacking masculine presence and thus created feminine with culturally and socially specified manners (e.g. hair removal, dieting, makeup). In contrast, male bodies 'exist' without being forced to achieve their 'maleness'. To fulfil societal ideals of femininity, women disguise and conceal their 'natural' bodies and undergo a vast array of these bodily modifications, procedures, grooming habits and maintenance behaviours to conform to social norms of proper femininity. Moreover, another societal norm is embedded within body hair removal practices: the social maintenance of heterosexuality, or *appearing* heterosexual, and adhering to the body practices accompanying this norm (Nielsen et al., 2000). Indeed, body hair is something that in previous research has been associated with lesbian aesthetics and queer culture (e.g. Basow, 1991). Turning this thought the other way around, appropriating these non-normative gender performances and further aestheticising them can also be seen as investing in 'queer glamor' (Branfman, 2019).

When assessing the norms' strength and the possibility for resisting these norms, it is important to recognise that individuals do not choose the prevailing beauty ideals. Individuals can choose the extent to which they conform to them, but the extent to which this can be done is also limited by the dominance of the ideal. Moreover, women who do succeed in rejecting and resisting the beauty ideal either do so at a significant cost and effort, or they are protected from the costs of nonconformity by membership in a community that endorses some other competing beauty ideal or other ideals that oppose the dominant beauty ideal. These communities are increasingly rare and often privileged (Widdows, 2018). However, it must be taken into account that non-obedience to existing beauty ideals can also benefit some individuals. Giselinde Kuipers's (2015) study on different taste repertoires and physical appearance confirmed that the more educated, younger, metropolitan informants prefer a beauty that is 'interesting' or 'authentic', defining their cultural capital. This confirms the possibility for only privileged individuals or groups to successfully aestheticise appearances that are considered subordinate in broader society or contest the prevailing norms and ideals.

Activism and Commodity Culture in Social Media

Today, social media is an inherent part of many everyday lives (See Åberg & Koivula, Chapter 7 in this book). It is also an important platform for activism (See Puhakka, Chapter 8 in this book). The contemporary media culture, and particularly in social media environments, have become the primary site for social movements and selfies established as a dominant practice of resisting bodily norms (e.g. Gill & Elias, 2014) and hetero-normativity (e.g. Tiidenberg, 2014). The movements, such as body positivity, challenge contemporary society's narrow beauty ideals and the visibility of bodies that do not fit mainstream beauty norms (Sastre, 2016). Through sharing and viewing selfies, the narrow standards of appearances are questioned, consumerist aspects of visual economy are rejected and thus control over the aesthetics of bodies is (re)claimed (Tiidenberg & Gomez-Cruz, 2015). In an article about portraying ageing femininities on Instagram, Tiidenberg (2018) considers selfie practices expanding community members' understanding of what Bourdieu and Whiteside (1996, p. 6) has referred to as 'photographable and unphotographable' about (women's) bodies.

Social media platforms have been widely used for different 'social movements', for example, movements such as 'Movember' and 'Decembeard' that focus on celebrating the male facial hair and simultaneously raise funds and awareness on prostate cancer or colon cancer. More recently, a movement called 'Januhairy' concentrated on reducing the stigma of women's natural hair growth and empowers its participants by encouraging them to explore how it feels to be *au naturel*. From well-known and large-numbered movements, such as 'Veganuary' or perhaps the more unfamiliar 'Masturbation May', the participation in any movement these days seems to be made easily achievable by packing them neatly as a 30-day experiment. This new lifestyle is reported occasionally, if not daily, by using the agreed hashtag devoted to reporting thoughts on the experiment or the results of the progress. Research on social media has found that women were more likely to have used social networking sites for a number of years. However, at the present day, women and men use social media at similar rates (Perrin, 2015). This previous gap may have implications for social movements, enabling women to become involved in social movements that they find thematically interesting as well as being more accustomed to sharing and discussing online personally relevant topics.

Thus, corroborating the previous claims, sharing pictures of hairy female bodies may expand the perception of female body parts that are worthy of being photographed, as well as resist the gender norms by aestheticising those 'forbidden' and othered parts. The fundamental aim of previously presented one-month-long social movements was to challenge the prevailing norms of, for example, femininity or acceptable bodies. However, the process of deciding what is worth photographing is indissociable from the system of values it claims autonomy from, more specifically, social class or profession.

Marketers and advertisers establish, follow and participate in these movements as well, trying to figure out the next big thing in modern capitalism and snoop around for customer values that could be turned into profits. This process has been described by coining the term 'commodity feminism' (Goldman et al., 1991), referring to the way feminist ideals and icons (such as Princess Nokia song or body hair) are appropriated for commercial purposes. Simultaneously, the practices are emptied of their political significance and offered back to the public in a commodified form – usually in advertising, as was the case of 'feminist razors' presented earlier in this chapter. Thus, the driving force of commodity culture lies in attaching disparate meanings to generate new sign values. In this context, feminism is a look, a sense of style or an established or a recognisable brand that signifies those values. The rise of commodified feminism has been distinguishable in modern consumer culture for quite some time, as chain stores such as H&M have started to sell clothing with feminist statements (e.g. Repo, 2020).

Research Questions

In the theory section, we have established firstly that the hairlessness norm is pervasive in modern society, despite it having been addressed for years. We have also found that social media is a perfect medium for questioning the prevailing appearance norms through user-created visual imagery, mainly selfies, that are also a central element of the studied Januhairy movement. Through these theoretical lenses, we ask: (1) How is the hairlessness norm challenged through images and texts in the Januhairy movement in social media? (2) How do people respond to these posts?

Data and Methods

Case #Januhairy

To study how the hairlessness norm is contested in online environments, we searched for publicly available content hashtagged with #januhairy on Instagram. This hashtag was part of a social media project created by a drama student, Laura Jackson. She started the project in January 2019 to encourage women to challenge social norms by going *au naturel* with their body hair for (at least) one month (Mettler, 2019). By May 2020, the page had over 33,000 followers and the hashtag had been included in 9,814 posts.

While browsing the content, we found connections between other hashtags centred on reducing body hair stigma, such as #noshamenoshave and #body-hairdontcare, or hashtags related to the body positivity movement such as #effyourbeautystandards. The majority of the posts had one thing in common: the imagery uses sexualisation as a strategy for opposing gendered beauty-related norms regarding body hair, but does not necessarily make verbal references to sexiness per se. Moreover, the objecting hashtags were often presented simultaneously with hashtags of famous brands, like Victoria's Secret or Ellesse swimsuits, attaching their feminist agenda to these brands. Another interpretation could be that the women wanted these brands usually associated with beautiful women with sexy bodies to be 'infected' with new meanings.

The images had distinctive features in other ways as well. Some of the people with more popular profiles did not just portray themselves casually with body hair, but instead were including extra layers to their hairy online performances. They were, for example, colouring their body hair with rainbow colours, which occasionally seemed even more time consuming than traditional shaving. Some of the participants were capturing their body hair in various environments, like forests and moors or presenting their body hair 'on the move', adding splits or yoga poses to their images to express other bodily capitals.

Study Sample

We gathered selfies posted under the hashtag #januhairy on Instagram that were written in English and initially posted by the holders of the accounts themselves, i.e. not reposted by other users or accounts. We randomly selected 100 pictures from those posted under the hashtag between January 2019 and June 2019.

Each post was posted by a different public account. After excluding duplicates, posts that were not available during the time we conducted the analysis in August 2020, and posts that included only a photo with no story attached, we were left with an analytical sample of 67 posts. Next, we asked each user for permission to use the user's photo and post in our study. In total, 21 users gave permission to analyse their photos, and a total of 34 users gave permission to analyse the captions and comments they had received to their post. Lastly, from the comments, we excluded duplicates and comments that were tagging other users without any content (e.g. @profile), resulting in 581 comments.

Ethical Considerations

All study subjects were asked for permission to analyse their photo and the story and comments attached to it. To ensure the privacy of our study subjects, we do not reference account URLs, user names or reproduce any images in this study. All the collected research materials will be deleted after this study is published.

Using hashtags is a part of the so-called attention economy on Instagram (Marwick, 2015) and makes it a publicly visible part of online body hair activism in ways that private or non-hashtagged accounts are not. It is important to note that the data are based on publicly visible and based on accounts that have decided to use hashtags, thus we do not claim to speak for all depictions of body hair on Instagram let alone outside the platform. It is likely that there would be private accounts, or public accounts, where they simply do not use hashtags, and thus are missed in this research. It is possible that including these accounts would have shown a wider range of themes and discursive elements than those presented here.

Methods

To study how the hairlessness norm was challenged by the Januhairy movement in social media, we conducted two analyses. In the first analysis, we used visual content analysis to search for key themes rising from the 21 images. In the second analysis, we conducted a content analysis to study the themes arising from the captions attached to the images ($n = 34$). To investigate how people responded to these images, we conducted a third analysis, where we used content analysis to study the comments ($n = 581$) the images ($n = 21$) received.

Content Analysis

Content analysis is an exploratory empirical method that can be described as 'a research technique for making replicable and valid inferences from texts (or other meaningful matter) to the contexts of their use' (Krippendorff, 2004). It can be applied to textual or visual content.

We followed Bengtsson's (2016) described content analysis process. This process is divided into four phases: decontextualisation, recontextualisation, categorisation and compilation. In the *contextualisation* phase, each identified meaning unit is labelled with a code that is related to the context. A meaning unit refers to the constellation of words or statements that relate to the same central meaning, such as words, sentences or paragraphs that share aspects related to each other (Graneheim & Lundman, 2004.). A researcher must choose to code either for manifest or latent content. The manifest content is explicit in an object (such as actual words) whereas latent content refers to more 'hidden' categories that rise from the text. The latter involves interpreting the text's underlying meaning, which is what we chose to use in this study. Next, in the *recontextual-isation* phase, the original text is re-read with the list of meaning units. Then, in the *categorisation* process, themes and categories are identified. The procedure in this phase varies, depending on whether a manifest analysis or a latent analysis is used. In this study, we used latent content analysis. Thus, the categories are traditionally referred to as themes in the latent analysis. A theme is an expression of the text's latent content. A meaning unit or category can fit into more than one category. Lastly, the *compilation* phase refers to the analysis and writing-up process.

To answer our first research question, we analysed the posts' written captions to study how the users seek to challenge the norms regarding body hair using online platforms. Using the total analytical sample, we coded and thematised the posts' written captions for the emergence of recurring themes and sub-themes. We used latent content analysis to examine how people commented on these posts. The analysis revealed two main themes and several sub-themes related to whether body hair is considered an acceptable or non-acceptable act, and thus, whether it could act as a form of capital.

Visual Content Analysis

The method of (visual) content analysis aims to count 'the frequency of certain visual elements in a clearly defined population of images and then analysing those frequencies' (Rose, 2016, p. 88). Each aspect of this process has certain requirements to achieve replicable and valid results.

We analyse this imagery, firstly, to see who is participating in this project and secondly, to understand what kind of visual and textual strategies are used in these posts. Finally, we explore how the content is textually framed and how the content is commented on. Visual Content analysis has been used previously for studying #fitspiration posts (Tiggemann & Zaccardo, 2018) and ageing femininities (Tiidenberg, 2018) on Instagram.

Results

Challenging the Norms?

Six themes arose from the visual content analysis and each photo could fall under multiple themes (Table 1). All 21 images were posted by females, around 15–30 years of age. Most images were of slender and white women showing their underarm hair. Most images were selfies exposing a hairy armpit and included the person's face, three images were taken of a hairy leg and three of only armpit with no full face. Over half of the images represent a theme: 'slim', 'aesthetic' and 'white.' Aesthetic points to the artisticness of the photo – the person in the photo wore makeup or fancier clothes, posed in a photogenic position and/or the lightning and colours of the photo were edited. In almost half of the pictures, the person incorporated typical Western beauty standards, i.e. thin, but feminine, firm, smooth and young (e.g. Widdows, 2018).

From the captions, we found eight themes (Table 2). Five captions were impossible to categorise into any of these themes either due to very short text. Most posts commented on #januhairy or the movement around female body hair directly (55.9%), while 44.1% of the posts did not comment on the movement at all. Around 23–29% of the captions described how empowering they felt taking part in this movement, discussed the importance of self-acceptance and the unnecessary shamefulness traditionally attached to female body hair. Some (23.5%) also underlined that female body hair is natural. Around 15% posted a photo of their body hair without giving any clear 'statement' on female body hair.

Table 9.1. The Names and Quantities of the Themes of the Images ($N = 21$).

	Slim	Aesthetic	White	Beauty	Feminine
N	20	18	17	9	9
%	95.2	85.7	81.0	42.9	42.9

Table 9.2. The Names and Quantities of the Themes Rising from the Captions.

	Does Not Comment	Brave/ Confident/ Empowering	Self-acceptance	Natural	Shame	Other's Acceptance	Doesn't Emphasize Hair	Other
N	15	10	9	8	8	8	5	5
%	44.1	29.4	26.5	23.5	23.5	23.5	14.7	14.7

Approval or Disapproval?

We explored how the images of female body hair were commented on. In total, out of the 581 comments, around 93% were categorised as positive (*N* = 542) and only a minority of the comments were negative (*N* = 39). This generally positive reception indicates that at least these users were not punished for challenging the beauty norms. Interestingly, one post received more negative comments than others, as one person of colour received a long message including multiple swastikas (Fig. 9.1).

We found four main themes under the 'positive' category (Table 3). Around 36.3% of all the positive comments, commented that the photo, its content or the user who posted it was 'beautiful' or 'lovely', or they commented only with a heart emoji. Of the total comments, 25.1% were generally positive and encouraging, while 17.4% commented on the 'sexiness' or 'attractiveness' of the user, her body hair or the picture. This category also included those who only posted emojis such

Fig. 9.1.   Wordcloud Form the Comments According to the Themes 'Positive' Comments (Left) and 'Negative' Comments (Right).

Table 9.3. The Names and Quantities of the Sub-themes Rising from the Comments.

	Positive						Negative		
	Natural and Normal 1	Sexy 2	Proud and Brave 3	Beautiful 4	Encouraging 5	Other	Unhygienic	Gross	Other
Total N	55	101	103	216	146	35	3	14	21
Total %	9.5	17.4	17.7	37.2	25.1	6.0	0.5	2.4	3.6

Codes for the themes: 1 Natural, healthy, normal, 2 Sexy/attractive/goddess/tongue, kissing or drooling smiley, 3 BeYourSelf/Brave/Proud/Queen, Yass, Amen, 4 beautiful/lovely/only heart emoji, 5 Encouraging emojis or comments that cannot be categorised into other categories.

as drooling smiley or a tongue. Around 18% praised the user of being 'brave' or 'encouraging'. This category also included comments like 'queen', 'yass', 'praise it' or 'tell them sis' that can be interpreted as encouraging comments with an idea of being 'proud and brave' (Branfman, 2019). Of the comments, 9.5% were either pointing out that female body hair is 'natural', 'healthy' or 'normal'. The category 'other' mainly consisted of neutral comments that were not clearly categorisable, for example, posts asking for permission to share the photo.

From the negative comments, we discovered two main themes: unhygienic and gross. However, only a couple of the comments pointed out that not shaving is unhygienic. The rest (the 'other' category) consisted mainly of comments such as 'no' or 'ridiculous'.

Discussion

Who Can Contest the Hairlessness Norm?

At first glance, despite the alleged inclusiveness of the Januhairy movement, the imagery generated in the project is young, thin, white and 'pretty'. It seems that while the photographs aimed to broaden the norms of performing femininity, they responded to what the traditional male gaze (for objectification theory, see Fredrickson & Roberts, 1997) or what the postfeminist girlfriend gaze (Winch, 2013), portraying the women as objects to be looked at, constructing their self-worth on how other people see them. Otherwise, participants seemed to represent the demographics of Instagram and were in line with the prevailing Western beauty standards: young, white and slim. The content also revealed that it seems possible only to contest one norm at a time.

Some of the visual imagery could also be interpreted as 'commodity feminism'. The uploaded content was made 'Instagrammable' and aestheticised the body hair. Uploading this kind of visual imagery on Instagram is challenging the hairlessness norm by portraying body hair in a new light: not affecting one's sexiness, or even improving one's looks by daring to look different.

The themes found in the captions and in the comments were mostly overlapping. One explanation for this is that possibly most of the comments were written by like-minded followers. Many of those who posted a story under the #januhairy also commented on other posts under this tag. Both captions and comments often discussed how female body hair is natural and should be more acceptable in today's society. Many also described the shame they had experienced before taking part of this social movement and how they had grown to accept themselves during this hair-growing period. Similarly, many comments discussed these same topics.

An interesting contradiction between the themes found in the captions and in the comments was about sexualisation. While no captions wrote about sexuality, it was one of the most common themes among the comments. Some users and commentators were annoyed by the number of comments that fetishised and sexualised the user's female body hair. However, since these were the first posts under #januhairy, it is possible that the later posted captions commented on the sexualisation. Also, it is possible that we are socialised to interpret young girls showing their underarms sexually alluring, or that a pose of lifting one's arm gets interpreted as sexual even if it is accompanied by something that contrasts the prevailing social norms regarding physical appearance.

The uploaded content was obviously seen by at least two different groups with different interests. In essence, the group of emerging cultural capitalists with similar taste patterns, shared aesthetics and feminist agenda, but also a community of body hair fetishists, who might use the content differently than intended by the person posting it. An example of the gradual (male) appreciation of the naturalness of the female body can be found in the following comment:

> I have just discovered your page and it is all beautiful, also...I'm just going to go ahead and say something that will probably make me very unpopular. I personally can no longer find women who shave their bodies attractive. I've always had a love for natural women...at first just the lower regions, then armpits became something I accepted...and now, a women with hair in all the places it grows is far more attractive to me than a woman who wears societies [*sic*] fake mask of 'beauty' never ever be ashamed. #Bareshaveisboring

However, women's body hair is seen as something that needs to be accepted either by society or by men, while no interest is laid on women's own experiences. Despite employing a discourse of naturalness and referring to a fake mask of beauty, it seems that this comment encourages women to free their bodies for men to enjoy, paying little attention to what women themselves want.

While most women received affirmations, refusing to shave body hair was considered unhygienic or disgusting by some commentators. It seems that it is not only about women shaving their body hair or photographing themselves but also social media encourages people to comment on each other's appearance. This reduces women to being equal to their appearance and intensifies the ugly–beautiful spectrum that others define. On one end of the spectrum is an empowered hairy lady who has 'chosen' this stigmatised appearance and is otherwise so beautiful that body hair does not diminish that beauty. On the other end of this spectrum is a woman socially deemed less appealing, pressured to shave her body hair to avoid the social stigma of being possibly interpreted as 'monstrous, grotesque, disgusting, aggressive, antisocial and mad' (Lesnik-Oberstein, 2006).

The construction of a similar spectrum was apparent especially in the negative comments that mainly focused on one post. The person had an open profile and approximately as many followers as the other selected posts, but somehow she had received more negative commentary than the others. It might be that she perhaps aesthetically represented a more 'girl next door', one who is ordinary looks. In addition to vomiting emojis, the commentators accused her of being a cliché, and not shaving being already tested by feminists and proven absurd: 'This new age feminism is ridiculous...' and '...shave your fucking pits'. It seemed that body hair was seen even as a personal attack towards gender order, and it should be stopped immediately by telling them about this issue's ridiculousness. The alleged naturalness of body hair was also conflated with not showering and being dirty. It seems that these negative comments are mostly in line with Leslik-Obestein's (2006) previously presented interpretations about social stigmas attached to body hair.

Body Hair as Classed Aesthetics

Contesting traditional appearance norms and looking normatively less beautiful may also seem 'cool' in certain groups of people, more specifically among the urban young, as Giselinde Kuipers (2015) establishes in her study. Evidently, the participants under these hairy hashtags are negotiating their appearance norms, which act as a capital in their social world, young women with similar social background and similar taste patterns. However, appreciating body hair might also be an example of lessening pressure on women to hide their 'unruly' bodies, but also implies that 'female masculinity' (see also Halberstam, 1998) or 'queer glamour', as Branfman (2019) refers to it, may only be acceptable when packaged and presented in appealing ways.

Moreover, although the photos seem to dispute the norm, they do so conventionally. It seems that while contesting the prevailing norms, women are again endorsing another norm, i.e. reducing themselves to the visual. That visual ought to always stick to beauty norms or perform sexy to be acceptable, even when trying to fight the very same beauty norms. Secondly, the content focuses mainly on one part of the body, underarm hair, not all body hair, as some body hair might be less easily accepted (for example, a moustache). Furthermore, it seemed that it was possible only to contest one norm at the time. The participants seemed otherwise to conform to the demographics and the prevailing Instagram beauty standards, that is young, slim and pretty. This sets the standards of hairy beauty high, making the standards as hard to attain as usual. Despite the good intentions, this might again cause appearance-related pressures, both inside and outside the activist group. This sets the beauty threshold higher, where only those who are cool enough for making a feminist statement, beautiful despite the hair or whose hair is aesthetic enough for being deemed as beautiful despite breaking the prevailing norm.

Capitalising the Dreaded Otherness?

It is evident that the 'capitalness' of body hair is situational and relational. This raises a question whether these are privileged young females who are allowed to expand societal perceptions of what is considered beautiful. Is body hair only allowed for those who have already accumulated other types of capital(s) and is body hair seen as only adding an intriguing nuance on their aesthetic capital (see also, Kuipers, 2015)?

In the future, it would be interesting to study how the visual presentations of body hair, the captions, the comments and the participants have further developed after this 'first wave'. People who participate in the first wave of social media movements tend to consist mostly of influencers and to some extent people familiar with the phenomenon. Further, later participants can consist of 'less-influential' people who the movement has encouraged. Another interesting point of a future study was influenced by the participants, who stressed the (occasionally sexual, but also other) content of the private messages they received, and the networks that are built between the commenters. Those inbox messages would be an interesting study as well.

Conclusion

With this chapter, we have focused on how the hairlessness norm is challenged in an online social movement, and how this challenge is received by online audiences. The results reveal that despite the aims of the Januhairy movement, such as inclusiveness and broadening the norms of performing femininity, the images the participants posted consisted of traditionally (in Western standards) 'beautiful' slim, white and young women. The analysis of the captions revealed that the users were knowingly challenging the hairlessness norm. The captions discussed the 'naturality' of female body hair and the importance of liberation from the shame imposed by family, the opposite sex and society. Most of the comments were encouraging and agreeing, discussing the same themes on naturalness, self-acceptance and liberation from the norms. However, a relatively large proportion of the comments discussed the sexiness of the female body hair, which was often not expected or welcomed by the posters.

Whether the participants were traditionally beautiful because they have 'less to lose' (as the social punishment for the non-obedience of the hairlessness norm is probably smaller for them than, for example, older, overweight and women of colour), or because these demographics are also descriptive for this social media platform, remains unclear. However, when elaborating our results in the light of capital theory, it seems evident that body hair in itself cannot be considered as a form of capital, but becomes such by accentuating the already existing assets appreciated in this platform. Few possible explanations for body hair accentuating the existing forms of capital are that it makes its bearer more aesthetically arousing, ideologically similar by exhibiting a visible marker of feminist orientation or lastly, imposing a certain 'wildness', i.e. sexual uninhibitedness and promiscuity.

From the perspective of appearance-oriented society, our findings seem contradictory. On one hand, it seems that more fragmented looks have become appreciated and promoted in certain environments. On the other hand, it possibly broadens the surface area of the female body that has social significance and needs to become groomed in socially approved ways. Moreover, it can be seen as inducing an even more nuanced form of appearance related to inequality, as it simultaneously offers freedom of choice for hair removal for some and offers possible benefits for it. Simultaneously, this ambiguity makes the hairlessness norm even more pervasive for others, as it is even harder for others to grow or cultivate it the right way.

Acknowledgements

We thank all the study subjects who gave us the permission to use their photos and/or posts for this study.

References

Basow, S. A. (1991). Women and their body hair. *Psychology of Women Quarterly*, *15*(1), 83–96.

Bengtsson, M. (2016). How to plan and perform a qualitative study using content analysis. *NursingPlus Open*, *2*, 8–14. https://doi.org/10.1016/j.npls.2016.01.001

Bourdieu, P., & Whiteside, S. (1996). *Photography: A middle-brow art*. Stanford University Press.

Branfman, J. (2019). "Plow him like a queen!": Jewish female masculinity, queer glamor, and racial commentary in broad city. *Television & New Media*. https://doi.org/10.1177/1527476419855688

Fahs, B. (2011). Dreaded "otherness" heteronormative patrolling in women's body hair rebellions. *Gender & Society*, *25*(4), 451–472.

Fredrickson, B. L., & Roberts, T. A. (1997). Objectification theory: Toward understanding women's lived experiences and mental health risks. *Psychology of Women Quarterly*, *21*(2), 173–206.

Gill, R., & Elias, A. S. (2014). 'Awaken your incredible': Love your body discourses and postfeminist contradictions. *International Journal of Media and Cultural Politics*, *10*(2), 179–188.

Goldman, R., Heath, D., & Smith, S. (1991). Commodity feminism. *Critical Studies in Communication, 8*(3), 333–351.

Graneheim, U. H., & Lundman, B. (2004). Qualitative content analysis in nursing research: Concepts, procedures and measure to achieve trustworthiness. *Nurse Education Today, 24*, 105–112. https://doi.org/10.1016/j.nedt.2003.10.001

Halberstam, J. (1998). *Female masculinity*. Duke University Press.

Herzig, R. (2015). *Plucked: A history of hair removal*. New York University Press.

Krippendorff, K. (2004). *Content analysis: An introduction to its methodology*. Sage Publications Inc.

Kuipers, G. (2015). Beauty and distinction? The evaluation of appearance and cultural capital in five European countries. *Poetics, 53*, 38–51.

Lesnik-Oberstein, K. (Ed.). (2006). *The last taboo: Women and body hair*. Manchester University Press.

Marwick, A. E. (2015). Instafame: Luxury selfies in the attention economy. *Public Culture, 27*(1–75), 137–160.

Mettler, L. (2019). 'Januhairy' encourages women to grow their body hair for a month. *Today's Office*, January 8. https://www.today.com/style/januhairy-encourages-women-grow-their-body-hair-month-t146345. Accessed on November 17, 2020.

Nielsen, J. M., Walden, G., & Kunkel, C. A. (2000). Gendered heteronormativity: Empirical illustrations in everyday life. *The Sociological Quarterly, 41*(2), 283–296.

Nokia, P., & Ramirez, G. (2017). "Tomboy" [Recorded by princess Nokia]. On 1992 deluxe [digital]. Rough Trade Records.

Perrin, A. (2015). Social media usage. Pew Research Center, pp. 52–68.

Repo, J. (2020). Feminist commodity activism: The new political economy of feminist protest. *International Political Sociology, 14*(2), 215–232. https://doi.org/10.1093/ips/olz033

Rose, G. (2016). *Visual methodologies: An introduction to researching with visual materials*. Sage.

Sastre, A. (2016). Towards a radical body positive: Reading the online body positive movement. *Feminist Media Studies, 14*(6), 929–943.

Smelik, A. (2015). A close shave: The taboo on female body hair. *Critical Studies in Fashion & Beauty, 6*(2), 233–251.

Synnott, A. (1987). Shame and glory: A sociology of hair. *British Journal of Sociology, 38*(3), 381–413.

Tiggemann, M., & Hodgson, S. (2008). The hairlessness norm extended: Reasons for and predictors of women's body hair removal at different body sites. *Sex Roles, 59*(11–12), 889–897.

Tiggemann, M., & Kenyon, S. J. (1998). The hairlessness norm: The removal of body hair in women. *Sex Roles, 39*, 873–885.

Tiggemann, M., & Lewis, C. (2004). Attitudes toward women's body hair: Relationship with disgust sensitivity. *Psychology of Women Quarterly, 28*(4), 381–387.

Tiggemann, M., & Zaccardo, M. (2018). "Strong is the new skinny": A content analysis of #fitspiration images on Instagram. *Journal of Health Psychology, 23*(8), 1003–1011.

Tiidenberg, K. (2014). Bringing sexy back: Reclaiming the body aesthetic via self-shooting. *Cyberpsychology: Journal of Psychosocial Research on Cyberspace, 8*(1).

Tiidenberg, K. (2018). Visibly ageing femininities: women's visual discourses of being over-40 and over-50 on Instagram. *Feminist Media Studies, 18*(1), 61–76. https:// doi.org/10.1080/14680777.2018.1409988

Tiidenberg, K., & Gómez Cruz, E. (2015). Selfies, image and the re-making of the body. *Body & Society, 21*(4), 77–102.

Widdows, H. (2018). *Perfect me: Beauty as an ethical ideal.* Princeton University Press.

Winch, A. (2013). *Girlfriends and postfeminist sisterhood.* Palgrave Macmillan.

Conclusion

Outi Sarpila, Iida Kukkonen, Tero Pajunen and Erica Åberg

Physical appearance can be approached as a form of capital. To some extent, this form of capital can be accumulated and converted into economic and social rewards. However, the logic of the aesthetic work done to accumulate physical appearance -related assets is far from straightforward. The same applies to composition and the convertibility of physical appearance as a form of capital as well. In this book, we have shown how different cultural, institutional, group-specific and situational norms regulate the possibilities of accumulating and converting aesthetic capital.

This finding constitutes the central contribution of this book. In contemporary consumer culture, physical appearance is often represented as a meritocratic form of capital that everyone can accumulate and use as a ticket to success. This gospel of aesthetic self-expression and self-improvement comes with undertones of responsibility, particularly in discourses around working life. As the chapters in this book have shown, the gospel clashes in many ways with cultural ideals and gendered, aged and classed norms. Although everyone carries a responsibility for his or her appearance, not everyone is allowed equal agency with regard to his or her physical appearance. Furthermore, not everyone has equal opportunities to convert such a form of capital into other forms (e.g., economic capital).

In very recent considerations, however, physical appearance has been approached as an independent form of capital (e.g., Shilling, 2004; Anderson et al., 2010; Hakim, 2010; Green, 2013; Mears, 2015; see also Holla & Kuipers, 2015). Early scholarship employing this theoretical stance examined the bodily and physical capital, particularly in terms of movement and strength (Shilling, 2004; Wacquant, 1995). Other researchers focussed on sexual and erotic capital (Green, 2008; Hakim, 2010; Martin & George, 2006). More recently, scholars have focussed on the gendered forms of the body as capital, such as girl capital (Mears, 2015), and they have made attempts to draw together the scattered scholarship on physical appearance and inequality using the term 'aesthetic

Appearance as Capital, 165–172

doi:10.1108/978-1-80043-708-120210011

capital' (Anderson et al., 2010; Holla & Kuipers, 2015; Sarpila et al., 2020; see also Kukkonen, Chapter 1).

In this book, we have approached physical appearance as aesthetic capital – a bundle of resources that includes the facial features, shape and size of the body, as well as personal styles of (body) hair, dressing and grooming (Anderson et al., 2010). We posited that aesthetic capital may work as a 'primary' form of capital (Kukkonen, Chapter 1; see also Neveu, 2018): that is, rather than being conditioned solely by class (as embodied cultural capital), it shapes class. While physical appearance per se has gender, age, ability and ethnicity as axes of inequality, it is also part and parcel of class (i.e., a combination of economic, social, cultural and aesthetic capital). Capital is mobilised in particular fields through reflexive practices that individuals with certain 'habitus', in Bourdieusian terms, have adopted. However, the abovementioned axes of (dis)advantage also shape individuals' opportunities in contemporary societies. In this book, we have argued and shown how social norms regarding the accumulation and conversion of aesthetic capital function as 'fences' that mostly advantage those already in advantageous positions (cf. Devine & Savage, 2005; Friedman & Laurison, 2020).

Thus, without mitigating the value of any strand of research on physical appearance and inequality, the book has joined an emerging body of research that takes a critical stance towards an economics-inspired analysis of physical appearance, with physical appearance being described as simply 'beauty' or 'attractiveness' based on a universally definable value standard for individuals. We argue that the term 'aesthetic capital' used in this book is useful in many ways. It not only leaves room for appearance-related qualities to be considered but also recognises the possibility of their accumulation and convertibility to other forms of capital. In terms of meritocracy, the concept thus recognises both accumulated and ascribed forms of aesthetic capital as problematic. This approach leaves no room for a simple economistic view of physical appearance as beauty based on monetary investments (see Mears, 2014).

Previous sociological studies examined physical appearance as an independent form of capital, and they focussed on the power relations defining the value of aesthetic capital (e.g., Mears, 2011, 2020). However, this book has explicitly focussed on the regulative and negotiable norms embedded in the social space or social fields, where individuals accumulate and convert their aesthetic capital. That is, this book has invited scholars to consider the manifestations of power relations in terms of social norms. As Vandebroeck (2017) points out with respect to the issues of inequality and physical appearance, approaching physical appearance only from inherited qualities can lead to the misrecognition of class-based physical appearance -related inequalities. He calls for broader insight into the privileges and advantages that physical appearance shapes:

> Moreover, unlike the stigmatization of relatively 'ascribed' physical traits (skin colour, sex or age[,] for instance), class-based physical differences provide a much less stable foundation for the development of an assertive 'counter-culture'. In fact, whereas critiques of sexual or ethnoracial domination can more

easily invoke the unjust and anti-meritocratic nature of social mechanisms of exclusion on the basis of factors over which agents ultimately have little or no control, physical markers of class [...] are more often deemed to be a simple matter of 'lifestyle-choice' and hence of individual responsibility.

(Vandebroeck, 2017, p. 232)

In line with Vandebroeck, we have shown how physical appearance -related traits are not simple matters of lifestyle choice and individual responsibility. This is not only because they mostly have to do with the mechanisms of exclusion that are beyond individuals' control but also it is because even when individuals are seemingly allowed to choose their aesthetic practices and lifestyles, the enactment of lifestyles and practices is socially controlled and sanctioned. We argue that the capital metaphor can be useful in revealing and challenging both larger societal mechanisms of exclusion and the more local, field-specific normativisation of bodies and their appearances.

Moreover, considering physical appearance as an independent form of capital allows for the recognition and analysis of physical appearance -related inequalities even in social spaces where cultural capital is considered to play a less significant role in producing and maintaining inequalities. In this book, we focussed our lens on Finland, a country that never had a feudal nobility that 'could have slowly cultivated different tastes and distinctions vis-à-vis the lower classes' (Purhonen et al., 2010, p. 269). Indeed, Purhonen et al. (2010) conclude in their study on taste preferences in Finland that 'Finland is a democracy of taste'. Finland is known for its welfare states policies, and the Finnish educational system is known for producing a rather large amount of educational mobility compared with other OECD countries (for a discussion, see Heiskala et al., 2020). Further, Finland is commonly indexed as a comparatively gender-equal society and is lauded for it (see Introduction chapter).

Despite this, or perhaps precisely because of this, we claim that Finland has become what we call an appearance society. By this, we mean a society in which aesthetic capital plays a key part in shaping an individual's class position – that is, a society in which physical appearance acts as a form of capital in itself. As cultural and economic capital are supposedly democratic, and as gender seemingly does not matter, appearance is at centre stage as Finns engage in global consumer culture and social media. However, the findings of this book suggest that a focus on appearance does not actually smooth over previous inequalities. Rather, it seems to enhance them, particularly in terms of gender.

The findings in this book suggest that the norms that guide the accumulation and, to some extent, the conversion of aesthetic capital are first and foremost gendered. Focussing on one's appearance is strongly coded as feminine, and gender differences in consumption have remained remarkably stable in Finland (see Sarpila, Chapter 3). This has consequences for both women and men. Although Finnish women and men equally endorse a belief in appearance as a currency – a ticket to success or social mobility – this belief gains a very gendered practical meaning: for women, the belief is straightforwardly linked to daily appearance work, whereas for men, no straightforward connection exists between beliefs and practices (see Kukkonen, Chapter 2). It is possible that even if men believe that appearance is important for achieving success, focussing on appearance does not even appear to be a possibility for them. The continued genderedness of physical appearance -related practices may be viewed as limiting men's choices and experiences as much as it limits those of women. This becomes clear in the fourth chapter of this book, where an elderly man narrates how the opportunity to buy his own clothes appeared to him for the first time at old age, and how nice it was. When he got to select his own corduroys, it seems that a new world opened up before him. Previously, the women in his life – his mother, his wife – had always bought his clothes. In a sense, women have a monopoly over appearance-related practices and consumption (whether they like it or not).

This is not to belittle the ways in which the gendered norms concerning physical appearance are hard on women. This monopoly drives particularly women to invest a tremendous amount of not only effort but also resources in terms of time and money on appearance. These efforts are looked down upon as vanity and are rarely taken seriously. Although appearance-related practices can certainly be enjoyable, light-hearted, frivolous and even vain, they can – in their repeated and mundane forms – also be regarded as appearance work, a form of labour which is also taxing and consuming (see Kukkonen, Chapter 2).

The book clearly shows how even in such a country as Finland, which is viewed as highly gender equal, aesthetic capital works together with the gender and normative expectations related to it. Although it would be tempting to interpret Finland as a 'lower-bound estimator' compared with other cultural contexts, this is hardly the case. As the chapters that go beyond the national context indicate, a very similar gendered normative logic crosses not only different fields but also different social spaces more generally. Thus, it seems clear that gender does not have to be taken into account when one is analysing the processes of the accumulation and conversion of aesthetic capital. However, it has to be integrated into the Bourdieusian analysis of fields and social space. Theoretically, this could also mean moving beyond the traditional conceptions of intersectionality (for a discussion, see Vandebroeck, 2018).

The second point of theoretical integration that the chapters in this book stress is that the roles of a consumer and worker can no longer be separated in terms of appearance work and consumption. As consumers and workers, or as aesthetic labourers, all individuals are expected to enhance their aesthetic capital to some extent (see also Pettinger, 2008; van den Berg & Arts, 2019; Elias et al., 2017). As Tero Pajunen's analysis (Chapter 5) clearly shows, the general societal norms and contextual norms do not always match, and even the social fields that one worker crosses during a day at work may have different appearance-related norms that the worker has to juggle. Although previous research on aesthetic labour and aesthetic norms in the workplace focussed on how employers normatively regulate the physical appearances of employees (see, however, Mears, 2020; Vonk, 2020), Pajunen shows how normative aesthetic regulation at work happens as an interplay among employers, customers and co-workers. Hence, no particular type of appearance acts as capital. Instead, the appropriateness of an appearance is determined in interaction.

Although this is a commonsensical statement, it is poorly understood in scholarship on working life as well as in recruitment and management. It appears that employers may prescribe and maintain appearance norms that are against anyone's profit, based on poor knowledge about how appearance actually works in social interaction, or appearance acts as capital in a particular social field. In line with the logic of the service industry, workers are possibly commodified and forced to fit the logic of the standardised 'customer knows best' model of service. Pajunen illuminates how norm disobedience can actually help with interaction in working life. Pajunen also argues that loosening appearance norms in working life could actually serve workers, customers and profit-making employers.

Yet, paradoxically, the loosening of norms may place even more stress on workers trying to get it right. 'Getting it right' is far from easy, as context and situations matter. Moreover, as underlined in Iida Kukkonen's chapter (Chapter 2), appearance work is also resource-consuming backstage work that is sometimes paired with an empty promise of social mobility.

The interplay of general norms and contextual norms is perhaps most clearly present in the chapters which are integrated into the analysis of social media. Erica Åberg and Aki Koivula suggest that generally among Finnish social media users, and particularly among young Finnish women on Instagram, social media use drives appearance dissatisfaction, which again drives online content creation, which again drives appearance dissatisfaction. However, it is also clear that social media offers to some individuals a virtual space in which they can challenge and negotiate the prevailing norms on valuable bodies and appearances. Simultaneously, it seems that particular individuals with cultural capital and other privileges, including whiteness, are allowed to develop and showcase reflexivity on their aesthetic practices on social media. Anna Puhakka shows in her analysis of Danish fat activist Sofie Hagen how she applies certain strategies to challenge prevailing appearance-related norms. As discussed previously, challenging physical traits that are commonly regarded in terms of lifestyle, choice and individual responsibility is not an easy task. It is worth asking what strategies can be deployed to develop what Vandebroek (2017) terms 'an assertive "counter-culture"'. Furthermore, what capital does one have to possess to join the counter-culture in which prevailing appearance ideals are contested? What does challenging aesthetic norms take? For example, is fatness more acceptable from a funny woman? A white woman? Åberg and Salonen show how the challenging of the hairlessness norm online typically comes with the package of youth, whiteness and slimness. It seems that even though singular appearance norms can be disobeyed, the disobedience has to be done in 'the right way'. In the context of social media, the diverse outcomes (i.e., likes, comments, harassment) of breaking such general norms is unpredictable due to the blurring boundaries of fields – the vantage points from which aesthetic assets are evaluated on.

Although social media platforms allow for the voice of certain, often young and somewhat privileged, white and female voices to be heard on the topic of appearance-related norms, it is clear that appearance and appearance-related norms impact just about everyone's life. Although a great deal of contemporary research on physical appearance has dealt with social media or working life, negotiations of the value of appearance and the content of appearance-related norms are ongoing offline as well (see Chapter 6). Importantly, appearance-related capital does not necessarily carry any less value outside of working life than it does therein: appearance matters for capital exchange among the 'economically inactive' population as well.

In the Finnish context, it is particularly clear that the appearance society is not only a gendered society but also an ageing society. In societies that put youthful looks on a pedestal, everyone's aesthetic capital erodes with ageing. However, this 'erosion' is felt most heavily by the elderly. In a society, such as Finland, that is ageing fast (see the introduction of this book), the largest and fastest growing proportion of the population face this dilemma, and this tendency may somewhat paradoxically increase the value of aesthetic capital rather than lead to its devaluation. According to the logic of consumer capitalism, money goes where 'loose money' is available, and as the chapters in this book show, the appearance-related insecurities that ageing people face have already been tapped into. Being seen and not being reduced to an invisible and marginalised part of society is a pressing concern, which also has to do with the attainment of social services.

Overall, the studies in this book make certain key points. First, the studies in this book highlight the deep entanglement of physical appearance and gender. Any discussion on physical appearance -related inequality is also a discussion on gender – whether we like it or not. It is not enough to regard gender as one control variable or to mention it in passing. We are dealing with phenomena so inherently gendered that gender indeed needs to be integrated in analyses.

Second, the studies in this book help one to think of appearance-related inequality not just in terms of an economic fatality but also as an endless series of actual social situations in which people interact and have agency. Although strong and persuasive social norms – universal, national and more field-specific ones – guide the practices that we undertake and the valuations we make, the studies in this book highlight that these norms are constantly negotiated and challenged. Norms change and can be changed. From this perspective, physical appearance -related inequality is not a natural law but rather is something that can be acted upon and changed.

Third, the studies in this book show how very different methods, methodologies and data can be used in the study of appearance-related inequality. Strength exists in such a diversity of approaches. Clearly, no one particular approach can illuminate the ways in which physical appearance engenders and deepens social and economic inequality. To develop a deeper and more multifaceted understanding of the phenomenon, it is therefore crucial to develop a dialogue between various methodological approaches within sociology, on the one hand, and between the various disciplines that grapple with the topic, on the other hand. It is also important to see that there is more to physical appearance -related inequality than just socioeconomic outcomes.

This book has presented many approaches to physical appearance and has invited its readers to 'a smorgasbord of appearance studies'. We can guarantee for a fact that the role of physical appearance in society will not plummet or diminish in the following years. In the future, we suggest comparative studies among countries to explore whether the Finns truly differ from other counties in terms of, for example, their appearance orientation and consumer attitudes. Additionally, the boundaries between cultural and aesthetic capital invite more theoretical discussion. In addition to conducting more research on the outcomes of appearance, norms should be integrated into appearance research. Norms should not just be considered to be an explanatory framework for appearance studies. Rather, we encourage the creation of new directions for studying the normative regulation of accumulating and exploiting aesthetic capital. Appearance has multiple possible directions for research, and room exists for more enthusiastic researchers.

References

Anderson, T. L., Grunert, C., Katz, A., & Lovascio, S. (2010). Aesthetic capital: A research review on beauty perks and penalties. *Sociology Compass*, *4*(8), 564–575. https://doi.org/10.1111/j.1751-9020.2010.00312.x

van den Berg, M., & Arts, J. (2019). The aesthetics of work-readiness: Aesthetic judgements and pedagogies for conditional welfare and post-Fordist labour markets. *Work, Employment and Society*, *33*(2), 298–313. https://doi.org/10.1177/0950017018758196

Devine, F., & Savage, M. (2005). The cultural turn, sociology and class analysis. In F. Devine, M. Savage, J. Scott, & R. Crompton (Eds.), *Rethinking class: Culture, identities and lifestyle* (pp. 1–23). Palgrave Macmillan.

Elias, A., Gill, R., & Scharff, C. (2017). Aesthetic labour: Beauty politics in neoliberalism. In A. S. Elias, R. Gill, & C. Scharff (Eds.), *Aesthetic labour: Rethinking beauty politics in neoliberalism* (pp. 3–49). Palgrave Macmillan.

Friedman, S., & Laurison, D. (2020). *The class ceiling: Why it pays to be privileged*. Policy Press.

Green, A. I. (2008). The social organization of desire: The sexual fields approach. *Sociological Theory*, *26*(1), 25–50. https://doi.org/10.1111/j.1467-9558.2008.00317.x

Green, A. I. (2013). 'Erotic capital' and the power of desirability: Why 'honey money' is a bad collective strategy for remedying gender inequality. *Sexualities*, *16*(1–2), 137–158. https://doi.org/10.1177/1363460712471109

Hakim, C. (2010). Erotic capital. *European Sociological Review*, *26*(5), 499–518. https://doi.org/10.1093/esr/jcq014.

Heiskala, L., Erola, J., & Kilpi-Jakonen, E. (2020). Compensatory and multiplicative advantages: Social origin, school performance, and stratified higher education enrolment in Finland. *European Sociological Review*, *34*(2), 171–185. https://doi.org/10.1093/esr/jcaa046

Holla, S., & Kuipers, G. (2015). Aesthetic capital. In L. Hanquinet & M. Savage (Eds.), *International handbook for the sociology of art and culture* (pp. 290–304). Routledge.

Martin, J. L., & George, M. (2006). Theories of sexual stratification: Toward an analytics of the sexual field and a theory of sexual capital. *Sociological Theory*, *24*(2), 107–132. https://doi.org/10.1111/j.0735-2751.2006.00284.x

Mears, A. (2011). *Pricing beauty: The making of a fashion model.* University of California Press.

Mears, A. (2014). Aesthetic labor for the sociologies of work, gender, and beauty. *Sociology Compass, 8*(12), 1330–1343. https://doi.org/10.1111/soc4.12211

Mears, A. (2015). Girls as elite distinction: The appropriation of bodily capital. *Poetics, 53*, 22–37. https://doi.org/10.1016/j.poetic.2015.08.004

Mears, A. (2020). *Very important people: Status and beauty in the global party circuit.* Princeton.

Neveu, E. (2018). Bourdieu's capital(s). In T. Medvetz & J. J. Sallaz (Eds.), *The Oxford handbook of Pierre Bourdieu* (pp. 347–374). Oxford University Press.

Pettinger, L. (2008). Developing aesthetic labour: The importance of consumption. *International Journal of Work Organisation and Emotion, 2*(4), 327–343. https://doi.org/10.1504/IJWOE.2008.022495

Purhonen, S., Gronow, J., & Rahkonen, K. (2010). Nordic democracy of taste? Cultural omnivorousness in musical and literary taste preferences in Finland. *Poetics, 38*(3), 266–298.

Sarpila, O., Koivula, A., Kukkonen, I., Åberg, E., & Pajunen, T. (2020). Double standards in the accumulation and utilisation of 'aesthetic capital'. *Poetics, 82.* https://doi.org/10.1016/j.poetic.2020.101447

Shilling, C. (2004). Physical capital and situated action: A new direction for corporeal sociology. *British Journal of Sociology of Education, 25*(4), 473–487. https://doi.org/10.1080/0142569042000236961

Vandebroeck, D. (2017). *Distinctions in the flesh: Social class and the embodiment of inequality.* Routledge.

Vandebroeck, D. (2018). Toward a European social topography: The contemporary relevance of Pierre Bourdieu's concept of 'social space'. *European Societies, 20*(3), 359–374. https://doi.org/10.1080/14616696.2017.1371469

Vonk, L. (2020). Peer feedback in aesthetic labour: Forms, logics and responses. *Cultural Sociology, 15*(2), 213–232. https://doi.org/10.1177/17499755209623

Wacquant, L. J. (1995). Pugs at work: Bodily capital and bodily labour among professional boxers. *Body & Society, 1*(1), 65–93. https://doi.org/10.1177/1357034X95001001005

Appendices

Appendix 1. Descriptive Statistics of Analytical Sample: Weighted Proportions of Categorical Variables, Weighted Means and Standard Deviations, as Well as Minimum and Maximum Values of Continuous Variables.

	N	Mean/ Proportion	Std.dev.	Min	Max
Daily time in front of the mirror	1,587	14.92	16.67	0	150
Belief in appearance as currency	1,580				
Disagree	83	5.28			
Somewhat disagree	199	12.60			
Neither agree nor disagree	482	30.53			
Somewhat agree	646	40.88			
Agree	169	10.71			
Gender	1,595				
Male	802	50.30			
Female	793	49.70			
Age group	1,589				
15–24	239	15.02			
25–34	269	16.91			
35–44	256	16.11			
45–54	282	17.72			
55–64	288	18.12			
65–74	256	16.11			
Area of living	1,568				
Urban	1,253	79.90			
Rural	315	20.10			
Partner status	1,528				
Partnered	1,105	72.30			
Single	2,423	27.70			

Appendix 1. *(Continued)*

	N	Mean/ Proportion	Std.dev.	Min	Max
Subjective class position	1,600				
Upper/upper middle class	403	25.20			
Lower middle class	450	28.13			
Working class	411	25.67			
None/other	336	21.00			

Appendix 2. Descriptive Statistics of Analytical Samples: Weighted Proportions of Categorical Variables, Weighted Means and Standard Deviations, as Well as Minimum and Maximum Values of Continuous Variables.

Finland Surveys

	N	Mean/Proportion
Appearance attitude		
Outcome 1	935	11.57
Outcome 2	2,519	31.17
Outcome 3	3,344	41.38
Outcome 4 (original categories 4 and 5)	1,284	15.89
Year		
1999	1,987	24.59
2004	2,937	36.34
2009	902	11.16
2014	980	12.13
2019	1,276	15.79
Gender		
Female	4,431	54.83
Male	3,651	45.17
Age group		
Older (31–64-year-olds)	6,116	75.67

Appendix 2. *(Continued)*

Finland Surveys

	N	Mean/Proportion
Younger (18–30-year-olds)	1,966	24.33
All	8,082	

(Only respondents who had valid scores on independent and dependent variables, non-weighted values)

The Household Budget Surveys

	N	Proportion/ Mean	Std.dev.	Min.	Max
Proportional share of personal hygiene and beauty care consumption expenditure	3,327	0.019	0.032	0	0.338
Year					
1998	642	19.30			
2001	828	24.89			
2006	588	17.67			
2012	546	16.41			
2016	723	21.73			
Gender					
Female	1,665	50.05			
Male	1,662	49.95			
Age	3,327	41.34	14.46	18	64
Place of residence					
Helsinki metropolitan area	664	19.96			
Other	2,663	80.04			
Education					
Non-academic	3,036	91.25			
Academic	291	8.75			
All	3,327				

(Only respondents who had valid scores on independent and dependent variables, weighted values)

Linear regression of personal hygiene and beauty care consumption (share of total consumption expenditure).

Gender (*ref. female*)	
Male	-0.020*** (0.001)
Year (*ref. 1998*)	
2001	0.000 (0.002)
2006	0.002 (0.002)
2012	-0.001 (0.002)
2016	-0.000 (0.002)
Age (*centred*)	-0.0002** (0.000)
Education (*ref. non-academic*)	
Academic	0.003 (0.002)
Place of residence (*ref. other*)	
Helsinki metropolitan area	0.004* (0.002)
Constant	0.028*** (0.002)
N	3,327
R^2	0.114

Note: Standard errors in parentheses
*$p < 0.05$, **$p < 0.01$, ***$p < 0.001$.

Index

Able-bodiedness, 4–5, 73–75
Accumulation of aesthetic capital,
    32–33, 39, 57–58
Activism in social media, 152–153
Admiration, 5–6
Aesthetic capital, 8, 10, 24, 28, 103,
    106, 117–118, 135, 138
    externalised forming of, 78–80
    grammar of exchanging, 30–33
    mechanisms, 106
    sociological conception, 103
    theory of, 149–150
Aesthetic labour, 28–29
Ageing, 71
    age-based collective consciousness,
        72
    body, 71–72
    gender and appearance-related
        consumption, 72–73
Anti-ageing products, 75
Appearance. *See also* Physical
    appearance
    appearance-related consumption,
        72–73
    different formulations of
        appearance-related capital,
        26–29
    dissatisfaction, 169
    as medium for inclusion and
        exclusion, 109–111
    norms, 136–137
    relation to psychological well-being,
        111–112
    as symbol of making an impression,
        107–109
Appearance satisfaction, 119–121
    on different social media platforms,
        121–122

social media platforms and gender,
    122–123
Appearance work, 39
    belief in appearance as currency,
        40–41
    significance of gendered appearance
        work, 41–43
Attention economy, 122, 154–155
Authentic self-presentation, 95
Authenticity, 73, 79, 81, 95

Beauty, 4, 24, 27–28, 30, 39–41, 71,
    108, 166
    care brands, 1
    fake mask, 159
    ideals, 120, 150
    ideology, 41
    logics, 6
    myth, 41
    perks and penalties, 8
    physical attractiveness, 4–5
    skin care and hair, 75–76
    standards, 5
    Western beauty ideal, 135
    work, 45–46
Belief in appearance as currency,
    40–41
Benevolent sexism, 41
Bodily capital, 24, 26–27
Body hair as classed aesthetics,
    160–161
Body management, 72–73
Bourdieu, Pierre, 4, 7, 24–26, 28, 31,
    39, 103–105, 152
Bourdieusian capital metaphor, 23
Bourdieusian tradition, 4–5
    forms of capital and body, 24–26
    theory, 105

Capital. *See also* Aesthetic capital, 24, 30
    Bourdieu's forms of, 24–26
    economist approach to, 27–28
    metaphor, 24
Capitalisation of physical appearance, 3–6
Clothing, 78–80
Colleagues monitoring, 96–97
Commodity culture in social media, 152–153
Content creation, 119–121
    on different social media platforms, 121–122
    social media platforms and gender, 122–123
Conversions of aesthetic capital, 32–33
Cosmetic procedures, 13
    non-surgical cosmetic interventions, 73
Cultural capital, 25–26, 32, 81, 99, 149–150, 159, 167

Decontextualisation, 155
Deep acting, 95
Dialogic thematic analysis, 138
Diet, 76–78
Disgust, 5–6
Distancing strategy, 74
Doing fatness wrong, 141–142
Dreaded otherness, 161

Economic capital, 8, 25, 167
Economist approach to capital, 27–28
Emotional labour, 28–29
Employer, 92–94
Exclusion, appearance as medium for, 109–111

Facebook, 119, 121–122, 125, 135–136, 140
Fat
    activism, 135, 137–138, 140
    activists, 140, 145
    good fatty, 136–137
    stigma, 136–137

weight discrimination, 136–137
Fatphobia, 136–137
Femininity, 40–41
Finland, 1, 6, 10, 43–44, 51, 61, 168, 170
    class structure, 11
    ethnic diversity, 12
    Finnish context, 7–8, 10, 13, 170
    Finnish culture, 45–46
    streetscape, 13
Finnish culture, 45–46
Flaunting, 139

Gender, 7, 24, 27–29, 46, 72–73, 122–123, 166
    'non-market' activity, 42
    differences in, 10
    gender-comparative perspective, 63
    gendered capital and labour, 28–29
    gendered form of capital, 6–8
    inequality, 41
    studies, 4
Generational habitus, 72
Geographical peculiarities, 11–13
Goffman, Erving, 2, 88
    dramaturgy, 90–91
    framework of impression management, 98–99
    Goffmanian lens, 8–9
    Goffmanian theatre metaphor, 87–88
    Goffman-inspired methodology, 91
Grooming, 4, 29, 41–43, 50, 58, 166
    skin care and hair, 75–76

Habitus, 105
Hagen, Sofie, 9, 135–142, 169
Hairless beauty ideal, 149
    (un) hairy female body, 150–152
    activism and commodity culture in social media, 152–153
Hairlessness, 149, 158, 160
    (un) hairy female body, 150–152
    activism and commodity culture in social media, 152–153
    hairless beauty ideal, 149

norm, 149, 158, 160
Hakim, Catherine, 3–4, 23, 28, 33, 68, 165–166
   idea of erotic capital, 28
   theory, 28

Impression management with work costumes, 88–90
Inclusion, appearance as medium for, 109–111
Instagram, 121–122, 127

#Januhairy, 149–150, 152–154

Kuipers, Giselinde, 3–5, 23, 26–28, 32, 43–44, 103–105, 151–152, 160, 165–166

Luxury-act, 11

Masculinity, 41, 57
   female, 160
   hypothesis, 58
   idealisation of performative masculinity, 76–78
   traditional man, 59–60
   traditional masculinity, 59–60
Mears, Ashley, 4, 6–8, 23, 27–30, 33, 43, 50–51, 104, 165–166, 168–169
Metrosexual, 57, 59, 61
   Metrosexual Masculinities, 57–58
   metrosexuality, 57–59, 68

Non-surgical cosmetic interventions, 73
Norms, 5, 87, 156
   normative aesthetic regulation, 168–169
   normative body, 135
   norm-breaking fat body, 135
   social norms, 24

Objectification theory, 119, 122–123
Offensive resistance, 138, 140–141

Performative masculinity, idealisation of, 76–78
Physical appearance, 1, 103–104, 165
   as aesthetic capital, 166
   capitalisation, 3–6
   in Finnish Context, 10–13
   importance, 1–3
   physical appearance -related traits, 167
Physical capital, 26–27
Physical exercise, 76–78
Psychological well-being, appearance relation to, 111–112

Self-projection, 95
Selfies, 2, 119–121, 128–129, 152, 154, 156
Sexual capital, 26–27
Shame, 5–6, 122–123, 129, 150, 159
Social capital, 25, 32–33, 113, 149–150
Social comparison theory, 119, 122–123
Social media. *See also* Facebook; Instagram, 2–3, 117–118
   activism and commodity culture in, 152–153
   appearance satisfaction and content creation on, 121–122
   effects of, 119
   gender, 122–123
   platforms, 122–123, 169–170
   social network site, 125
Social movements, 152

Working life, 8–9, 33, 87, 169–170
   aesthetic norms in, 93–94
   effects of, 4
   everyday, 87, 98–99, 110
   experiences, 6–7